AI PROMPT ENGINEERING

From Scratch to Professional Prompt Writer

The Beginner's Guide

By

Dr. Hesham Mohamed Elsherif

Dr. Salwa Elmeawad

About the Author

Dr. Hesham Mohamed Elsherif stands at the forefront of library management, research, and the practical implementation of Artificial Intelligence (AI) in educational and library systems. With over 22 years of dedicated service in the field, he brings a wealth of expertise that bridges the worlds of technology, organizational leadership, and scholarship.

Dr. Elsherif's academic credentials are as diverse as they are impressive. He holds two doctoral degrees - one in **Management and Organizational Leadership** and the other in **Information Systems and Technology**. This dual specialization has equipped him with a holistic perspective on how institutions can effectively integrate emerging technologies, particularly AI, to optimize resource allocation, streamline operational processes, and enrich learning experiences.

A recognized authority in **empirical research methodology**, Dr. Elsherif specializes in **qualitative approaches** and **action research**. His mastery of these methodologies has not only bolstered his own scholarly work but has also allowed him to pioneer new ways of investigating and implementing AI-driven solutions in school, academic, and public libraries. Whether he is designing user-centric AI tools or conducting in-depth studies on technology adoption, Dr. Elsherif's methodical and data-driven approach consistently yields impactful, real-world results.

Over the years, he has made significant strides in shaping the academic community - not just as a **professional researcher**, but also as an **Adjunct Professor**. In the classroom, Dr. Elsherif has a remarkable ability to translate complex theories into accessible insights, thereby training a new generation of thought leaders and specialists in both library science and technology. This multifaceted role, spanning teaching, research, and practice, has cemented his status as a **pioneer** whose influence extends well beyond traditional academic boundaries.

Dr. Elsherif's expertise and passion are truly global in scope. He has served as a **consultant to numerous educational institutions worldwide**, offering guidance on best practices, AI integration strategies, and effective management models. His international collaborations speak to the versatility of his knowledge, which is informed by a deep understanding of how AI can enhance resource discovery, user engagement, and scholarly communication across cultural and institutional contexts.

Central to Dr. Elsherif's mission is the belief that **innovative technologies**, including AI, must be harnessed responsibly and ethically. This commitment is evident in his approach to library management and educational technology, where he advocates for solutions that are inclusive, data-secure, and aligned with the core values of academic freedom and public service. By focusing on ethical implementation, he ensures that advancements in AI serve learners, educators, and researchers effectively and fairly.

Today, Dr. Elsherif continues to break new ground in **library innovation**, **academic research**, and **technology leadership**. Combining a passion for education with an unparalleled depth of knowledge, he remains a guiding force - **inspiring, educating, and leading** in library systems, educational institutions, and beyond. Through his work, he illuminates the path toward a future where AI seamlessly complements human expertise, thereby enriching the academic and public spheres for generations to come.

About the Contributor

Dr. Salwa Elmeawad stands out as a luminary in both the academic and community service spheres. With an illustrious career at the helm of adult services manager at Queens Library, she has profoundly impacted the field of information access and literacy. Dr. Elmeawad's educational journey is marked by not one, but two doctoral degrees, showcasing her dedication to lifelong learning and expertise in both organizational leadership and information systems and technology.

Her commitment extends beyond the academic realm into spirited community service. As the Distinguished Lieutenant Governor for the Kiwanis Queens East Division, Dr. Elmeawad plays a pivotal role in steering community-focused initiatives and fostering a spirit of service. Her role as a board member of the KPTC further exemplifies her dedication to impactful community work, particularly in areas of pediatric care and trauma prevention.

Dr. Elmeawad's passion for mentorship and youth development is evident through her involvement with the Benjamin Cardozo High School Key Club. As a lead mentor, coach, and advisor, she guides young minds in their personal and professional development, instilling in them the values of leadership and community service.

Her multifaceted expertise and unwavering commitment to both academic excellence and community service make Dr. Salwa Elmeawad a distinguished figure in her field and an inspiration to many.

Preface

AI can write, summarize, brainstorm, translate, code, plan, tutor, and critique. The surprising part is not what it can do, it is how often it fails in ways that feel random. You ask for one thing and get another. You request a format and receive a wall of text. You need accuracy and get confident nonsense. You try again, and the second answer is magically better, but you cannot explain why.

That gap between "AI is powerful" and "AI is dependable" is where prompt engineering lives.

This book is a practical guide to turning AI from a sometimes-helpful chatbot into a reliable professional tool. Prompt engineering, as we will use the term here, is not about secret phrases or clever tricks. It is a communication discipline. You are learning how to specify goals, supply the right context, define constraints, control output formats, and build repeatable workflows that survive real-world messiness. The same way a great brief improves a design, and a clear spec improves a build, a well-constructed prompt improves an AI outcome.

Who this book is for

This book starts at the beginning. If you are new to AI tools, you will learn the fundamentals without needing a technical background. If you have been using AI for a while, you will likely recognize many of the problems, but you may not yet have a systematic way to solve them. By the end, you should be able to write prompts that are clear, testable, reusable, and aligned with professional standards.

The examples and workflows are designed to serve a wide range of roles, including students, researchers, writers, marketers, analysts, product teams, customer support, and software developers. You do not need to be a programmer to benefit from this book, but you will learn to think like a designer of instructions, tests, and processes.

What this book will teach you

You will learn how to:

- Translate a vague request into a precise objective with measurable success criteria.
- Add the context an AI needs, without drowning it in irrelevant detail.
- Control tone, style, structure, and length so outputs match what you actually need.
- Use proven prompting patterns, including question-first prompts, few-shot examples, multi-step workflows, and critique loops.
- Debug prompts like you would debug a process, by isolating variables and testing changes.
- Reduce hallucinations by requesting uncertainty, verification steps, and grounded outputs.
- Build a reusable prompt library, with templates, rubrics, and evaluation test sets you can use over time.

Most importantly, you will learn a mindset: prompting is not a one-shot request. It is an iterative craft, guided by feedback and validation.

What this book is not

This is not a collection of "magic prompts" to copy blindly. You will find templates and ready-to-use recipes, but the goal is to help you understand why they work, when they fail, and how to adapt them to your own domain.

This is also not a book that pretends AI is always right. Professional use means acknowledging limits, managing risk, and choosing the right tasks for the tool. You will learn how to ask for uncertainty when needed, how to verify, and how to keep human judgment in the loop.

How to use this book

You can read straight through, but the fastest progress comes from doing the exercises.

- If you are a beginner, start with the foundations and complete the drills. You are building core instincts.

- If you are experienced, skim the early chapters, then focus on patterns, debugging, reliability, and evaluation. This is where professional results become repeatable.
- If you want immediate results for work, jump to the domain chapters, pick a workflow, and then return to earlier chapters to strengthen your fundamentals.

A simple rule will serve you well: every time you get a weak output, do not just try again. Diagnose why it happened and improve the prompt using a method. This book gives you that method.

A note on responsible use

AI systems can generate errors, biased language, or content that sounds authoritative without being accurate. Treat high-stakes domains like medicine, law, finance, and safety with extra care. Do not paste sensitive or confidential data into tools that are not approved for it. When accuracy matters, verify with reliable sources and subject matter expertise.

Prompt engineering is not only about performance. It is also about professionalism.

The promise of this book

By the time you finish, you should be able to sit down with a blank page and produce a prompt that looks and behaves like a professional deliverable. You will have a set of templates you trust, a workflow for improving them, and a practical understanding of how to guide AI toward outcomes that are useful, consistent, and aligned with your goals.

Let's begin.

Dr. Hesham Mohamed Elsherif

Dr. Salwa Elmeawad

Table of Content

Quick start in 20 minutes

The simplest prompt formula: Goal + Context + Output format + Constraints + Examples

If you only learn one thing from this book, learn this: most "bad AI answers" come from vague instructions, missing context, unclear formatting, or weak boundaries. The fastest way to fix that is a prompt that behaves like a professional brief.

Here is the simplest formula that reliably upgrades your results:

Goal + Context + Output format + Constraints + Examples

Think of it as five knobs. Turn each knob just enough to make the task unambiguous, then let the model do the work.

1) Goal

What you want, and what "done" looks like

Goal is the single sentence that defines the task. It should answer:

- What are you producing?
- Who is it for?
- What is the purpose?

A strong goal is specific and testable.

Weak goals

- "Write about prompt engineering."
- "Help me with my resume."
- "Summarize this."

Strong goals

- "Write a 900 to 1,100 word chapter introduction explaining prompt engineering to beginners, with 3 real examples and a short summary."
- "Rewrite my resume bullets for a data analyst role, emphasizing impact metrics and ATS-friendly keywords, without inventing facts."

- "Summarize the attached article into 7 bullets: problem, approach, key findings, and limitations."

Professional tip

Add a success signal to your goal. For example:

- "The reader should be able to do X after reading."
- "The output is ready to paste into X."
- "Use a checklist that I can follow step-by-step."

Goal mini-template

- Task: …
- Audience: …
- Purpose: …
- Success criteria: …

2) Context

The background the model needs to do the right thing

Context is the information that prevents wrong assumptions. Include only what affects decisions.

Common context types:

- Audience knowledge level (beginner, intermediate, expert).
- Domain constraints (industry, region, tools, policies).
- Inputs (your notes, text, data, requirements).
- Definitions (what specific terms mean in your situation).
- Prior decisions (what you have already chosen, what you rejected).

Bad context

- 6 paragraphs of unrelated history.
- No data or examples, then expecting precision.
- Missing definitions, then complaining the model "misunderstood."

Good context examples

- "Audience: first-year university students, non-technical."
- "Use US English. Tone: friendly and clear, not salesy."
- "I'm applying to roles in healthcare analytics."

- "Here are 6 bullet points I want included."
- "Do not assume I have access to paid tools."

Context mini-template

- Audience and level: …
- Situation: …
- Inputs: …
- Definitions: …
- Assumptions allowed: …

Rule of thumb

If the model might reasonably guess wrong, include the detail.

3) Output format

The shape of the answer, so it is usable immediately

Many prompts fail because the model does not know what form you need. Saying "be detailed" is weaker than specifying structure.

Good format instructions include:

- Length limits (words, bullets, sections).
- Specific headings.
- Order of sections.
- Table vs bullets vs JSON.
- Style requirements (tone, reading level, voice).

Examples

- "Return a markdown outline with H2 and H3 headings."
- "Create a table with columns: Step, Why it matters, Example prompt."
- "Output valid JSON matching this schema."
- "Write exactly 10 bullets. Each bullet starts with a verb."

Format mini-template

- Structure: …
- Length: …
- Tone: …
- Required sections: …

- Output type: bullets/table/JSON/markdown: …

Format guardrail

If you need the output to be copy-pasted into a document, specify the format as if you are the editor approving it.

4) Constraints

Boundaries that prevent common failures

Constraints tell the model what it must do, and what it must not do. They reduce irrelevant content, hallucinations, and overreach.

Common constraint categories:

- Scope: what to cover, what to exclude.
- Accuracy: "Do not invent facts. If missing, ask questions or state assumptions."
- Style: tone boundaries, forbidden phrases.
- Compliance: privacy, sensitive data, policy limits.
- Quality: "Include risks and limitations," "include citations," "include edge cases."
- Process: "Ask 3 clarifying questions before drafting," or "Draft then critique then revise."

Examples

- "Do not include pricing, brand names, or medical advice."
- "If you are uncertain, list what you would need to verify."
- "Avoid jargon. Define any technical term in one sentence."
- "No more than 2 sentences per bullet."
- "Include at least 2 counterarguments."

Constraint mini-template

- Must include: …
- Must avoid: …
- Accuracy rules: …
- Scope limits: …
- Quality checks: …

Power move
Add a self-check:

- "Before finalizing, verify you met every constraint and list any that were not met."

5) Examples

Show the model what you mean, not just what you want

Examples dramatically improve reliability, especially for style, formatting, and edge cases. Even one example can outperform paragraphs of explanation.

Types of examples:

- Input-output pairs (best).
- "Good vs bad" outputs.
- A mini style sample you want it to emulate.
- Counterexamples (what to avoid).

Example mini-template

- Example 1 (good): …
- Example 2 (good): …
- Example 3 (bad, avoid): …

Short example

- "Example bullet style: 'Reduce report generation time by 35% by automating SQL pipelines.'"

Important
Your examples act like training data. Keep them consistent with your constraints.

The complete 20-minute workflow

Minute 1 to 3: Write the Goal

Write one sentence that includes task, audience, and success signal.

Minute 4 to 7: Add Context

List only what changes decisions. Paste relevant source text if needed.

Minute 8 to 10: Define Output format

Specify headings, length, tone, and exact structure.

Minute 11 to 14: Add Constraints

List must-haves, must-not, accuracy rules, and scope boundaries.

Minute 15 to 20: Add Examples

Give 1 to 3 short examples. If you do not have examples, create one "gold" example yourself.

A copy-ready master template (use this everywhere)

Prompt

- Goal: …
- Context: …
- Output format: …
- Constraints: …
- Examples: …

You can paste that skeleton into any AI tool and fill it in.

Two before-and-after transformations

Example 1: Writing a professional section for a book

Before (weak)
"Write a section about prompt engineering for beginners."

After (professional using the formula)

- Goal: Write a 700 to 900 word section that teaches beginners the simplest prompt formula and how to use it.
- Context: Audience is non-technical. This is for a book called "AI Prompt Engineering." Readers want practical templates.
- Output format: Use markdown with headings. Include a short checklist and two examples.
- Constraints: No jargon without definitions. Do not mention proprietary tools. Must be actionable.

- Examples:
  - Good: "Goal: Draft a polite follow-up email to a recruiter, 120 to 160 words, confident tone."
  - Good output style: "Checklist: 1. Define audience… 2. Specify format…"

Example 2: Extracting structured info from text

Before (weak)
"Summarize these meeting notes."

After (professional using the formula)

- Goal: Extract decisions and action items from meeting notes so they can be tracked.
- Context: Stakeholders are product and engineering. Notes may be messy.
- Output format: Table with columns: Item type, Description, Owner, Due date, Risks.
- Constraints: Do not infer owners or dates. If missing, mark "Unknown."
- Examples:
  - Decision: "Adopt feature flag rollout for release."
  - Action item: "Create test plan for onboarding flow."

Common mistakes and fast fixes

Mistake 1: Goal is unclear

Fix: add audience, deliverable type, and success criteria.

Mistake 2: Context is missing or too long

Fix: include only decision-changing info. Use bullets.

Mistake 3: Output is not usable

Fix: specify structure, headings, length, and order.

Mistake 4: The model invents facts

Fix: add an accuracy constraint. "If missing, ask questions or say Unknown."

Mistake 5: Style is inconsistent

Fix: add 1 to 3 examples that demonstrate the style you want.

Practice drills (10 minutes total)

1. Turn this into a professional prompt:
   "Help me study for an exam."
   Include goal, context, format, constraints, examples.
2. Turn this into a professional prompt:
   "Write social media posts for my business."
   Specify audience, brand voice, number of posts, platform, and constraints.
3. Turn this into a professional prompt:
   "Make a plan for my project."
   Require milestones, risks, dependencies, and a verification checklist.

Your first "professional prompt" (fill-in exercise)

Copy and fill:

- Goal:
- Context:
- Output format:
- Constraints:
- Examples:

When you finish, you will already be prompting like a professional.

Two "before and after" transformations

A fast way to learn professional prompting is to watch weak prompts become strong prompts in real situations. Below are two complete transformations you can copy, adapt, and reuse. Each one shows:

- The **before** prompt (typical, vague, inconsistent).
- The **after** prompt (professional, structured, reusable).
- Why the "after" works, and how to remix it for your own tasks.

Transformation 1: From "Write something" to a publish-ready section

Before (weak prompt)

"Write a section about AI prompt engineering for beginners."

What typically goes wrong

- The model guesses the audience's level and your preferred tone.
- The output is generic, or too technical, or too long.
- No structure, no examples, no practical steps.
- You cannot easily reuse the prompt to write the next section.

After (professional prompt you can paste)

Task: Write a book section that teaches beginners how to write effective AI prompts from scratch.

Audience: Absolute beginners, non-technical readers.

Goal: Produce a 900 to 1,100 word section that a reader can apply immediately to improve results in any AI chat tool.

Context:

- This section belongs in a book titled "AI Prompt Engineering."
- The reader has used AI casually but gets inconsistent results.
- They need a repeatable method, not theory or hype.

Output format (strict):

1. Title (1 line)
2. 1-paragraph introduction (no more than 120 words)
3. The core method in 5 steps (Goal, Context, Output format, Constraints, Examples)
4. Checklist (8 to 12 items)
5. Two mini examples (bad prompt, improved prompt)
6. Common mistakes (at least 5) with quick fixes
7. Short conclusion (2 to 3 sentences)

Constraints:

- Use plain language, define any technical term in one sentence.
- Do not mention proprietary tools or brand-specific features.

- Do not invent statistics or claims.
- Keep paragraphs short (max 4 lines).
- Prioritize practical guidance and concrete phrasing.

Examples of tone and style:

- Write like a helpful instructor.
- Use direct sentences and actionable verbs.
- Use real-world examples like email writing, summarization, planning.

Verification:

Before finalizing, confirm you followed the output format and list any missing elements.

Why the "after" prompt works

- **It removes guesswork.** Audience and goal are explicit.
- **It controls structure.** The model cannot drift into a vague essay.
- **It reduces hallucinations.** "Do not invent statistics or claims" prevents fake authority.
- **It is reusable.** You can keep this prompt and swap the topic of the section.

Quick remix options

Replace only these parts to create a new section prompt:

- "Task" topic (example: "prompt debugging," "few-shot examples," "format control").
- Output length.
- Required elements (add a table, add a rubric, add a case study).

Transformation 2: From "Analyze this" to a decision-ready business output

Before (weak prompt)

"Analyze this data and tell me what it means."

What typically goes wrong

- The model makes assumptions about what "meaning" you want.
- You get a summary without decisions, actions, or priorities.
- You might get confident explanations unsupported by the data.

- The output is not in a format you can send to stakeholders.

After (professional prompt you can paste)

Task: Turn the following metrics into an executive-ready weekly performance update.

Audience: Business leaders, non-technical.

Goal: Explain what changed, why it likely changed, and what we should do next. The update must be clear enough to paste into an email.

Context:

- Time period: Week over week comparison (this week vs last week).
- Business type: Subscription app.
- Metrics provided: signups, activations, trial-to-paid conversion, churn, revenue, support tickets.
- Stakeholders care about trends, risks, and recommended actions.

Inputs:

Paste metrics in this format (example):

- Signups: 12,450 (last week 13,200)
- Activations: 6,980 (last week 7,500)
- Trial to paid: 18.2% (last week 17.5%)
- Churn: 3.4% (last week 3.1%)
- Revenue: $412,000 (last week $421,000)
- Support tickets: 1,340 (last week 1,050)
  [Replace with my actual metrics below.]

Output format (strict):

1. Headline summary (3 bullets max)
2. KPI table with columns: Metric, This week, Last week, Change, Interpretation
3. "What changed and why" (4 to 6 bullets)
4. Risks and watch-outs (at least 3 bullets)
5. Recommended actions (5 bullets), each with: action, owner role, expected impact, urgency
6. Questions to investigate next (3 to 5 questions)

Constraints:

- Do not invent causes. If a cause is uncertain, label it as a hypothesis.
- Use only the numbers provided. If you need more data, list what is needed.
- Keep the tone objective, not promotional.
- Avoid jargon.
- If changes are small, say so.

Examples (style):

- Good: "Support tickets rose 27.6% week over week, which may indicate a product issue or billing friction. We should review top ticket categories within 24 hours."
- Avoid: "Users disliked the UI," unless the data supports it.

Verification:

After writing, check that every recommendation is linked to at least one metric change.

Why the "after" prompt works

- **It defines what "meaning" is.** Leaders want decisions, risks, actions.
- **It forces accountability.** Recommended actions include owner role and urgency.
- **It prevents fabricated explanations.** Hypothesis labeling reduces overconfidence.
- **It produces a usable deliverable.** Email-ready structure, not a generic analysis.

Quick remix options

To use the same prompt for other situations:

- Swap the "Business type" and metrics list.
- Change the output sections to match your meeting style (example: add "Opportunities," remove "Questions").
- Add a constraint for length (example: "must fit on one screen").

The pattern you should notice (the "upgrade recipe")

Both transformations follow the same upgrade recipe:

1. Make the **deliverable** explicit (section, email, report, table).
2. Specify **audience and purpose** (who reads it, what they need).
3. Provide **inputs and definitions** (numbers, text, scope).
4. Lock the **output format** (headings, sections, table columns).
5. Add **constraints** (no invention, label uncertainty, length limits).
6. Include **examples** that show tone and quality.

If you apply that recipe consistently, your prompting quality jumps fast, and your results become repeatable.

Practice: do your own transformation (5 minutes)

Take any weak prompt you have used recently and rewrite it:

Before:
"One sentence that feels vague."

After:

- Task:
- Audience:
- Goal:
- Context:
- Output format:
- Constraints:
- Examples:
- Verification:

A one-page cheat sheet

Use this cheat sheet as your always-on prompt upgrade tool. You can print it, pin it near your desk, or keep it as a note. If you follow it, your prompts will become clearer, more consistent, and easier to reuse.

The One-Page Prompt Engineering Cheat Sheet

The Core Formula

Goal + Context + Output format + Constraints + Examples

If you only add one thing to your prompt, add **Output format**. If you add two, add **Constraints**.

1) Goal

Write one sentence that defines "done"

Include:

- Deliverable: what you want produced.
- Audience: who it is for.
- Purpose: what it will be used for.

Goal template

- "Create a [deliverable] for [audience] to achieve [purpose]."

Good goal examples

- "Draft a 150-word follow-up email to a recruiter to confirm next steps."
- "Create a 10-slide outline for a training session on prompt debugging."
- "Summarize this article into 8 bullets for an executive update."

Goal quality test

If someone else read your goal, could they tell whether the result is correct?

2) Context

Give only the information that changes decisions

Include:

- Background: what is happening and why.
- Inputs: paste the text, data, notes, or constraints.
- Definitions: clarify terms that could be misunderstood.
- Assumptions: what is safe to assume, what is not.

Context checklist

- Who is the reader or user?
- What is the scenario or business setting?
- What source material should be used?

- What should not be assumed?

Fast context prompt

- "If anything is unclear, ask up to 5 clarifying questions before drafting."

3) Output format

Specify the shape so it is usable immediately

Choose:

- Structure: headings, bullet lists, table columns, JSON schema.
- Length: word count, number of bullets, number of steps.
- Tone: formal, neutral, friendly, persuasive, technical.
- Ordering: what comes first, second, third.

Format templates

- "Return a table with columns: A, B, C."
- "Use markdown with H2 headings and bullet points."
- "Write exactly 10 bullets, each 12 to 18 words."
- "Output valid JSON matching this schema: {…}."

Format quality test

Could you paste the output directly into the place you need it?

4) Constraints

Prevent the most common failure modes

Common constraints

- Accuracy: "Do not invent facts. If unknown, say 'Unknown' and list what you need."
- Scope: "Cover X and Y. Do not cover Z."
- Style: "Avoid jargon. Define terms in one sentence."
- Safety and privacy: "Do not include personal or confidential data."
- Reasoning discipline: "State assumptions. Separate facts from hypotheses."

Constraint starter pack

- "Do not fabricate details."
- "If you are unsure, ask questions or state assumptions."
- "Stay within the provided inputs."
- "Keep it concise and structured."
- "Include limitations and edge cases."

Constraint quality test
Does your prompt clearly say what the model must avoid doing?

5) Examples

Show what good looks like

Examples teach:

- Tone and voice.
- Formatting conventions.
- Depth level.
- Edge cases.

Example types

- Good output sample.
- Bad output sample to avoid.
- 1 to 3 input-output pairs.

Examples template

- "Example (good): …"
- "Example (bad, avoid): …"
- "Match the style of this sample: …"

Examples quality test
If the model copied your example style, would you be happy?

The 30-Second Prompt Builder

Copy and fill:

- **Task (Goal):**
- **Audience:**
- **Context / Inputs:**

- **Output format:**
- **Constraints:**
- **Examples:**
- **Verification:**

The 60-Second Prompt Debugger

When output is wrong, diagnose the cause:

1. **Wrong content?** Add missing context and definitions.
2. **Too generic?** Add constraints and examples.
3. **Wrong shape?** Tighten output format and ordering.
4. **Invented facts?** Add accuracy rules and a verification step.
5. **Too long?** Add length limits and bullet requirements.
6. **Too complex?** Ask for an outline first, then expand.

Debug prompt

- "List 5 reasons your output might not match my intent, then propose a revised prompt."

Professional Prompt Patterns (pick one)

Pattern A: Direct deliverable

- "Create X in Y format with Z constraints."

Pattern B: Question-first

- "Ask up to 5 clarifying questions, then produce the deliverable."

Pattern C: Plan then write

- "First outline, then draft, then check constraints."

Pattern D: Extract then transform

- "Extract structured fields first, then write a summary from those fields."

Pattern E: Critique and revise

- "Generate draft, critique against rubric, revise, present final."

Reliability Guardrails (use when accuracy matters)

Add one or more:

- "Separate facts from hypotheses."
- "Cite sources if you used any external claims."
- "If data is missing, list what is needed."
- "Provide a short confidence note: high, medium, low."
- "Run a self-check against the constraints before finalizing."

"Upgraded prompt" examples (tiny but powerful)

Example 1: Email

Weak: "Write an email asking for a meeting."
Upgraded: "Write a 120 to 160 word email to a busy manager requesting a 20-minute meeting next week. Tone: confident and respectful. Include 3 time options and a clear subject line. Do not sound salesy."

Example 2: Summary

Weak: "Summarize this."
Upgraded: "Summarize into 7 bullets: problem, method, key results, limitations, and what to do next. Use only the text provided. If something is unclear, mark it as unknown."

Example 3: Planning

Weak: "Make a plan for my project."
Upgraded: "Create a 4-week plan with milestones, dependencies, risks, and owners by role. Output as a table. Include a brief risk mitigation strategy for each major risk."

Final reminder

If your prompt does not specify the output shape, the model will choose one for you. If your prompt does not define boundaries, the model will guess. Your job as a professional prompt writer is to replace guessing with specification.

Part 1. Foundations, the mental model

Chapter 1. What an AI model is and is not

Tokens, context window, and why phrasing matters

To prompt like a professional, you need a simple mental model of what an AI language model is doing when it "reads" your message and produces an answer. This does not require advanced math. It requires understanding three ideas:

The model processes text as tokens, not as words.

The model only "sees" a limited amount of text at once, called the context window.

The model predicts what comes next based on patterns, so phrasing changes outcomes.

When you understand these, many confusing behaviors become predictable, and you start writing prompts that are clearer, more stable, and easier to debug.

1) Tokens: what the model actually reads

Tokens are pieces of text

A token is not exactly a word. It is a chunk of text that might be:

a whole word,

part of a word,

punctuation,

whitespace,

a number or symbol.

For example, a long word might be split into several tokens. A short common word might be one token. Numbers and code can tokenize in unintuitive ways. This matters because the model's "reading" and "writing" happen token by token.

Why tokens matter for prompting

Tokens affect three practical things:

A) Length limits
Every AI model has a limit on how many tokens it can process at once. Your prompt plus the model's response must fit inside that limit. If your prompt is huge, you may get:

truncated responses,

missing sections,

the model ignoring earlier instructions,

reduced quality due to competing instructions.

B) Cost and speed in many systems
In many AI products and APIs, usage is measured in tokens. More tokens often means more time and more cost.

C) Precision and ambiguity
Because the model is predicting the next token, small changes in wording can change the distribution of likely next tokens. That is why prompts that look "similar" to humans can produce noticeably different results.

A practical rule you can use

If the output is drifting or incomplete, reduce token load:

remove irrelevant context,

move long references to a short summary,

ask for an outline first, then expand.

2) Context window: what the model can consider at one time

The context window is the model's working text

The context window is the maximum amount of text the model can attend to at once. It includes:

your prompt,

prior messages in the conversation,

system instructions in the tool,

any documents or pasted text,

and the model's own draft output as it generates.

Once the context window is full, older content falls out, or the system compresses it in some way. When that happens, the model can no longer "see" earlier details, even if you think they are still part of the conversation.

What context window is not

The context window is not memory in the human sense. The model does not "remember" a fact like a person does. It simply uses the text currently available to generate the next tokens.

This explains common experiences:

"It forgot what I said earlier."

"It changed the format halfway through."

"It ignored the policy I mentioned at the start."

"It contradicts something it said earlier."

Often, the reason is not stubbornness. It is context competition, where the model has too many instructions and examples to satisfy at once.

Context competition: the hidden enemy

Within the available context, not all text has equal influence. Instructions can compete with each other. If you include:

multiple roles,

conflicting constraints,

long background narratives,

many examples with inconsistent style,
the model may produce a compromise that pleases none of them.

Professional tip
When you want the model to follow a rule, place it:

clearly,

early,

and again near the output request,
but avoid repeating it in 10 different ways. Redundancy can create confusion if wording changes slightly each time.

The two-step workflow for long tasks

For any large document or complex task, use a two-step approach:

Compress the context. Ask the model to create a structured summary of the important points.

Work from the compressed summary. Generate the deliverable using that summary as the primary source.

This keeps the "working set" small and consistent.

3) Why phrasing matters: the model predicts, it does not understand like a human

The core behavior: next-token prediction

A language model generates text by predicting the most likely next token given the context. That does not mean it has intentions, beliefs, or deep understanding in the human sense. It has learned patterns from training data and uses those patterns to produce plausible continuations.

This has two important consequences:

A) It is sensitive to framing
The prompt sets a frame that guides what "likely" looks like. The same task can be framed as:

a casual request,

a formal specification,

a checklist,

a rubric-driven evaluation,

an expert consultation.

Each frame activates different patterns.

B) It is sensitive to cues
Words like "draft," "policy," "email," "rubric," "table," "JSON," "step-by-step," or "for executives" are strong cues that change structure and tone.

"Be detailed" vs "Include these sections"

"Be detailed" is a weak instruction because it does not define where detail belongs or how it should be organized. The model will guess.

Compare:

Weak: "Explain prompt engineering in detail."

Strong: "Explain prompt engineering using 5 sections: definition, why prompts fail, the core formula, two examples, and a checklist. Keep it under 900 words."

The second prompt gives the model a clear path. The first gives it freedom, and freedom often produces inconsistency.

Ambiguity words that cause inconsistent results

Be cautious with words that require interpretation:

best, optimal, improve, modern, strong, professional, simple, detailed, robust, comprehensive.

If you use them, define them with measurable criteria:

"professional" means "neutral tone, concise, no slang, structured headings."

"comprehensive" means "cover A, B, C, include examples and edge cases."

"simple" means "grade 8 reading level, define terms, short sentences."

Instruction clarity beats intensity

Adding forceful language does not necessarily help:

"Do this perfectly!"

"Follow strictly!"

"Very very important!"

Professional prompts rely on clarity and structure, not emphasis.

What works better:

a precise output format,

explicit constraints,

and a verification step.

4) Professional techniques that use this mental model

Technique 1: Put critical instructions in a "control block"

Create a small section in your prompt that is easy to follow:

Goal:

Output format:

Constraints:

Inputs:

This reduces ambiguity and limits token waste.

Technique 2: Replace long context with a short "facts and assumptions" list

Instead of pasting pages, write:

Facts:

Assumptions allowed:

Unknowns:

This makes the model less likely to invent details.

Technique 3: Use "first outline, then expand"

Outlines are cheap in tokens and powerful in control. Once the outline is approved, expansion is straightforward.

Technique 4: Ask for a self-check

Add:

"Before finalizing, verify you followed each constraint and each required section."

This catches common failures automatically.

5) Mini examples: phrasing that changes outcomes

Example A: Summarization

Weak: "Summarize this document."

Strong: "Summarize into 8 bullets: problem, approach, key results, limitations, and next steps. Use only the text provided. Mark unknowns as Unknown."

Example B: Writing

Weak: "Write a professional introduction."

Strong: "Write a 120 to 150 word introduction for beginners. Tone: clear and confident. Include one simple analogy. Avoid jargon."

Example C: Analysis

Weak: "Analyze these metrics."

Strong: "Create an executive update with: headline summary (3 bullets), KPI change table, hypotheses labeled clearly, risks, and 5 recommended actions linked to the metrics."

Summary:

The mental model in one paragraph

An AI language model processes your message as tokens, considers only a limited amount of text inside its context window, and generates output by predicting the next token based on patterns and cues. That is why long prompts can crowd out important instructions, why the model can appear to "forget," and why small phrasing changes can shift results. Professional prompting is about controlling what the model sees, reducing ambiguity, structuring outputs, and adding constraints and verification so the model does less guessing and produces more reliable work.

Why models "sound right" even when wrong

People are often surprised by how confidently an AI can deliver an incorrect answer. It reads smoothly, uses the right buzzwords, follows a logical structure, and sometimes even includes numbers or citations-like phrasing. That "sounds right" quality is called **fluency**. Fluency is not the same thing as **truth**.

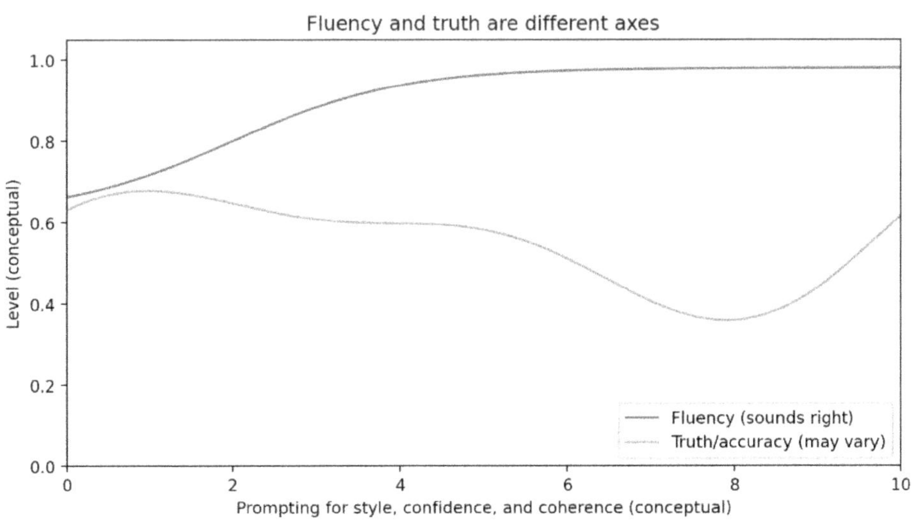

The Figure above explains the Fluency and truth are different axes. A response can be highly fluent while accuracy varies.

A useful mental model is this: **language models are optimized to produce plausible text, not guaranteed facts**. When your prompt asks for something that resembles patterns the model has seen, it can generate a convincing response even if the underlying facts are missing, outdated, or unknowable from the provided context.

The core reason: next-token prediction creates believable narratives

A language model generates text by repeatedly predicting the next token that best fits the context. If the prompt implies that an answer exists, the model often continues the pattern of "answering" rather than stopping to say, "I don't know." This is not dishonesty; it is pattern completion.

That is why a model can:

- write a confident explanation for an event that never happened,
- invent references or details when asked for "sources,"
- produce a coherent plan that ignores a hidden constraint,
- give a clean definition that is subtly wrong in your domain.

Why "coherence" is easy and "correctness" is hard

Humans judge writing quality using signals like clarity, structure, and confidence. Models are very good at those signals because they are common in training data. Correctness often requires additional ingredients that may not be present:

1. **Grounding to reliable sources**
   If the model is not connected to a database, documents, or tools, it cannot verify facts. It can only generate what seems likely from patterns.
2. **Distinguishing what is known vs assumed**
   Many prompts do not specify what to do when information is missing. The model then fills gaps with plausible defaults.
3. **Specialized domain constraints**
   In medicine, law, engineering, finance, or niche technical fields, small details matter. Fluency can mask subtle errors.
4. **Pressure from the prompt**
   Prompts like "Give me the best answer" or "Explain in detail" push

the model toward confident completion. If you also demand a single final answer, the model is less likely to flag uncertainty.

5. **Sampling and variability**
   Even with the same prompt, small randomness can change wording and sometimes facts. The model is not retrieving a stored answer. It is generating one.

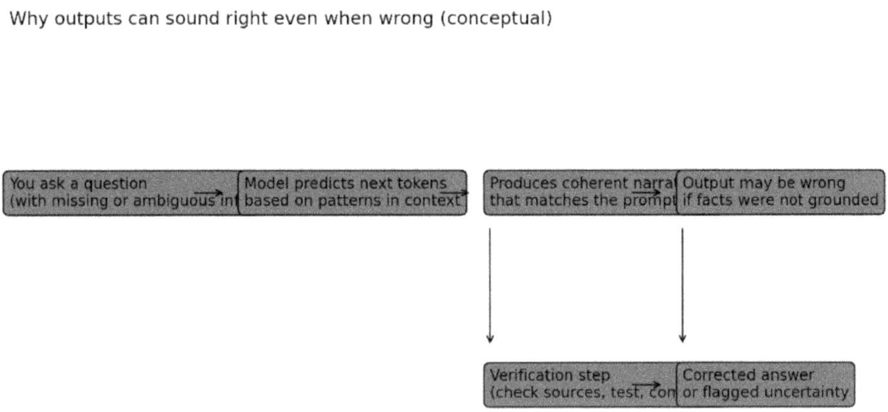

The figure above shows how an ungrounded question can produce a coherent narrative, and how verification changes the outcome.

The most common mechanisms behind "sounds right but wrong"

1) Gap-filling, the model completes missing pieces

If you provide partial details, the model may infer the rest. This is helpful for brainstorming, but risky for factual tasks.

Example

- You: "Write a bio for Dr. Mo, include awards."
- Risk: It invents awards because bios often contain awards.

Fix

- "Use only the details I provide. If an award is not provided, write 'Not specified.'"

2) Overgeneralization from typical cases

The model has seen many "typical" versions of a thing and may produce the common case, not your case.

Example

- You: "Write the policy for PTO."
- Risk: It outputs a generic PTO policy that conflicts with your organization's rules.

Fix

- "Ask clarifying questions about jurisdiction, accrual rules, carryover, and exceptions before drafting."

3) Confusing plausibility with evidence

The model can generate a strong causal story from weak signals. Humans love explanations, and models have learned that style.

Example

- You: "Support tickets increased. Why?"
- Risk: It states a cause as fact without proof.

Fix

- "List 3 hypotheses, label them hypotheses, and state what data would confirm or reject each."

4) "Citation-shaped text" that is not real support

If you ask for citations, the model may produce something that looks like a citation even when it cannot truly verify.

Fix

- "If you cannot verify a source, say so. Provide a search plan and the exact queries you would use."

5) Instruction conflict and context overload

When a prompt includes many goals at once, the model may satisfy the easiest ones first, often style and structure, then miss factual precision.

Fix

- Split into steps: outline, extract facts, then write; keep each step focused.

How to spot when an answer only sounds right

Use these red flags:

- **Overconfidence without boundaries**: no mention of uncertainty where uncertainty is expected.
- **Specific numbers without origin**: precise percentages, dates, or counts with no source.
- **Generic phrasing**: "studies show," "experts agree," without who or where.
- **Too smooth**: complex topics summarized with suspicious certainty and zero caveats.
- **No alternative explanations** when the situation is ambiguous.
- **No testable next steps**: recommendations that cannot be validated.

Professional guardrails to reduce "sounds right" failures

Guardrail A: Force a known/unknown split

Add to your prompt:

- "Separate your response into: What we know from the input, What we are assuming, What we need to verify."

Guardrail B: Require hypotheses, not conclusions

- "Provide 3 possible explanations, label confidence (high, medium, low), and list the data needed to confirm."

Guardrail C: Ask for a verification plan

- "Give a checklist to validate the answer. Include steps like cross-checking sources, sanity checks, and edge cases."

Guardrail D: Use extraction before generation

For documents and data:

1. "Extract facts into a table."
2. "Write the narrative using only that table."

This prevents the model from quietly inserting new facts.

Guardrail E: Add a self-check against constraints

- "Before finalizing, confirm you did not introduce any facts not present in the input."

Two mini prompt upgrades you can reuse

1) Factual explanation prompt (safe version)

"Explain X using only the information provided. If key facts are missing, list them. Provide hypotheses separately from confirmed statements. End with a verification checklist."

2) Decision support prompt (safe version)

"Summarize the situation, then give options with tradeoffs. Label assumptions. For each recommendation, state what evidence would change your recommendation."

<u>Determinism, randomness, temperature in plain language</u>

When people say an AI is "random," they usually mean this: they asked the same question twice and got two different answers. That can be frustrating in professional work, but it is also a feature when you want creativity.

To control this, you need a simple model of how text generation works:

- The model does not pull a single fixed answer from a database.
- It generates the response one token at a time.

- At each step, it has a set of possible next tokens, each with a probability.
- The system then either picks the most likely token every time (more deterministic), or samples among likely tokens (more varied).

This is where determinism, randomness, and temperature come in.

1) Determinism. Same input, same output

What determinism means

A deterministic setting behaves like a strict rule:

- If you give the same prompt, you get the same output (or extremely close), every time.

In practice, determinism depends on how the system chooses the next token:

- **Deterministic choice:** always pick the most likely next token.
- **Stochastic choice:** sometimes pick a less likely token to increase variety.

Why you may not get perfect determinism in real tools

Even if temperature is low, you can still see variation because of:

- tiny internal numerical differences,
- system prompt changes, model updates, or safety layers,
- different context from earlier conversation turns,
- tool or retrieval results that change between runs.

So, think of determinism as a goal you approach, not always a guarantee.

2) Randomness. Variety comes from sampling

What "randomness" actually is here

Randomness is not the model "making things up on purpose." It is the sampling step selecting among plausible next tokens.

If multiple next tokens are reasonably likely, sampling can produce different phrasings, different examples, and sometimes different conclusions, especially when the prompt is vague.

Randomness affects:

- word choice and tone,
- ordering of points,
- which examples get used,
- how confidently the model commits to one path.

This is why two answers can be:

- both well-written,
- both plausible,
- but not identical.

3) Temperature. The main knob that controls variety

Temperature in plain language

Temperature controls how "peaked" or "flat" the model's next-token probabilities are.

- **Low temperature:** the model strongly prefers the top choice. Output becomes more consistent, sometimes more rigid.
- **Medium temperature:** balanced. Usually coherent and reasonably consistent.
- **High temperature:** more exploration. More variety, more surprises, and more risk of drifting off format or making mistakes.

A helpful analogy:

- Low temperature is like choosing the safest sentence that fits.
- High temperature is like brainstorming with less filtering.

Temperature does not create knowledge. It changes how adventurous the wording and choices are.

4) What temperature changes, and what it does not

Temperature changes

- phrasing and style variation,
- creativity and novelty,
- likelihood of unusual wording,
- chance of format drift when prompts are weak,
- probability of rare token choices that can introduce mistakes.

Temperature does not change

- what the model "knows" in a factual sense,
- whether a claim is true,
- whether an answer is grounded in your data.

A high temperature answer can still be correct. A low temperature answer can still be wrong. Temperature is about selection behavior, not truth.

5) Practical guidance. Which temperature should you want

Use **lower temperature** when you need:

- consistent formatting (reports, tables, JSON),
- policies, SOPs, checklists, summaries,
- compliance-sensitive writing,
- technical instructions, code with tests,
- anything you will reuse as a template.

Use **medium temperature** when you need:

- general writing help,
- explanations for learning,
- drafting where you will edit,
- balanced brainstorming and structure.

Use **higher temperature** when you want:

- many creative options,
- slogan and naming ideas,
- story prompts, ad variants, fresh angles,
- divergent thinking before you converge with a rubric.

Professional workflow tip: **diverge then converge**. Start higher for idea generation, then go lower for final drafting and formatting.

6) How to reduce randomness without "turning creativity off"

Even when you cannot control temperature directly (some chat products hide it), you can still get consistency by prompting in a deterministic style:

Add structure

- "Use exactly these headings in this order."

- "Write exactly 8 bullets, each 12 to 18 words."

Add constraints

- "Do not invent facts. If unknown, say Unknown."
- "Use only the information in the input."

Add examples

Examples act like a mini style guide and reduce drift.

Add a verification step

- "Before finalizing, check each constraint and confirm compliance."

These techniques often matter more than temperature.

7) Mini experiments you can do in 3 minutes

Experiment A. Measure variability

1. Ask the same prompt 5 times in new chats.
2. Compare outputs for:
    - structure, length, tone, and claims.

If variation is high, your prompt is under-specified. Tighten output format and constraints.

Experiment B. Find your "stable prompt"

Use this prompt and re-run it:

- "Draft the answer, then rewrite it to match this exact outline and length."

This forces convergence even if the first draft varies.

Experiment C. Two-phase prompting

- Phase 1 (creative): "Generate 20 options, be original."
- Phase 2 (deterministic): "Select the best 3 using this rubric, then rewrite them in a consistent style."

8) Professional takeaways

- Determinism means repeated runs look the same. You get it by reducing sampling freedom and by specifying structure.
- Randomness comes from sampling among plausible tokens. It is useful for creativity, risky for precision.
- Temperature is the main control for variety. Lower for reliability and structure, higher for exploration.
- When quality matters, do not rely on temperature alone. Use clear goals, strict output format, constraints, examples, and verification.

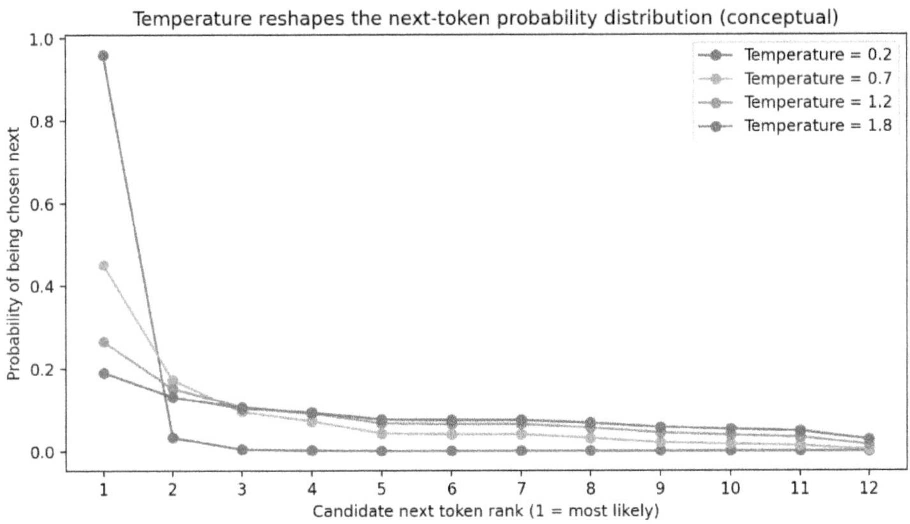

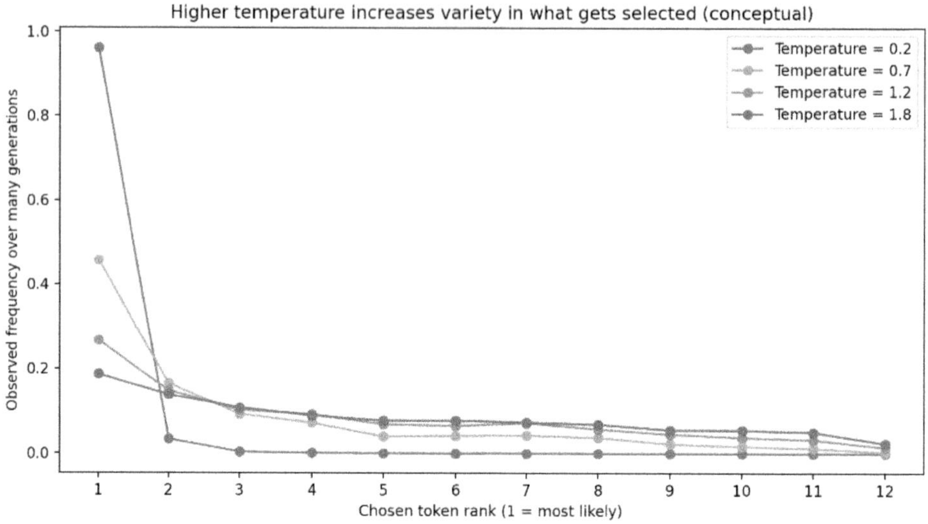

Instruction hierarchy and why your prompt sometimes gets ignored

One of the most confusing experiences in prompting is this: you clearly asked for something, but the model did something else. Sometimes it ignores your format. Sometimes it refuses. Sometimes it follows a different instruction that you never typed.

This happens because your prompt is not the only instruction the model is following. In most AI systems, instructions have a **hierarchy**. Higher-priority instructions override lower-priority ones, even if you never see them.

1) The instruction hierarchy in plain language

Think of the model as receiving multiple layers of guidance at the same time:

1. **System instructions (highest priority)**
   Platform-level rules such as safety policies, privacy rules, and core behavior. These are not written by you and usually are not visible.
2. **Developer instructions**
   Instructions set by the application or product that is hosting the model. Examples: tool use rules, formatting requirements, tone defaults, refusal style, or "always cite sources" behavior.

3. **Tool or retrieved context**
   Information inserted by tools (search results, documents, function outputs). This content can strongly influence the answer, but it does not override system or developer rules.
4. **User instructions (your prompt)**
   Your request, constraints, and preferences. This is powerful, but it sits below the layers above.
5. **Model completion (the output)**
   The final text is the result of the model trying to satisfy all layers without violating higher-priority rules.

Key idea: your prompt is "in charge" only when it does not conflict with higher layers.

2) The most common reasons your prompt gets ignored

Reason A: It conflicts with higher-priority rules

If your prompt requests disallowed content, the model must refuse or redirect. This can feel like "ignoring," but it is a policy override.

Example

- User: "Give step-by-step instructions for wrongdoing."
- Result: refusal or partial help.

Reason B: Your prompt conflicts with itself

Models often follow the *most recent*, *clearest*, or *most specific* instruction. If your prompt contains contradictions, something will be dropped.

Example

- "Be extremely concise and include a detailed explanation with examples and edge cases."

Fix

- Decide which constraint wins, or separate into steps:
  - "First provide the concise version (6 bullets). Then provide the detailed version (with examples)."

Reason C: The prompt is under-specified, so the model fills gaps

If you do not specify output shape, scope, or audience, the model guesses. Guessing can look like ignoring.

Example

- "Write a report about this."
- You expected: executive summary, KPIs, recommendations.
- It outputs: a generic essay.

Fix

- Lock the format: headings, bullet counts, sections, tables.

Reason D: Context overload, your key instruction gets buried

Long prompts, many examples, and multiple tasks can cause your most important instruction to lose influence.

Symptoms

- It follows your early instructions at first, then drifts.
- It forgets a constraint mid-answer.
- It returns partial sections.

Fix

- Put critical constraints in a short "control block" near the end, right before "Output:".
- Remove anything that does not change decisions.
- Use a two-step workflow: outline first, then expand.

Reason E: Tool outputs dominate the narrative

When tools inject large blocks of text, the model may anchor on them and treat them as the main instruction or truth source, even if the tool text is irrelevant or incomplete.

Fix

- Tell the model how to use tool content:
    - "Use the tool output only for facts. Ignore opinions."
    - "If sources conflict, list the conflict and do not choose without evidence."

Reason F: The model is optimizing for "helpfulness" over strict compliance

If your prompt is polite but vague, the model may choose what it thinks is most helpful, even if it is not what you wanted.

Fix

- Add a verification step:
    - "Before finalizing, check each requirement and confirm compliance."

3) How to write prompts that survive the hierarchy

Technique 1: Put a "priority block" in your prompt

This reduces ambiguity and makes your intent easy to follow.

Priority block template

- Highest priority: follow the output format exactly.
- Next priority: do not invent facts, mark unknowns as Unknown.
- Next priority: keep within length limits.
- If conflict occurs: ask clarifying questions.

This works because it teaches the model how to resolve conflicts inside your own prompt.

Technique 2: Restate constraints right before the output instruction

Models respond strongly to the most recent clear instructions.

Bad:

- Constraints buried in paragraph 3.

Good:

- A short checklist right before "Output now."

Technique 3: Split complex jobs into stages

Instead of one mega-prompt, use a chain:

1. Clarify requirements.
2. Draft outline.
3. Draft output.

4. Self-check against constraints.
5. Revise.

This reduces instruction competition and increases compliance.

Technique 4: Ask for "compliance reporting"

This is a professional trick when format matters.

Add:

- "After your answer, include a checklist showing which requirements you satisfied."

If the model cannot check a box, it often reveals what would have been ignored.

4) Prompt patterns that fix "ignored instructions" fast

Pattern A: Format-first prompting

"Output must follow this structure exactly:

1. …
2. …
3. …

   Do not add extra sections."

Pattern B: Constraint-first prompting

"Rules:

- Use only the provided input.
- If missing info, ask questions.
- Do not invent facts.

   Now perform the task."

Pattern C: Ask-first prompting

"Before answering, ask up to 5 clarifying questions. After I answer, produce the final output using the specified format."

Pattern D: Self-check prompting

"Draft the output. Then verify it against the requirements. Then provide the final version."

5) Quick diagnostic. When your prompt is ignored, check these in order

1. Did you request something that might violate platform or safety rules?
2. Did you include contradictory instructions?
3. Did you specify output format clearly and strictly?
4. Did you overload the prompt with irrelevant context?
5. Did tool content or examples conflict with your constraints?
6. Did you add a self-check and requirement checklist?

6) A ready-to-copy "anti-ignored prompt" template

Task: …
Output format (must follow): …
Rules:

- Use only the provided inputs.
- If uncertain, state assumptions or ask questions.
- Do not invent facts or citations.
- If a rule conflicts, follow this priority order: format, accuracy, length, style.
  Inputs: …
  Verification: After drafting, check each rule and list any unmet items.

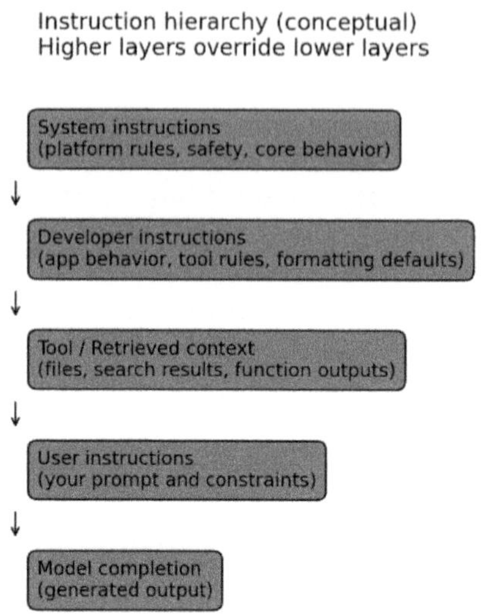

Mini lab: "Same prompt, different outputs", and how to stabilize

This mini lab teaches a professional habit: when outputs vary, do not keep re-rolling answers and hoping. Instead, measure variation, diagnose why it happens, then patch the prompt until it becomes stable and reusable.

What you will learn in 20 minutes

- Why the same prompt can produce different answers.
- How to detect what is actually varying (facts, structure, tone, scope).
- How to stabilize outputs using format control, constraints, examples, and a verification loop.
- How to turn a "good prompt" into a reusable template.

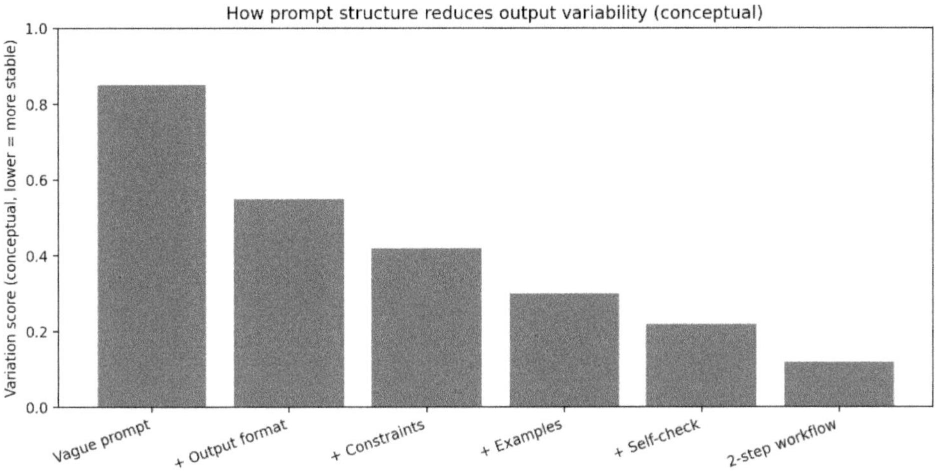

The Figure above shows each added control, format, constraints, examples, self-check, reduces variability

Part A. The experiment: run the same prompt multiple times

Step 1: Start with a deliberately vague prompt

Use a prompt like:

Prompt (V1, vague)
"Write a professional introduction about AI prompt engineering for beginners."

Step 2: Run it 3 to 5 times

Do this in new chats or with the same chat if it does not carry a lot of earlier context.

Step 3: Compare outputs using a simple scorecard

Create a quick checklist and score each run as Pass or Fail:

- Did it match the intended audience level (beginner)?
- Did it stay within the expected length?
- Did it include practical steps or just theory?
- Did it follow a structure you can reuse?

- Did it introduce facts or claims you did not request?
- Was the tone consistent across runs?

What you will usually observe

Even with the same prompt, answers often vary in:

- length and level of detail,
- structure (bullets vs paragraphs),
- examples chosen,
- confidence and specificity,
- invented facts or vague filler.

This variation happens because your prompt leaves many decisions open. When decisions are open, the model samples different valid paths.

Part B. Diagnose variation: what is changing?

Use this fast diagnostic. Circle what varied between runs.

1) Format drift

Symptoms:

- sometimes a list, sometimes an essay,
- headings appear randomly,
- the order of ideas changes.

Cause:

- output format was not specified.

Fix:

- specify headings, bullet counts, table columns, and order.

2) Scope drift

Symptoms:

- one answer focuses on basics, another jumps to advanced patterns,
- too broad, too narrow, or includes unrelated topics.

Cause:

- the prompt does not define boundaries.

Fix:

- define what must be included and what must be excluded.

3) Tone drift

Symptoms:

- one answer sounds academic, another sounds salesy.

Cause:

- tone not defined, or examples not provided.

Fix:

- define tone and include a short style example.

4) Fact risk or invented detail

Symptoms:

- confident claims, statistics, or references appear without support.

Cause:

- the prompt implies "authority" but provides no grounding or accuracy rules.

Fix:

- add accuracy constraints and an "Unknown" policy, plus verification prompts.

Part C. Stabilize: patch the prompt in controlled steps

You will now upgrade the prompt in small increments, re-run 2 to 3 times after each patch, and watch variation drop.

Version 2: Add output format

Prompt (V2)

"Write an introduction for beginners about AI prompt engineering.
Output format:

- Title (1 line)
- Intro paragraph (80 to 120 words)
- 5 bullet points explaining the core ideas
- Closing sentence (1 line)."

What this stabilizes:

- structure, length, ordering.

Version 3: Add constraints

Prompt (V3)

"Write an introduction for beginners about AI prompt engineering.
Output format: Title, 80 to 120 word intro, 5 bullets, closing sentence.
Constraints:

- No jargon without a one-sentence definition.
- Do not invent statistics or cite sources.
- Keep tone neutral and instructional.
- Focus only on beginner fundamentals, not advanced tooling."

What this stabilizes:

- scope and accuracy behavior.

Version 4: Add examples

Prompt (V4)
"Write an introduction for beginners about AI prompt engineering.
Output format: Title, 80 to 120 word intro, 5 bullets, closing sentence.
Constraints: No invented stats, define jargon, neutral tone, beginner scope only.
Style example (match this clarity):
'Prompt engineering is the skill of giving clear instructions so an AI produces usable results. A good prompt tells the AI what you want, what it should use, and how the answer should look.'"

What this stabilizes:

- tone, phrasing, and level.

Version 5: Add a self-check

Prompt (V5, stable)
"Write an introduction for beginners about AI prompt engineering.
Output format: Title, 80 to 120 word intro, 5 bullets, closing sentence.
Constraints: No invented stats, define jargon, neutral tone, beginner scope only.
After writing, verify:

1. Word count is within range,
2. Exactly 5 bullets,
3. No statistics or citations,
4. Jargon is defined,
5. Beginner scope only.
   If any check fails, fix it and output only the corrected final version."

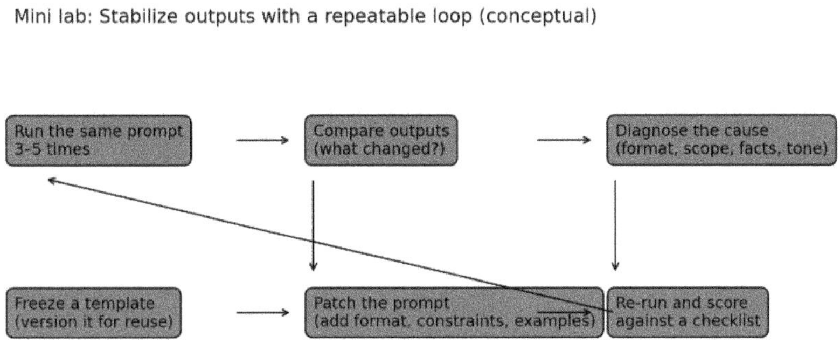

What this stabilizes:

- compliance with requirements, reduces drift.

Part D. The stabilization loop you can reuse for any task

This loop is your professional method:

1. **Run** the same prompt 3 to 5 times.
2. **Compare** outputs and mark what changed.
3. **Diagnose** the cause (format, scope, tone, facts).
4. **Patch** the prompt with the smallest fix.
5. **Re-run** and score against a checklist.
6. **Freeze** the prompt as a template and version it.

If you repeat this loop, you stop relying on luck and start building dependable prompts.

Extra stabilization tricks (when variation still happens)

Trick 1: Force a plan first

"First produce an outline that matches the format. Wait. After I approve, write the full draft."

Why it works:

- it locks structure before content expands.

Trick 2: Extract then write

For long inputs:

1. "Extract key facts into a table."
2. "Write the summary using only the table."

Why it works:

- reduces invented details.

Trick 3: Add "decision rules" for conflicts

"If there is a tradeoff between being concise and being complete, prioritize conciseness and list missing details as questions."

Why it works:

- prevents inconsistent choices.

Trick 4: Ask for two drafts with different goals

"Produce Draft A optimized for brevity, Draft B optimized for completeness. Then produce a final balanced version."

Why it works:

- separates competing objectives.

Chapter 2. The anatomy of a professional prompt

Prompt components:

Objective

In professional prompt engineering, the **Objective** is the single most important component. It is the "north star" that tells the model what success looks like. If the objective is vague, the model has to guess, and guessing produces unstable, generic outputs.
A professional objective is not a topic. It is not a wish. It is a clear deliverable statement that includes what you want, who it is for, and how you will judge whether it is correct.

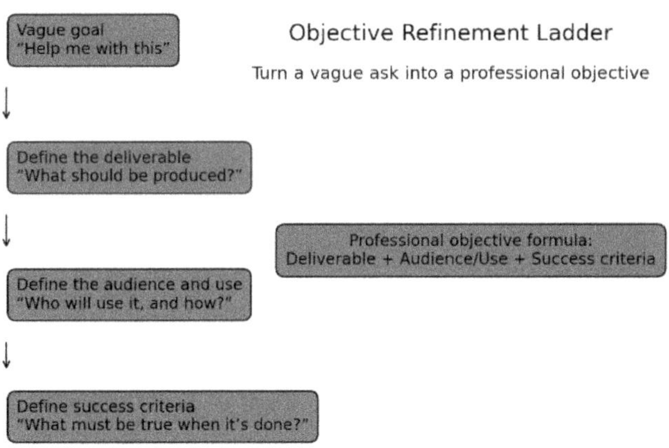

The figure above shows Objective Refinement Ladder. Turn a vague ask into a professional objective by specifying deliverable, audience/use, and success criteria

What "Objective" means in prompting

Objective is the specification of the outcome

The objective answers three questions:

1. **Deliverable**: What exactly should be produced?
2. **Audience and use**: Who will use it, and where will it be used?
3. **Success criteria**: What must be true when the task is done?

When those three pieces are present, the model stops guessing and starts executing.

The professional objective formula

Deliverable + Audience/Use + Success criteria

Objective examples (strong)

- "Create a 1-page cheat sheet for beginners that they can use while writing prompts, including a checklist and 2 examples."
- "Draft a 140 to 170 word email to a hiring manager requesting an interview follow-up, with a confident tone and 3 time options."
- "Turn these meeting notes into action items and decisions in a table with owners and due dates. If missing, write Unknown."

Objective examples (weak)

- "Help me write something professional."
- "Explain prompt engineering."
- "Make this better."
- "Give me the best answer."

Weak objectives fail because they do not define the deliverable and do not define what "better" or "best" means.

Objective quality checklist

A good objective is:

- **Specific**: names the deliverable type (email, outline, table, script, rubric).
- **Bounded**: has length limits or scope boundaries.
- **Audience-aware**: states who it is for and what they need.
- **Measurable**: includes success criteria you can check quickly.
- **Non-conflicting**: does not demand contradictory outcomes (for example "extremely short and very comprehensive" unless you define priorities).

Fast test: If a colleague read only your objective, could they judge whether the output is correct?

How to write an objective from scratch in 60 seconds

Step 1: Name the deliverable

Use nouns, not verbs:

- "A 10-bullet brief"
- "A table"
- "A 3-section report"
- "A step-by-step SOP"
- "A JSON object with these fields"

Step 2: Name the audience and the usage context

- "for executives"
- "for first-year students"
- "for a customer support response"
- "to paste into a slide"
- "to send as an email"

Step 3: Add success criteria that are easy to verify

Pick 2 to 5 checks:

- exact number of bullets
- required sections and order
- word range
- must include examples
- must avoid invented facts
- must output in a specific structure

Turn it into one sentence

- "Create a [deliverable] for [audience/use] that meets [success criteria]."

Common objective mistakes and fixes

Mistake 1: Objective is a topic, not an outcome

- Topic: "Prompt engineering"
- Objective: "Write a 900 to 1,100 word beginner chapter section that teaches the prompt formula with two examples and a checklist."

Mistake 2: Objective misses the audience

- "Explain tokens"
- Fix: "Explain tokens to non-technical readers using one analogy and one practical example for prompt writing."

Mistake 3: Objective is not testable

- "Make it professional"
- Fix: "Write in a neutral, business tone, avoid slang, keep to 150 to 180 words, include a clear call-to-action."

Mistake 4: Objective is overloaded

- "Write a detailed report, make it short, include everything, and be creative."
- Fix: split into phases:
  - Phase 1: outline with headings and bullet counts.
  - Phase 2: write the final version within length limits.

Objective templates you can reuse

Template A: Writing

"Draft a [type of document] for [audience] to achieve [purpose]. Keep it to [length]. Include [required elements]."

Template B: Analysis

"Analyze [inputs] to produce a [deliverable] for [audience]. Output must include [sections]. If evidence is missing, label claims as hypotheses."

Template C: Extraction

"Extract [fields] from the text into a table. Use only the provided text. If a field is missing, write Unknown."

Template D: Teaching

"Teach [topic] to [audience level] so they can [skill outcome]. Include [examples] and a [checklist]."

Audience

If the **Objective** tells the model what to produce, the **Audience** tells it how to produce it. Audience is the difference between a response that is correct in theory and a response that is useful in practice.

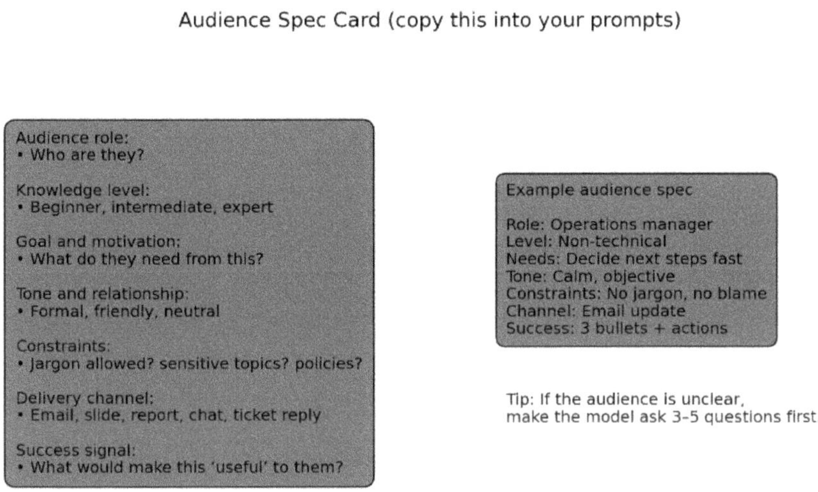

The figure above shows Audience Spec Card. A compact checklist you can paste into prompts to control depth, tone, constraints, and channel.

When audience is missing, the model has to guess:

- how much background to include,
- what tone is appropriate,
- what format is easiest to consume,
- how formal or casual to sound,
- what level of detail is expected.

That guessing is a major cause of "this is not what I wanted" results.

What "Audience" means in prompting

Audience is a set of design decisions

Defining audience is not just naming a person. It is specifying the reader's:

- **Role** (student, executive, developer, customer, researcher)

- **Knowledge level** (beginner, intermediate, expert)
- **Goal and motivation** (learn, decide, buy, approve, troubleshoot)
- **Context and constraints** (time pressure, sensitivity, policy rules)
- **Preferred style** (brief, structured, narrative, technical)
- **Delivery channel** (email, slide, ticket reply, report, chat)

A professional prompt uses audience to reduce the number of choices the model must invent.

Why audience control makes outputs better

1) It sets the right depth

- Beginners need definitions, analogies, and step-by-step structure.
- Experts need precision, assumptions, edge cases, and minimal filler.

If you do not specify audience level, the model often lands in a middle zone that satisfies nobody.

2) It sets the right tone

A "friendly tutor" voice is wrong for a compliance memo. A strict policy tone is wrong for a creative brainstorm. Audience tells the model which voice to use.

3) It sets the right format

Executives often prefer:

- headline summary,
- key risks,
- recommended actions.

Engineers often prefer:

- steps,
- inputs and outputs,
- test cases,
- constraints and edge cases.

4) It reduces hallucination pressure

When you specify a real audience and use case, you can add realistic constraints like:

- "Do not invent facts, label unknowns."
- "Use only the provided notes."
- "If information is missing, ask questions."

This reduces confident filler.

Audience quality checklist

A strong audience specification answers these questions:

- Who is the reader, specifically?
- What do they already know?
- What do they need to do after reading?
- What tone fits the relationship?
- What is the delivery channel?
- What should be avoided (jargon, sensitive language, blame)?
- What does success look like for that audience?

If you can answer those in 30 seconds, your prompting results will improve immediately.

The "Audience Spec" you can paste into any prompt

Use this mini block exactly as written and fill it:

- **Audience role:**
- **Knowledge level:** beginner, intermediate, expert
- **Goal and motivation:**
- **Tone and relationship:** formal, friendly, neutral
- **Constraints:** jargon allowed, sensitivity, policies
- **Delivery channel:** email, slide, report, chat, ticket reply
- **Success signal:** what would make it useful

Example

- Audience role: Operations manager
- Knowledge level: Non-technical
- Goal and motivation: Decide next steps quickly
- Tone and relationship: Calm and objective
- Constraints: No jargon, no blame language
- Delivery channel: Email update
- Success signal: 3 bullets plus 5 actions

Common audience mistakes and fixes

Mistake 1: "Everyone" is the audience

If you write for everyone, the output becomes generic.

Fix:

- pick the primary audience, then add a note for secondary audiences:
    - "Primary: beginners. Secondary: managers who want a short summary."

Mistake 2: Audience role is specified, but knowledge level is not

"Write this for executives" is incomplete. Some executives are technical, many are not.

Fix:

- explicitly set knowledge level and time budget:
    - "Non-technical executive, 60-second read."

Mistake 3: Tone is not aligned with relationship

The same message sounds different when written to:

- a customer,
- a coworker,
- a direct report,
- a regulator.

Fix:

- specify relationship:
    - "Tone: respectful and firm, not apologetic."
    - "Tone: warm and supportive, no corporate jargon."

Mistake 4: Channel is missing

A slide needs short bullets. A report can handle paragraphs. A support ticket needs empathy and policy alignment.

Fix:

- always name the channel:
    - "Deliverable will be pasted into a slide."
    - "This will be sent as a customer support reply."

Professional patterns that use audience well

Pattern A: Dual-layer output for mixed audiences

When you have two audiences, ask for two layers:

- "Start with an executive summary (3 bullets)."
- "Then provide a technical appendix (steps, edge cases)."

Pattern B: Audience-first question mode

When you do not know the audience, make the model ask:

- "Before drafting, ask 3 to 5 questions to confirm audience, tone, and channel. Then write the final output."

Pattern C: Reading-level control

- "Write at grade 8 reading level."
- "Avoid acronyms unless defined on first use."

Context and assumptions

After Objective and Audience, the next reason prompts fail is missing or messy **Context**. Context is the information the model needs to make correct decisions. Assumptions are the rules that tell it what to do when information is missing.

Professional prompting is not about stuffing more text into the prompt. It is about giving the model the *right* context and controlling its assumptions so it does not guess in harmful ways.

What "Context" means in prompting

Context is decision-making information

Context is anything that changes the best answer. It includes:

- **Inputs**: the text, data, notes, requirements, or examples you want it to use.
- **Background**: what situation you are in, what has already happened, what is already decided.
- **Definitions**: how you use terms in your domain.
- **Constraints**: limits that shape the output (time, scope, tone, policy).
- **Environment**: tools, region, audience setting, format destination (email, slides, report).

A simple rule:

If removing a detail would change the answer, it is context worth including.

The problem with context: either too little or too much

Too little context creates guesswork

When critical details are missing, the model fills gaps with plausible defaults. Examples:

- "Write my resume bullet" without role, industry, or achievements.
- "Summarize this report" without what the reader cares about.
- "Create a plan" without timeline, constraints, or resources.

Too much context creates noise and conflicts

When you paste everything, you often add:

- irrelevant history,
- multiple competing requirements,
- repeated instructions in different wording,

- long references that bury the actual task.

This makes the model less consistent because it has to decide what matters. The professional solution is to reduce context to a "working set."

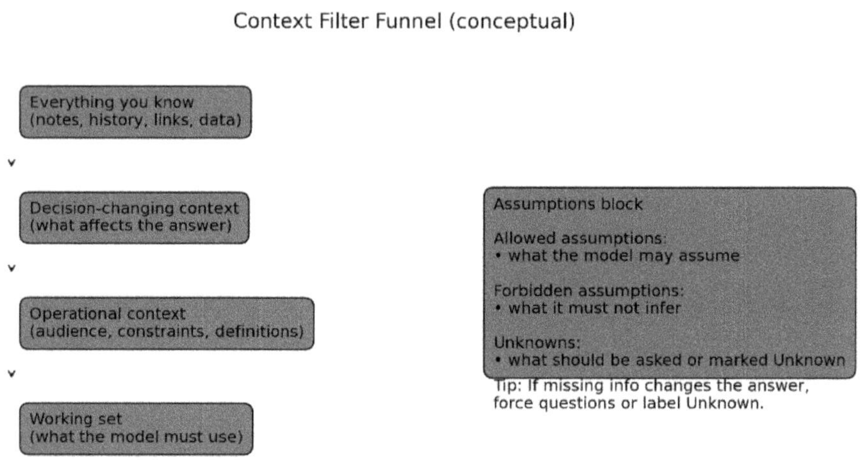

The figure above shows Context Filter Funnel. Reduce raw information into a compact working set, and control assumptions to prevent guesswork

Context filtering: how to provide the right amount

The "Context Filter Funnel"

Use this funnel to compress raw information into what the model should actually operate on:

1. **Everything you know**
   Notes, links, raw text, data dumps.
2. **Decision-changing context**
   Only what affects the outcome.
3. **Operational context**
   Audience, constraints, definitions, formatting needs.
4. **Working set**
   The final, compact block the model should rely on.

If you do this, your prompts become shorter, clearer, and more stable.

Assumptions: the hidden source of hallucinations

What assumptions are

Assumptions are what the model believes it is allowed to fill in. If you do not define assumptions, the model chooses them.

That is why it may:

- invent missing details in a bio,
- choose a country, policy, or legal standard you did not specify,
- pick a tech stack you did not mention,
- fabricate a citation-like reference.

Why assumptions matter more than you think

Many prompts sound complete but contain missing variables.

Example:

"Write a customer support reply for this issue."

Missing variables:

- product name, policy, refund rules, tone constraints, escalation rules, customer segment, region.

The model will guess those unless you control assumptions.

The "Assumptions Block" (copy and paste)

Add this to any professional prompt where missing info would change the answer:

- **Allowed assumptions:**
  What the model may assume if not provided.
- **Forbidden assumptions:**
  What it must not infer or fabricate.
- **Unknown handling:**
  If something is missing, should it ask questions, mark Unknown, or provide options?

Example

- Allowed assumptions: Use US English, neutral professional tone, general audience.
- Forbidden assumptions: Do not invent policies, prices, dates, or personal details.
- Unknown handling: If a missing detail affects the recommendation, ask up to 5 clarifying questions. Otherwise mark Unknown.

Three levels of "unknown handling" you can choose

Level 1: Mark Unknown (fastest, safest)

Use when you need structured outputs and cannot wait for questions.

- "If data is missing, write Unknown."

Best for:

- extraction tables,
- compliance summaries,
- meeting action items.

Level 2: Ask questions first (best quality)

Use when requirements are unclear.

- "Ask 3 to 5 clarifying questions before producing the final output."

Best for:

- plans,
- policies,
- stakeholder communications.

Level 3: Provide options with labeled assumptions (best when you need progress)

Use when you want forward movement even with gaps.

- "Provide 2 to 3 options. For each option, list assumptions."

Best for:

- strategy,
- product decisions,
- architecture proposals.

Common context and assumption mistakes, and fixes

Mistake 1: Context is implied, not stated

- "Write a policy" (which country, which organization type, which constraints?)

Fix:

- Add: "Jurisdiction, organization type, intended audience, enforcement style."

Mistake 2: You paste everything without a working set

Fix:

- Ask the model to compress first:
  - "Summarize the inputs into a working set of facts and constraints, then use only that for the final output."

Mistake 3: Definitions are missing

Words like "professional," "comprehensive," "simple," "robust," "safe" are ambiguous.

Fix:

- Define them in measurable terms:
  - "Professional means neutral tone, structured headings, no slang, 150 to 200 words."

Mistake 4: Assumptions are not controlled

Fix:

- Add a strict rule:
  - "Do not invent facts. If not provided, ask or mark Unknown."

Practical templates

Template A: Context-first prompt block

- Objective:
- Audience:
- Context (facts):
- Definitions:
- Inputs:
- Constraints:
- Assumptions block:

Template B: Long document workflow

1. "Extract the key facts into a table."
2. "List unknowns and questions."
3. "Write the summary using only the fact table."

This keeps the model grounded and reduces invented details.

Constraints and non-goals

After you define **Objective**, **Audience**, and **Context**, the next step is to control the model's behavior with **Constraints** and **Non-goals**.

- **Constraints** tell the model what it must do and what rules it must follow.
- **Non-goals** tell the model what not to do, even if it seems related or tempting.

This pair is one of the fastest ways to reduce:

- rambling and irrelevant content,
- "helpful" additions you did not ask for,

- invented facts and confident speculation,
- format drift,
- scope creep.

If you want predictable, professional outputs, constraints and non-goals are not optional.

What constraints are

Constraints are explicit rules that shape the output. They are not general preferences like "make it good." They are specific requirements that can be checked.

Common categories of constraints:

1. **Format constraints**
    - number of bullets, headings, table columns, schema, order
    - word limits or character limits
2. **Scope constraints**
    - what to cover, what depth, which timeframe
3. **Accuracy constraints**
    - "use only the provided inputs"
    - "do not invent facts"
    - "label hypotheses clearly"
4. **Style constraints**
    - tone (neutral, friendly, formal), reading level, voice
    - banned phrases or wording
5. **Policy and compliance constraints**
    - privacy limits, sensitive topics, internal rules
6. **Process constraints**
    - "ask clarifying questions first"
    - "draft, then self-check against a checklist, then revise"

A good constraint is written so that a reviewer could say Pass or Fail.

What non-goals are

Non-goals are explicit exclusions. They define what is out of scope.

Non-goals prevent the model from:

- drifting into related topics,
- adding features, requirements, or sections you did not request,
- making assumptions that expand scope,
- turning an answer into a lecture.

Non-goals are especially important when the topic is broad, such as "prompt engineering," "business strategy," or "project planning," because broad topics invite drift.

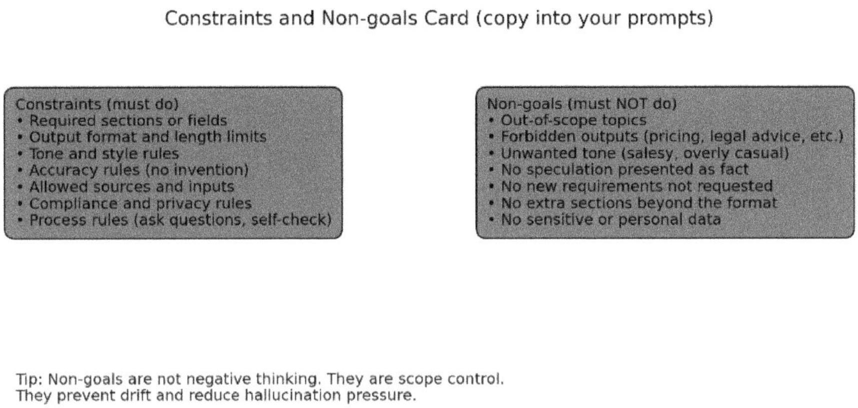

The figure above explains Constraints and Non-goals Card. A compact block to prevent drift and control accuracy, format, and scope.

The "Constraints and Non-goals" cards (copy and paste)

Use this block in your prompts:

Constraints (must do)

- Required sections or fields:
- Output format and length limits:
- Accuracy rules:
- Allowed sources and inputs:
- Tone and style rules:
- Compliance and privacy rules:
- Process rules (questions, self-check):

Non-goals (must not do)

- Out-of-scope topics:
- Forbidden outputs:
- Unwanted tone:
- No speculation presented as fact:
- No extra sections beyond the format:

- No sensitive or personal data:

The scope target mental model

Think of scope like a target:

- The **goal core** is what you are trying to produce.
- **Constraints** are the boundary you must stay within.
- **Non-goals** are the outer area you must avoid.

This framing helps you write non-goals without feeling like you are being "negative." You are simply protecting scope.

How to write strong constraints in 60 seconds

Step 1: Lock the output shape first

Choose one:

- "Return a table with columns: …"
- "Use markdown with these headings in order: …"
- "Write exactly 10 bullets, each 12 to 18 words."

Format constraints reduce variability immediately.

Step 2: Add accuracy and unknown handling

Pick one approach:

- "If missing, write Unknown."
- "Ask up to 5 clarifying questions before drafting."
- "List assumptions separately from facts."

Step 3: Add scope boundaries

Examples:

- "Cover only beginner fundamentals."
- "Do not discuss advanced tooling."
- "Focus on practical templates, not history."

Step 4: Add a self-check

- "Before finalizing, verify you followed every constraint. Fix any violations."

Examples: weak vs strong constraint sets

Weak constraint

"Make it professional and detailed."

Strong constraint set

- Output must include: definition, 5-step method, 2 examples, checklist.
- Length: 900 to 1,100 words.
- Tone: neutral, instructional, no hype.

- Accuracy: do not invent facts or statistics.
- Non-goals: no vendor names, no API details, no advanced topics.
- Verification: confirm each requirement is met before final output.

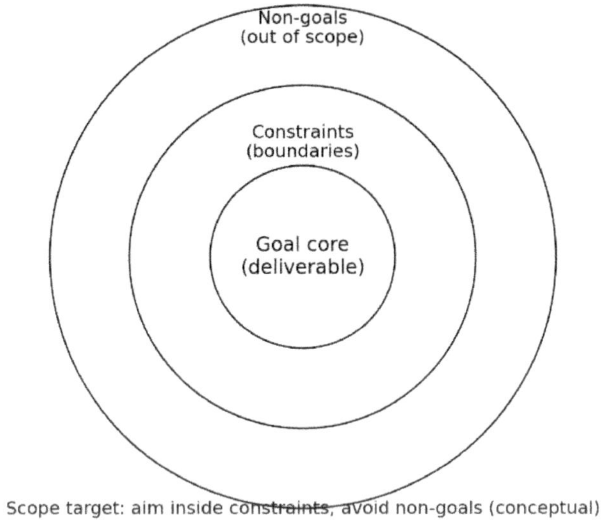

The figure above shows Scope target. Aim inside constraints and explicitly mark non-goals to avoid scope creep

Common mistakes and fixes

Mistake 1: Constraints are too abstract

- "Make it robust."
  Fix: specify what robust means:
- "Include edge cases, limitations, and a verification checklist."

Mistake 2: Non-goals are missing

The model adds bonus sections you did not ask for.

Fix:

- "Do not add extra sections beyond the specified format."

Mistake 3: Conflicting constraints

- "Be extremely short and fully comprehensive."
  Fix: set priority rules:

- "If there is a conflict, prioritize brevity and list missing items as questions."

Mistake 4: Constraints are buried in a long prompt

Fix:

- Put constraints in a dedicated block right before the "Output" line.

Reusable templates

Template A: Format-first constraint block

- Output format:
- Required sections in order:
- Length:
- Non-goals: no extra sections, no speculation, no invented facts.
- Verification: checklist and correction.

Template B: High-stakes accuracy block

- Use only provided inputs.
- Separate facts, assumptions, and hypotheses.
- If uncertain, ask questions or mark Unknown.
- Provide a short verification plan.

Output requirements

If the **Objective** defines what you want, **Output requirements** define what the deliverable must look like when it arrives. This is where professional prompting becomes predictable.

Most disappointing outputs happen because the model had to guess:

- the structure (essay vs bullets vs table),
- the length,
- the ordering of sections,
- the formatting (markdown, JSON, headings),
- what must be included vs optional,
- and how to present the information for the intended channel.

Output requirements remove guesswork. They turn "write something" into "produce a deliverable I can paste into my workflow."

What output requirements are

Output requirements are a concrete specification of the final response. They usually include:

1. **Output type**
   Email, outline, lesson plan, report, checklist, table, JSON, code, SOP.

2. **Structure (order matters)**
   Headings, section names, required fields, table columns, exact sequence.
3. **Length rules**
   Word range, number of bullets, sentence limits, max characters.
4. **Formatting rules**
   Markdown headings, plain text, numbering, schema, code fences.
5. **Content requirements**
   Must include, must avoid, allowed sources, citation behavior.
6. **Tone and reading level**
   Formal, neutral, friendly; beginner or expert; jargon rules.
7. **Acceptance tests**
   A checklist that proves the model complied.

If you define these clearly, the output becomes consistent across runs and easier to evaluate.

Why output requirements stabilize results fast

A model can produce many valid answers to the same prompt. Output requirements narrow the set of valid answers.

- Without requirements: the model chooses its own structure and length.
- With requirements: the model has a clear target and fewer degrees of freedom.

Professional teams treat this like a "contract." If the output does not meet the contract, it is not finished.

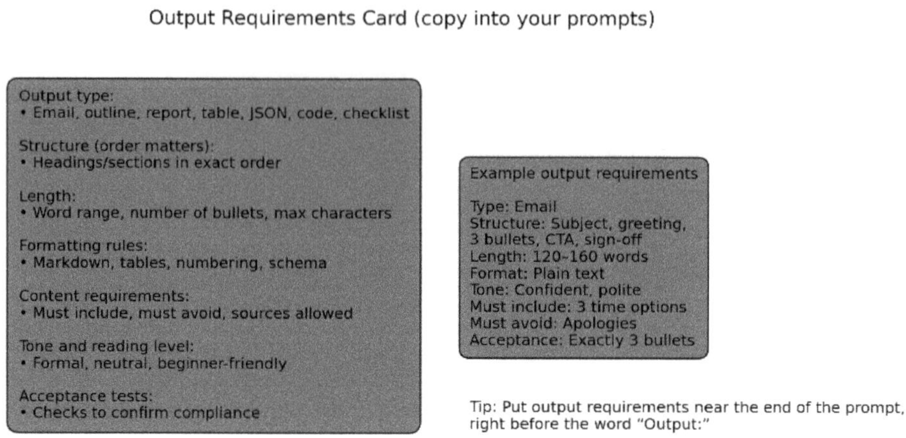

The figure above explains the Output Requirements Card. A compact specification that turns a prompt into a deliverable contract.

The Output Requirements block (copy and paste)

Use this block in your prompts:

- **Output type:**
- **Structure (exact order):**
- **Length:**
- **Formatting rules:**
- **Must include:**
- **Must avoid:**
- **Tone and reading level:**
- **Acceptance tests:**

Example (email)

- Output type: Email
- Structure: Subject, greeting, 3 bullets, call-to-action, sign-off
- Length: 120 to 160 words
- Formatting rules: plain text
- Must include: 3 time options
- Must avoid: apologies, filler
- Tone: confident, polite
- Acceptance tests: exactly 3 bullets, includes 3 time options

Use "output skeletons" when format must be exact

Sometimes you need a consistent structure every time, for example training material, SOPs, reports, or reusable templates. In those cases, give the model a skeleton it can fill.

A skeleton works like a form. It makes drift unlikely because the model is guided line by line.

Output Skeleton (a structure the model can follow)

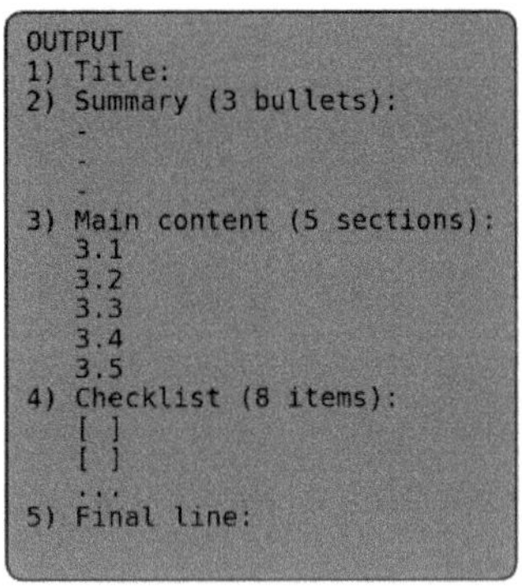

Use skeletons when format must be consistent across runs.

The above figure explains the Output skeleton. Provide a fill-in structure to enforce consistent formatting across runs.

Common output requirements patterns

Pattern A: Fixed sections in order

"Use these headings in this exact order:

1. …
2. …
3. …

Do not add additional headings."

Pattern B: Bullet and length discipline

"Write exactly 8 bullets. Each bullet is 12 to 18 words. No sub-bullets."

Pattern C: Table contract

"Return a table with columns: Field, Value, Evidence, Notes. No extra columns."

Pattern D: Schema output

"Output valid JSON matching this schema. Do not include commentary outside JSON."

Pattern E: Channel-based formatting

- Slides: short bullets, no paragraphs.
- Email: subject, greeting, scan-friendly bullets, clear CTA.
- Report: headings, rationale, recommendations, risks.

The "acceptance test" trick

When a model fails, it often fails quietly. Acceptance tests force the model to check itself.

Add:

- "Before finalizing, confirm you met each requirement. If not, revise."

Example acceptance tests:

- "Contains exactly 5 sections."
- "Word count between 900 and 1,100."
- "No invented facts."
- "Includes 2 examples and 1 checklist."
- "No extra headings beyond the required list."

This improves reliability without needing repeated retries.

Evaluation criteria

A professional prompt does not end at "write the answer." It ends at "write the answer that passes the test."

That test is your **evaluation criteria**. Evaluation criteria define how you will judge whether the output is acceptable. Without them, you end up relying on vibes, and you will re-roll outputs repeatedly hoping one looks right.

Evaluation criteria convert prompting from a one-shot request into a controlled process:

- generate,
- evaluate,
- revise,
- finalize.

This is how professional teams get consistent quality.

What evaluation criteria are

Evaluation criteria are explicit quality standards. They answer:

- What does "good" mean for this task?

- What must be present for the output to be accepted?
- What failures are unacceptable?
- How should the output be scored or checked?

Evaluation criteria can be:

- a checklist (pass/fail),
- a rubric (scored),
- test cases (inputs with expected outputs),
- schema validation (structure must match).

For most beginner-to-professional workflows, a **simple rubric + a minimum score** is enough.

Why evaluation criteria matter in prompt engineering

1) They reduce variability

If the model knows what it will be judged on, it is more likely to produce stable outputs.

2) They prevent silent failures

The model can produce something that looks polished while missing key requirements. Evaluation forces it to notice what is missing.

3) They make iteration efficient

Instead of "try again," you get targeted revision:

- "The output is missing section 3,"
- "Tone is too casual,"
- "Assumptions are not separated from facts."

4) They create reusable prompt systems

Once you have a rubric, you can reuse it across projects and teams to maintain consistent standards.

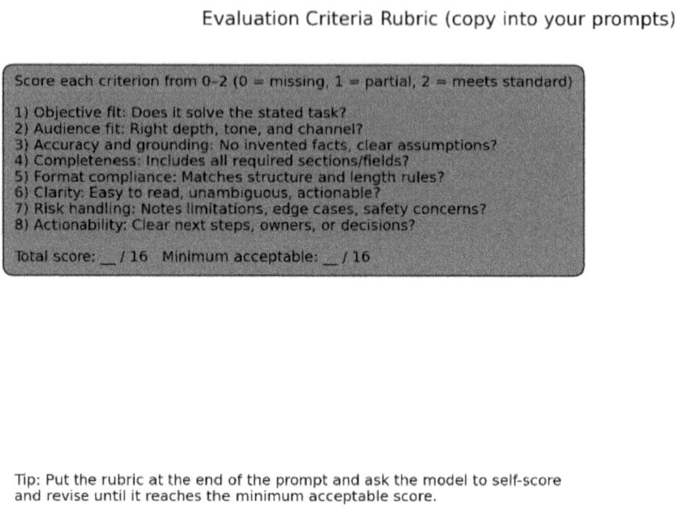

The figure above shows Evaluation Rubric Card. A reusable scoring framework for prompt outputs.

The Evaluation Rubric (copy and paste)

Use this in prompts where quality matters:

Scoring: 0–2 per criterion

0 = missing, 1 = partial, 2 = meets standard.

1. Objective fit: Does it solve the stated task?
2. Audience fit: Right depth, tone, and channel?
3. Accuracy and grounding: No invented facts, clear assumptions?
4. Completeness: Includes all required sections or fields?
5. Format compliance: Matches structure and length rules?
6. Clarity: Easy to read, unambiguous, actionable?
7. Risk handling: Notes limitations, edge cases, safety concerns?
8. Actionability: Clear next steps, owners, or decisions?

Total score: __ / 16

Minimum acceptable: __ / 16

How to use it in a prompt

Add these instructions:

- "Generate a draft."
- "Score it using the rubric."

- "Revise to reach at least 14/16."
- "Return only the final version and the final score summary."

This creates a built-in quality loop.

The Evaluate → Revise loop (professional workflow)

This is the simplest professional loop:

1. Generate a draft.
2. Score it against the rubric.
3. Identify gaps.
4. Revise specifically to close gaps.
5. Re-score.

   Stop when score meets the minimum acceptable threshold, or when the remaining gaps require human input or external verification.

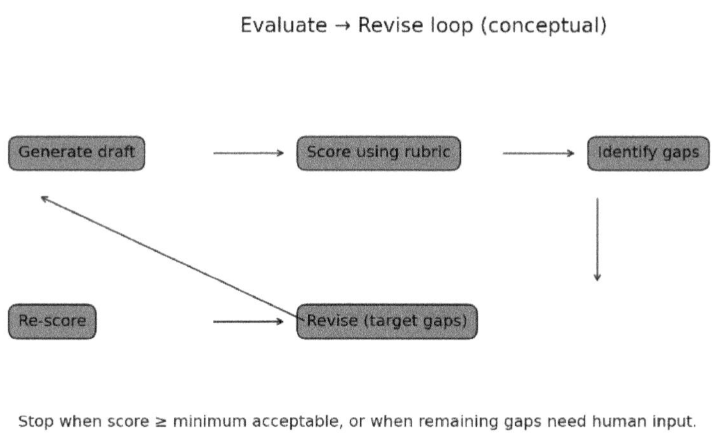

The figure above explains how to Evaluate → Revise loop. Use scoring to drive targeted revisions instead of random re-rolls.

Two types of evaluation criteria you should know

A) Compliance criteria (hard requirements, pass/fail)

Use for:

- formatting, structure, word count,
- "must include" sections,
- safety, privacy, and policy rules.

Example:

- "Exactly 5 bullets."
- "No extra headings."
- "No invented facts."
  If any fail, the output is rejected.

B) Quality criteria (soft requirements, scored)

Use for:

- clarity, usefulness, persuasion,
- depth level,
- reasoning quality and tradeoffs.

These can be improved by iteration.

Professional prompts typically combine both:

- First ensure compliance, then optimize quality.

Common mistakes in evaluation criteria, and fixes

Mistake 1: Criteria are vague

- "Make it better."
  Fix:
- define what better means:
  - "more concise," "more actionable," "more aligned to executives," "include risks."

Mistake 2: No minimum acceptable standard

Fix:

- set a threshold:
  - "Minimum acceptable score is 14/16."

Mistake 3: No instruction to revise

Fix:

- explicitly require revision:
  - "Revise until the minimum score is met."

Mistake 4: Criteria do not match the task

A creative brainstorm should not be judged by the same criteria as a compliance memo.

Fix:

- choose criteria that fit:
  - creativity criteria (novelty, variety, on-brief),
  - business criteria (clarity, feasibility, ROI assumptions),

- technical criteria (correctness, tests, edge cases).

The difference between "asking" and "specifying"

A beginner prompt often *asks* for help. A professional prompt *specifies* a deliverable.

That difference is the dividing line between:

- inconsistent outputs vs repeatable outputs,
- "try again" prompting vs systematic prompting,
- subjective results vs testable results.

When you ask, you are having a conversation. When you specify, you are writing a brief, a contract, or a set of requirements.

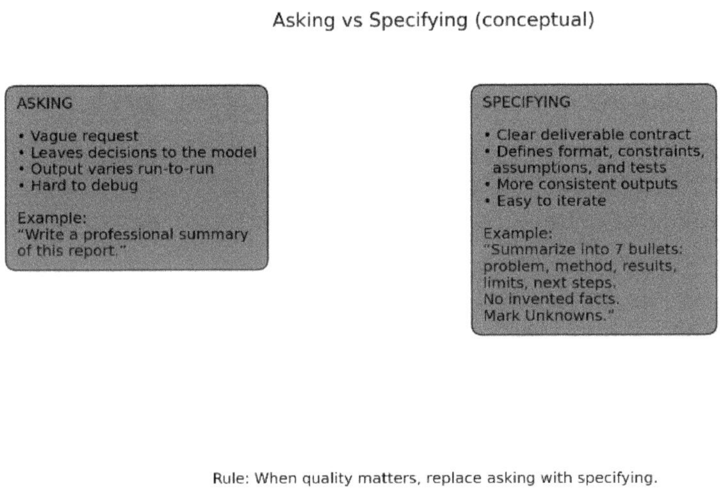

The figure above explains Asking vs specifying. Asking leaves decisions open, specifying creates a deliverable contract.

What "asking" looks like

"Asking" is an open-ended request where you leave key decisions to the model.

Typical signs of asking:

- vague verbs: "help," "improve," "make better," "write something," "analyze,"
- undefined quality terms: "professional," "best," "strong," "detailed,"
- no clear format or acceptance tests,

- no boundaries,
- no handling for missing information.

Asking is fine for:

- quick brainstorming,
- casual drafting,
- exploratory learning,
- when variation is acceptable.

Asking is risky for:

- business deliverables,
- compliance and policy,
- stakeholder communications,
- technical specs,
- anything you must reuse reliably.

What "specifying" looks like

"Specifying" is giving the model a target it can aim for. You define:

- the deliverable,
- the audience and use,
- the output structure,
- constraints and non-goals,
- how to handle unknowns,
- and how the output will be evaluated.

Specification does not mean writing long prompts. It means writing **clear constraints and structure**.

Why asking creates variability

When you ask, you leave decisions open. The model must decide:

- how long to write,
- what structure to use,
- what examples to pick,
- how confident to sound,
- what assumptions to make.

Different runs can make different "reasonable" choices. That is why your outputs change even when the prompt is identical.

Why specifying creates stability

When you specify, you reduce degrees of freedom. The model has fewer places to improvise because you told it:

- what sections must exist,

- what order to use,
- what to include and avoid,
- what to do if information is missing,
- what counts as success.

That leads to more consistent results and easier debugging.

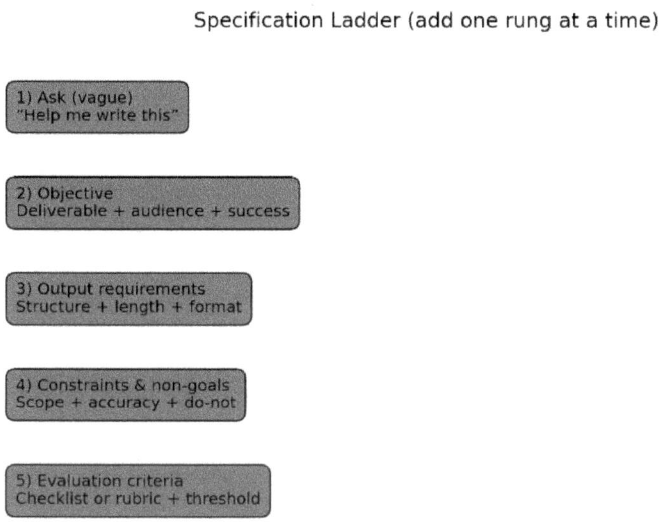

The figure above shows the Specification ladder. Upgrade prompts by adding objective, output requirements, constraints, and evaluation one rung at a time.

The fastest way to convert asking into specifying

A practical conversion recipe:

1. Replace "help me" with a concrete **deliverable**
2. Add **audience and channel**
3. Define **output requirements** (structure, length, format)
4. Add **constraints and non-goals**
5. Add **evaluation criteria** (checklist or rubric)

Two quick before-and-after conversions

Example 1: Summary

Asking

"Summarize this report professionally."

Specifying

"Summarize the report for a non-technical executive. Output exactly 7 bullets in this order: problem, approach, key results, limitations, risks, decisions needed, next steps. Use only the text provided. If something is missing, write Unknown. No extra sections."

Example 2: Planning

Asking

"Make a plan for my project."

Specifying

"Create a 4-week project plan for a marketing launch. Output a table with columns: Week, Milestone, Tasks, Owner role, Dependencies, Risks, Success metric. Keep each task to one sentence. Do not invent dates or resources. If inputs are missing, list up to 5 clarifying questions before the plan."

A useful rule: ask when exploring, specify when delivering

- Exploring: you want options, ideas, variety. Asking is fine.
- Delivering: you want something you can ship, paste, or send. Specify.

Professional work usually starts with asking and ends with specifying:

1. Ask for options.
2. Choose a direction.
3. Specify the final deliverable with constraints and evaluation.

<u>Professional prompt checklist</u>

A chapter on prompt anatomy should end with something the reader can use immediately. This checklist is that tool. It converts the concepts into a repeatable, professional workflow.

A professional prompt is not "long." It is **complete**. Completeness means the model does not need to guess the goal, the reader, the inputs, the boundaries, or what success looks like.

Use the checklist in two ways:

- **Before you prompt**: to write a strong prompt from scratch.
- **After you get a weak output**: to diagnose what you forgot to specify.

Professional Prompt Checklist (copy, fill, paste)

1) Objective

- Did you define the deliverable type?
- Did you include audience or use case?
- Did you define what "done" means?

Template:

- Objective: Create a [deliverable] for [audience/use] that meets [success criteria].

2) Audience

- Who is the reader (role)?
- What is their knowledge level?
- What tone fits the relationship?
- What is the delivery channel?

Template:

- Audience: role, level, tone, channel.

3) Context

- Did you provide decision-changing facts only?
- Did you paste the correct inputs?
- Did you define key terms?

Template:

- Context: facts, inputs, definitions.

4) Assumptions

- What is the model allowed to assume?
- What is forbidden to assume?
- How should unknowns be handled?

Template:

- Assumptions: allowed, forbidden, unknown handling (ask or mark Unknown).

5) Output requirements

- Structure and order specified?
- Length specified?
- Format specified (markdown, table, JSON, plain text)?

Template:

- Output requirements: structure, order, length, format.

6) Constraints and non-goals

- Must include list present?
- Must avoid list present?
- Non-goals clearly marked?

Template:

- Constraints: must include, must avoid, non-goals.

7) Quality rules

- Clarity rules (short paragraphs, define jargon)?

- Safety or compliance rules?
- Style boundaries (no hype, no blame, no fluff)?

Template:

- Quality rules: clarity, safety, style boundaries.

8) Evaluation criteria

- Do you have a checklist or rubric?
- Did you define a minimum acceptable threshold?

Template:

- Evaluation: rubric + threshold, or pass/fail checklist.

9) Verification step

- Did you instruct the model to self-check and fix violations before final output?

Template:

- Verification: self-check against requirements, then revise.

10) Reusability

- Did you name the prompt?
- Did you version it so you can improve it over time?

Template:

- Template name + version (for example "ExecSummary_v1").

Optional power-ups (use when needed)

- Add 1 to 3 examples (good and bad).
- Use an output skeleton when formatting must be exact.
- Use a two-step flow: outline, then draft.
- Use an evaluate and revise loop until the threshold is met.

How to use the checklist for debugging

If the output is wrong, do not rewrite everything. Identify the missing checkbox:

- Wrong structure? Tighten output requirements.
- Too generic? Add constraints and examples.
- Invented facts? Add assumptions and accuracy rules.
- Not usable? Add channel-specific formatting and acceptance tests.
- Inconsistent quality? Add evaluation criteria and a verification step.

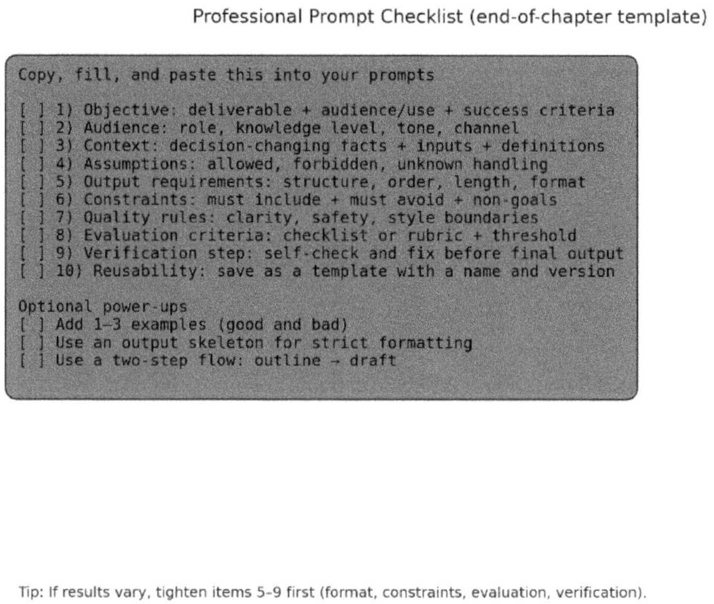

The figure above shows the Professional Prompt Checklist. A reusable end-of-chapter template for building and debugging prompts.

Exercises: rewrite 10 weak prompts into strong ones

This exercise trains the skill that separates casual prompting from professional prompting: turning a vague "ask" into a clear specification.

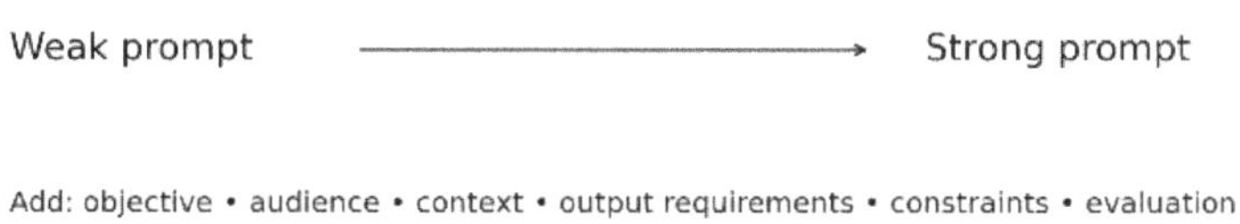

The figure above explains the Prompt upgrade flow. Strong prompts add objective, audience, context, output requirements, constraints, and evaluation.

Use the same upgrade recipe for every item:

- **Objective** (deliverable + purpose)

- **Audience** (role, level, channel)
- **Context** (inputs and definitions)
- **Output requirements** (structure, length, format)
- **Constraints and non-goals** (must do, must not do)
- **Evaluation** (checks or rubric)

How to do the exercise

1. Read the weak prompt.
2. Rewrite it as a strong prompt that a professional would reuse.
3. Compare your rewrite to the sample strong prompt (answer key) below.
4. Notice what you forgot, then revise.

Optional: print the worksheet and do it by hand.

Prompt Rewrite Worksheet (10 items)

	Weak prompt	Strong prompt (rewrite)
1.		
2.		
3.		
4.		
5.		
6.		
7.		
8.		
9.		
10.		

Prompt rewrite worksheet. Use this to rewrite weak prompts into strong, reusable templates.

The 10 weak prompts (student tasks)

Rewrite each into a strong prompt.

1. "Summarize this."
2. "Write a professional email."
3. "Make a plan for my project."
4. "Improve this paragraph."
5. "Explain prompt engineering."
6. "Analyze these numbers."
7. "Write social media posts for my business."
8. "Create interview questions."
9. "Write a policy for my team."
10. "Help me study for an exam."

Answer key: 10 strong prompts (sample solutions)

1) Weak: "Summarize this."

Strong prompt

"Summarize the text below for a non-technical executive. Output exactly 7 bullets in this order: problem, approach, key findings, evidence, limitations, risks, next steps. Use only the provided text. If a detail is missing, write 'Unknown.' No extra sections."

2) Weak: "Write a professional email."

Strong prompt

"Draft an email to a hiring manager requesting an update on my application. Audience: busy professional. Tone: confident and respectful. Length: 120–160 words. Structure: subject line, greeting, 3 bullets (value, interest, request), clear call-to-action, sign-off. Constraints: do not sound desperate, do not invent dates, include 3 time options for a quick call."

3) Weak: "Make a plan for my project."

Strong prompt

"Create a 4-week project plan for launching a beginner course on AI prompt engineering. Audience: project stakeholders. Output as a table with columns: Week, Milestone, Tasks, Owner role, Dependencies, Risks, Success metric. Constraints: keep tasks to one sentence each, include at least 5 risks with mitigations, do not assume budget or team size. If key inputs are missing, ask up to 5 clarifying questions before the table."

4) Weak: "Improve this paragraph."

Strong prompt

"Rewrite the paragraph below for clarity and professionalism. Audience: general readers. Keep meaning unchanged. Constraints: do not add new facts, keep within plus or minus 10 percent of the original length, use simple sentences, remove filler and repetition. Output: revised paragraph plus a 5-bullet list of what you changed and why."

5) Weak: "Explain prompt engineering."

Strong prompt

"Teach 'prompt engineering' to absolute beginners. Goal: the reader can write a basic professional prompt after reading. Output format: 1 short definition, 5-step method, 2 before-and-after examples, 10-item checklist. Constraints: avoid jargon or define it in one sentence, no vendor-specific features, no invented statistics. Length: 800–1,000 words."

6) Weak: "Analyze these numbers."

Strong prompt

"Turn the metrics below into an executive weekly performance update. Output format: (1) headline summary in 3 bullets, (2) KPI table with columns Metric, This week, Last week, Change, Interpretation, (3) 3 hypotheses labeled as hypotheses, (4) risks and watch-outs, (5) 5 recommended actions with owner role and urgency. Constraints: use only provided numbers, do not invent causes, if uncertain state what data would confirm. Inputs: [paste metrics]."

7) Weak: "Write social media posts for my business."

Strong prompt

"Write 12 social posts for LinkedIn promoting a beginner-friendly course on AI prompt engineering. Audience: professionals new to AI. Tone: helpful, not salesy. Output format: table with columns Post #, Hook, Body, CTA, Hashtags. Constraints: each post 60–120 words, no exaggerated claims, include 1 practical tip per post, vary angles (career, productivity, learning, mistakes, templates). Non-goals: no pricing, no competitor mentions."

8) Weak: "Create interview questions."

Strong prompt

"Create interview questions for a junior data analyst role. Output: 12 questions grouped into 4 categories (SQL, statistics, communication, problem-solving). For each question include: what a strong answer includes, a red flag answer, and difficulty level (easy/medium). Constraints: no trick questions, focus on practical work scenarios, avoid company-specific tools."

9) Weak: "Write a policy for my team."

Strong prompt

"Draft a one-page AI usage policy for an internal team. Audience: mixed technical and non-technical staff. Output format: Purpose, Allowed uses, Prohibited uses, Data handling, Verification requirements, Approval/escalation, Examples (3 allowed, 3 prohibited). Constraints: do not include legal advice, avoid jargon, clearly state that confidential data must not be pasted into external tools. Ask 5 clarifying questions first about industry, jurisdiction, and data sensitivity, then draft."

10) Weak: "Help me study for an exam."

Strong prompt

"Create a 7-day study plan for my exam on [subject]. Audience: student with limited time. Ask 3 questions first (topics, exam format, time per day). Then output: daily schedule table, key topics per day, practice questions plan, spaced repetition plan, and a final-day review checklist. Constraints: realistic workload, include at least one active recall activity per day, include two mock tests."

Chapter 3. Clarity beats cleverness

Avoid ambiguity. Define terms, scope, and boundaries.

A professional prompt is not impressive because it is clever. It is impressive because it is **clear**. Clear prompts are easier for the model to follow, easier for you to evaluate, and easier to reuse.

Clever prompts often rely on implication, inside jokes, or "you know what I mean" phrasing. That works with humans because humans share context and can ask follow-up questions naturally. Models can ask questions, but only if you tell them to, and they cannot reliably infer your intent when key details are missing.

Clarity beats cleverness because it reduces guesswork.

Why ambiguity breaks prompts

Ambiguity creates **multiple valid interpretations**. The model must pick one interpretation, often without knowing which you intended. Different runs can pick different interpretations, which produces inconsistent output.

Ambiguity usually enters through three doors:

1. **Ambiguous terms**: "professional," "simple," "comprehensive," "best," "robust."
2. **Ambiguous scope**: "cover prompt engineering," "explain this," "include everything."
3. **Ambiguous boundaries**: what to exclude, what not to assume, what to avoid.

If a word requires interpretation, it is not an instruction. It is a risk.

Ambiguity triggers. Replace vague words with measurable definitions.

Ambiguity triggers: replace or define them

Common vague terms and how to fix them

Instead of: "Make it professional."

Define: "Neutral business tone, no slang, short paragraphs, headings, 150 to 200 words."

Instead of: "Keep it simple."

Define: "Grade 8 reading level, short sentences, define jargon in one sentence, one example."

Instead of: "Make it comprehensive."

Define: "Cover A, B, and C, include 2 examples, include edge cases, include a checklist."

Instead of: "Analyze these metrics."

Define: "Output KPI table, list hypotheses, list risks, recommend actions with owners."

Professional prompts replace subjective words with measurable tests.

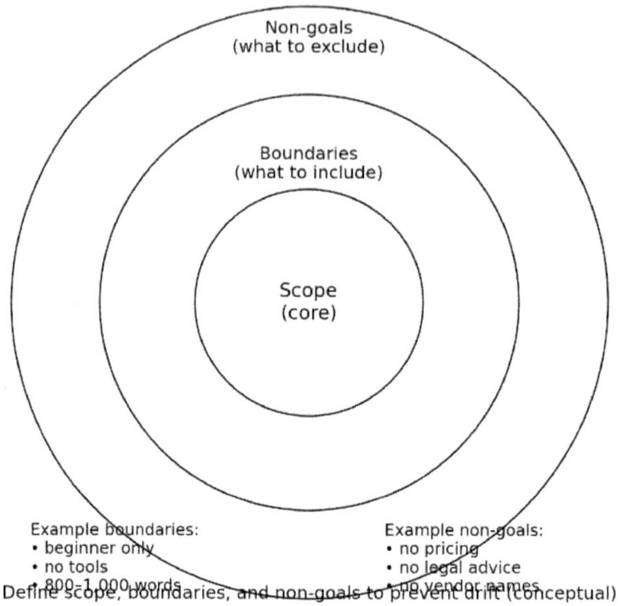

Scope and boundaries. Define what to include and what to exclude to prevent drift.

Define scope, boundaries, and non-goals

Many prompt failures are not about wrong facts. They are about scope drift. The model keeps writing because it is trying to be helpful, and without boundaries it will expand into adjacent topics.

Scope (what the work is about)

Scope defines the core topic and depth.

Examples:

- "Beginner-only explanation of prompt components."
- "Executive summary of the report, not the full report."
- "Focus on practical templates, not history."

Boundaries (what to include)

Boundaries are inclusion rules that stop the model from guessing what you want.

Examples:

- "Include exactly two before-and-after examples."
- "Include a checklist with 10 items."
- "Use only the provided text."

- "Only cover the last 30 days of data."

Non-goals (what to exclude)

Non-goals prevent drift and reduce hallucination pressure.

Examples:

- "Do not mention vendor names."
- "Do not provide legal advice."
- "Do not invent statistics."
- "Do not add extra sections beyond the structure."

The "define it as a test" technique

A reliable professional move is to turn ambiguous words into acceptance tests.

Example conversion

Ambiguous: "Write a strong introduction."

Defined as tests:

- 120 to 150 words,
- one analogy,
- one practical example,
- no hype words,
- ends with one-sentence takeaway.

This approach makes "strong" measurable, and measurability makes the output stable.

Practical templates you can reuse

Template A: Define key terms

"Definitions for this task:

- 'Professional' means: …
- 'Simple' means: …
- 'Comprehensive' means: …"

Template B: Scope and boundaries block

- Scope:
- Include:
- Exclude (non-goals):
- Unknown handling: ask questions or mark Unknown.

Template C: Ask questions when ambiguity is unavoidable

"Before drafting, ask up to 5 clarifying questions about audience, scope, and success criteria. Then produce the output using the final answers."

Quick self-check: the clarity test

Before sending a prompt, ask:

- Could two people interpret this differently?
- Did I define my ambiguous words as tests?
- Did I specify what to include and what to avoid?
- Did I tell the model what to do if information is missing?

If any answer is "no," tighten the prompt.

Replace abstract words with measurable instructions

Abstract words feel efficient, but they are expensive in practice. When you write "make it professional" or "keep it simple," you are outsourcing key decisions to the model. The model will choose a definition that seems reasonable, but your definition might be different. That gap is where inconsistent outputs come from.

Professional prompting replaces abstract words with **measurable instructions**. Measurable instructions are easy to follow and easy to verify. They also make your prompts reusable because the target stays stable across runs and across different models.

Why abstract words cause unpredictable outputs

Abstract words are not instructions, they are interpretations.

Examples of abstract words:

- professional, strong, better, simple, clear
- comprehensive, robust, optimized, modern
- concise, detailed, high quality

Each of these can mean multiple things:

- "professional" could mean formal tone, or it could mean structured headings, or it could mean short and direct.
- "comprehensive" could mean long, or it could mean covering specific categories, or it could mean adding examples and edge cases.
- "robust" could mean defensive checks, or it could mean handling edge cases, or it could mean being adaptable.

If you do not define the meaning, the model guesses. If the model guesses, results vary.

Replace abstract words with measurable instructions

Abstract word	What it usually means	Measurable instruction
professional	neutral, business tone	150-200 words; headings; no slang; 1 CTA
simple	easy to understand	grade 8 level; short sentences; define terms once
comprehensive	covers key areas	cover A,B,C; 2 examples; 5 pitfalls; checklist
concise	short, no fluff	max 120 words; 6 bullets; no paragraphs
detailed	adds depth	include steps; edge cases; assumptions; 2 scenarios
robust	handles variations	include constraints; failure modes; validation checks
best	optimize for a goal	rank 3 options by rubric; show tradeoffs; recommend 1

Tip: Write measurable instructions as constraints + counts + structure + acceptance tests.

The figure above shows Abstract to measurable. Replace interpretation words with structure, counts, boundaries, and tests.

The rule: define abstract words as tests

A measurable instruction should answer:

- What structure should the output have?
- How long should it be?
- What must be included?
- What must be avoided?
- How will we confirm it is correct?

If you can mark it Pass or Fail, it is measurable.

Quick conversion table: abstract to measurable

Use this pattern:

- Abstract word → what you really mean → measurable instruction.

Examples:

- "professional" → neutral business tone → 150–200 words, headings, no slang, one clear call-to-action.
- "simple" → easy to understand → grade 8 reading level, short sentences, define terms once, one example.
- "best" → optimize for a goal → compare 3 options using a rubric, show tradeoffs, recommend 1.

The measurable instruction formula

A reliable formula you can reuse:

Structure + Counts + Boundaries + Examples + Acceptance test

Structure

Tell the model the shape:

- headings in order, table columns, schema, bullet format.

Counts

Numbers reduce drift:

- word range, number of bullets, number of examples, max sentences.

Boundaries

Define scope and non-goals:

- what to include, what to exclude, what not to assume.

Examples

Give 1 to 3 examples when style matters:

- a mini example of the tone and format you want.

Acceptance test

Add verification:

- "Before finalizing, check all constraints and fix violations."

Measurable instruction formula:

Structure + Counts + Boundaries + Examples + Acceptance test

The figure above shows Measurable instruction formula. A compact recipe for turning vague requests into specifications.

Before-and-after conversions (practical)

Example 1

Abstract: "Write a professional summary."

Measurable:

"Write a summary for a non-technical executive. Output exactly 6 bullets. Each bullet is 12–18 words. Include: problem, approach, result, limitation, risk, next step. No invented facts. If missing, write Unknown."

Example 2
Abstract: "Make it concise."
Measurable:
"Max 120 words. Use 5 bullets only. No paragraphs. No filler phrases. End with one action sentence."
Example 3
Abstract: "Make it comprehensive."
Measurable:
"Cover exactly these 5 topics: A, B, C, D, E. Include 2 examples and 5 common pitfalls. End with a 10-item checklist. 900–1,100 words."
Common mistakes when making instructions measurable
Mistake 1: Only adding length limits
Length helps, but it does not control structure or content.
Fix:

- add structure, must include, must avoid, and acceptance tests.

Mistake 2: Using numbers without defining content
"Write 10 bullets" can still produce random bullets.
Fix:

- define what each bullet must represent or the categories they must cover.

Mistake 3: Measurable but conflicting constraints
"Write 100 words and include everything."
Fix:

- set priorities:
    - "Prioritize brevity. If something cannot fit, list it as questions."

<u>Add "success conditions" and "stop conditions"</u>

A clear prompt tells the model what to do. A professional prompt also tells it **when the job is finished** and **when to stop adding extra content**.
These two ideas solve a common problem: the model keeps expanding. It adds bonus sections, extra advice, additional examples, or a long conclusion. Sometimes that extra content is useful, but often it breaks your format, violates length limits, or drifts out of scope.

- **Success conditions** define what "done" means.
- **Stop conditions** prevent drift after the deliverable is complete.

Think of them as the finish line and the guardrail.

What are success conditions?

Success conditions are explicit requirements that must be true when the output is complete. They are the easiest way to turn vague quality into measurable completion.

Success conditions often include:

- required sections present in the correct order,
- exact counts (bullets, examples, steps),
- word range or character limit,
- required fields in a table or JSON schema,
- required elements included (risks, assumptions, next steps),
- verification or checklist included.

A success condition is written so you can verify it quickly.

Examples of success conditions

- "Done when the answer contains exactly 7 bullets in the specified order."
- "Done when output is valid JSON matching the schema."
- "Done when you include 2 before-and-after examples and a 10-item checklist."
- "Done when unknowns are labeled Unknown and assumptions are separated."

What are stop conditions?

Stop conditions are explicit limits and "do not do" rules that prevent the model from continuing beyond the deliverable.

Stop conditions often include:

- no extra sections beyond the defined structure,
- stop after the checklist or table,
- do not add commentary, prefaces, or explanations,
- do not exceed the word limit,
- do not include citations unless provided,
- do not speculate or invent facts.

Stop conditions are especially important when:

- you need strict formatting,
- you are producing content for slides, forms, or templates,
- you want predictable length and structure,

- you are extracting structured information.

Side-by-side examples: success vs stop

Use this pairing style:

- Success conditions tell the model what must exist.
- Stop conditions tell the model what must not happen after completion.

Success conditions and stop conditions

Success conditions (done when...)	Stop conditions (do NOT...)
All required sections present in order	Do not add extra sections
Word count 900-1,100; exactly 2 examples	Do not exceed 1,100 words
Uses only provided inputs; Unknown for missing	Do not invent facts or citations
Outputs valid JSON matching schema	Do not output commentary outside JSON
Ends with a checklist of 10 items	Stop after checklist; no appendices

The figure above shows Success vs stop conditions. Define "done" and define "do not continue."

The professional pattern: generate, check, stop

This is a powerful instruction to add near the end of a prompt:

- "Generate the output."
- "Check it against the success conditions."
- "If any condition fails, revise until all pass."
- "Stop immediately when all conditions are met."

It reduces drift and improves compliance.

How to write success and stop conditions (fast method)

Step 1: Convert requirements into tests

Instead of: "Make it detailed."

Write: "Include 5 steps, 2 examples, 3 edge cases."

Step 2: Add a finish line

Add: "Done when: …"

Examples:

- "Done when all required headings appear in order."
- "Done when the table has these columns and at least 8 rows."

Step 3: Add guardrails that prevent extra content

Add: "Do not: …"

Examples:

- "Do not add extra headings."
- "Stop after the checklist."
- "No appendices, no extra commentary."

Step 4: Add a self-check instruction

- "Before final output, verify every success condition. Fix violations."

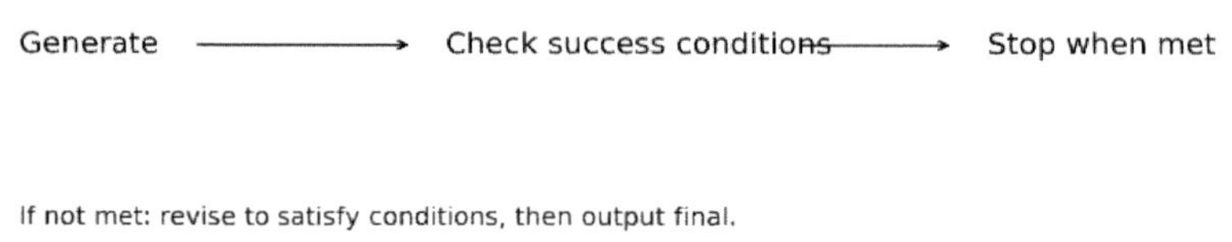

The figure above shows Generate → check → stop. Use verification to prevent drift.

Copy-paste block you can reuse

Success conditions (done when):

- Required structure present in order: …
- Length and counts satisfied: …
- Must include items present: …
- Accuracy rules satisfied: …
- Output is valid format: …

Stop conditions (do not):

- Do not add extra sections beyond structure.
- Do not exceed length limits.
- Do not invent facts, statistics, or citations.
- Stop after the final required section.
- Do not add commentary outside the requested format.

Verification:

- "Check success conditions, revise if needed, then output final and stop."

Common mistakes and fixes

Mistake 1: Only using stop conditions

If you only say "do not exceed 200 words," the model still does not know what must be included.

Fix:

- pair stop conditions with success conditions.

Mistake 2: Success conditions that are not measurable

- "Done when it is high quality."
  Fix:
- define quality using counts and structure.

Mistake 3: Conflicting completion criteria

- "Include everything" plus "max 150 words."
  Fix:
- set priority:
  - "Prioritize brevity. If something does not fit, list it as questions."

Common ambiguity traps

Some words look harmless, but they cause a huge percentage of prompt failures because they hide missing requirements. The model will still answer, but it will answer using its own default interpretation, which may not match yours.

Four of the biggest ambiguity traps are:

- **best**
- **optimize**
- **detailed**
- **quick**

Each one contains a hidden question. If you do not answer the hidden question in the prompt, you should expect variability.

The rule: expose the hidden question

When you see a trap word in your prompt, pause and ask:

- What decision is the model being asked to make?

- What criteria should it use?
- What constraints must it respect?
- What does success look like?

Then turn that into measurable requirements.

Ambiguity traps table

Use this table as a prompt-writing checklist: whenever you use one of these words, replace it with a measurable alternative.

Common ambiguity traps and how to fix them

Trap word	Hidden question	Measurable replacement
best	Best for what goal?	Rank 3 options by rubric; show tradeoffs; recommend 1
optimize	Which metric and constraints?	Maximize X under constraints Y; provide baseline and improved version
detailed	What details matter?	Include steps + examples + edge cases + assumptions; specify counts
quick	How quick and for whom?	60-second version: 5 bullets; 5-minute version: 1 page; specify time budget

The figure above shows Ambiguity traps. Replace "best," "optimize," "detailed," and "quick" by answering their hidden questions with measurable requirements.

Trap 1: "Best"

Why it causes ambiguity

"Best" always means "best according to a goal," but prompts often omit the goal. Best for speed? cost? quality? safety? simplicity? persuasion? compliance?

Hidden questions

- Best for what objective?
- Who is judging "best"?
- What tradeoffs are allowed?

Professional replacement patterns

- "Rank the top 3 options using this rubric, then recommend one."
- "Choose the best option for this audience and goal, and explain tradeoffs."

Copy-paste fix

"Provide 3 options. Score each 0–2 on: accuracy, clarity, cost, time, risk. Recommend the highest score and explain one tradeoff."

Trap 2: "Optimize"

Why it causes ambiguity

"Optimize" implies a measurable metric, but prompts often do not define the metric, baseline, or constraints. Without those, the model guesses what optimization means.

Hidden questions

- What metric are we maximizing or minimizing?
- What constraints must not be violated?
- What is the baseline?

Professional replacement patterns

- "Maximize X under constraints Y and Z."
- "Provide baseline and improved version, and explain changes."

Copy-paste fix

"Optimize for readability and speed of scanning. Constraints: 120–160 words, 5 bullets, no jargon. Provide: original, revised, and a checklist showing constraints met."

Trap 3: "Detailed"

Why it causes ambiguity

"Detailed" can mean longer, more technical, more examples, more steps, more edge cases, or more justification. The model picks one at random unless you specify what kind of detail you want.

Hidden questions

- What type of detail matters: steps, examples, edge cases, assumptions, data, rationale?
- How much detail is appropriate for the audience?
- What format should detail take?

Professional replacement patterns

- "Include steps + 2 examples + 5 edge cases + assumptions."

- "Give implementation steps, then risks and mitigations."

Copy-paste fix

"Write a step-by-step guide with: 7 steps, 2 worked examples, 5 common mistakes, and 1 checklist. Audience: beginners. Length: 900–1,100 words."

Trap 4: "Quick"

Why it causes ambiguity

"Quick" is meaningless without a time budget and audience. Quick for a developer might be different from quick for an executive.

Hidden questions

- How quick: 30 seconds, 2 minutes, 10 minutes?
- What format fits that time budget?
- Should it sacrifice completeness or detail?

Professional replacement patterns

- "Give a 60-second version in 5 bullets."
- "Give a 2-minute version, then provide a deeper appendix."

Copy-paste fix

"Create two versions:

1. 60-second version: 5 bullets, max 90 words.
2. 5-minute version: one page with headings and one example. Stop after version 2."

A simple practice drill

Take any prompt you wrote recently and search for these words:

- best, optimize, detailed, quick.

For each, answer the hidden question directly in the prompt using:

- measurable goals,
- structure and counts,
- constraints and non-goals,
- and acceptance tests.

You will see output consistency improve immediately.

<u>Lab, convert vague tasks into testable deliverables</u>

This lab trains a core professional skill: turning a vague request into a deliverable you can verify. You will practice converting "do something good" language into a clear contract with acceptance tests.

A **testable deliverable** has two properties:

1. You can tell if it is correct without debating taste.

2. Someone else could run the same prompt and get a similar result.

The lab goal

You will take vague tasks like:

- "Make this better,"
- "Give me the best approach,"
- "Write a quick summary,"

and convert them into:

- a specific deliverable type,
- a defined structure,
- measurable counts,
- clear boundaries and non-goals,
- and an acceptance checklist.

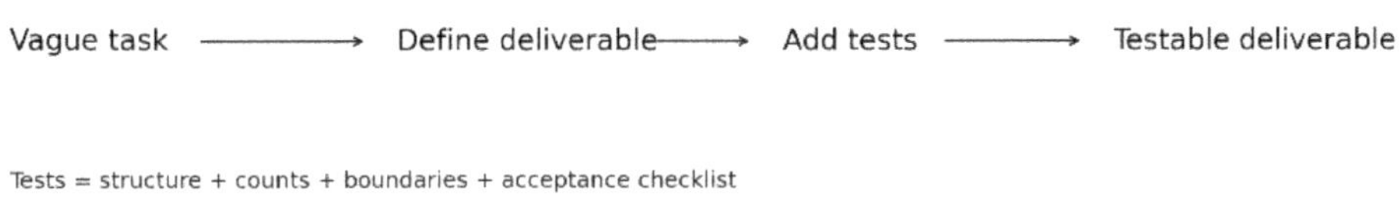

The figure above shows Vague to testable pipeline. Define the deliverable, then add acceptance tests.

The conversion pipeline

Use this simple pipeline every time:

1. **Vague task**
   Identify the abstract words (best, quick, detailed, professional).
2. **Define deliverable**
   Name the output type and its purpose.
   Examples: "executive email," "one-page cheat sheet," "table," "SOP," "JSON."
3. **Add tests**
   Tests = structure + counts + boundaries + acceptance checklist.
4. **Testable deliverable**
   You now have something you can evaluate objectively.

The worksheet

Print this page or recreate it in your notes and fill it out.

Columns:

- Vague task
- Testable deliverable
- Acceptance tests

Lab worksheet: convert vague tasks into testable deliverables

	Vague task	Testable deliverable	Acceptance tests
1.			
2.			
3.			
4.			
5.			

The figure above shows Worksheet. Convert vague tasks into testable deliverables with measurable acceptance tests.

Part A. Do the lab with 5 vague tasks

Below are five vague tasks. Rewrite each into a testable deliverable. Do not worry about perfect wording. Focus on making it measurable.

Task 1

Vague: "Summarize this quickly."

Convert to a testable deliverable:

- Deliverable: "60-second executive summary"
- Acceptance tests:
  - Exactly 5 bullets

- Max 90 words
- Bullets must cover: problem, approach, result, limitation, next step
- No invented facts, Unknown if missing
- Stop after the 5 bullets

Task 2

Vague: "Write the best introduction for my chapter."

Convert to a testable deliverable:

- Deliverable: "Chapter introduction for beginners"
- Acceptance tests:
  - 150 to 180 words
  - One definition sentence + one analogy + one practical example
  - Tone: neutral, instructional
  - No hype words, no promises
  - Ends with a one-sentence takeaway

Task 3

Vague: "Optimize this email."

Convert to a testable deliverable:

- Deliverable: "Rewritten email optimized for response rate"
- Acceptance tests:
  - Subject line included
  - 120 to 160 words
  - Contains one clear ask and one deadline
  - Contains exactly 3 bullets listing value or context
  - Removes filler, no repeated points
  - Provide final version only

Task 4

Vague: "Give me a detailed plan."

Convert to a testable deliverable:

- Deliverable: "4-week plan table"
- Acceptance tests:
  - Table columns: Week, Milestone, Tasks, Owner role, Dependencies, Risks, Metric
  - Exactly 4 rows for weeks, at least 3 tasks per week
  - Includes at least 5 risks total with mitigations

- Assumptions listed separately
- If missing key inputs, ask up to 5 questions first

Task 5

Vague: "Analyze these metrics."

Convert to a testable deliverable:

- Deliverable: "Weekly performance review"
- Acceptance tests:
  - KPI table with This week, Last week, Change, Interpretation
  - 3 hypotheses labeled as hypotheses
  - 5 recommended actions with owner role and urgency
  - No invented causes, list what data would confirm
  - Ends with a short "watch list" of 3 items

Part B. The template you should reuse

When you convert vague tasks, write your prompt using this structure:

- Objective: deliverable + purpose
- Audience: role, level, channel
- Inputs: paste or reference source material
- Output requirements: structure, order, length, format
- Constraints: must include, must avoid, non-goals
- Success conditions: done when...
- Stop conditions: do not...
- Acceptance tests: checklist

Part C. Quick scoring

For each rewritten prompt, ask:

- Can I verify it in 30 seconds?
- Does it remove abstract words or define them as tests?
- Does it include both success and stop conditions?
- Would a colleague interpret it the same way?

If not, add counts, structure, and boundaries.

Chapter 4. Controlling output format like a pro

How to request structure

Most "bad" outputs are not actually wrong, they are just the wrong shape. You wanted a checklist, you got an essay. You wanted JSON, you got commentary plus JSON. You wanted a table, you got mixed formatting. Professional prompting treats format as a **contract**:

- you specify the structure and rules,
- the model fills it in,
- you verify compliance,
- then you stop.

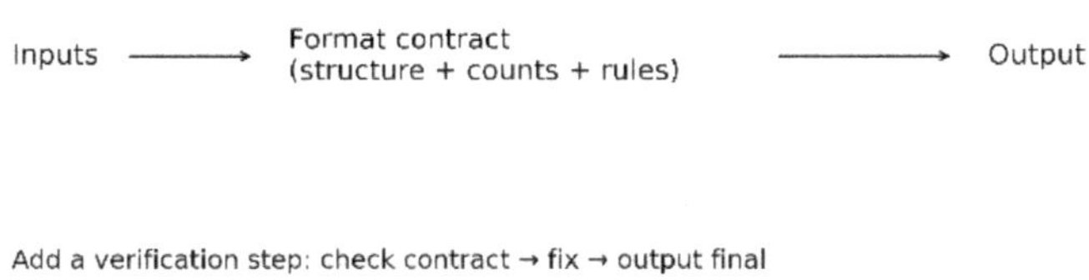

The figure above shows format contract. Define structure and rules, verify, then output and stop.

The core principle: structure is part of the objective

When you request structure, do not say "format it nicely." Say exactly what "nice" means:

- section names and order,
- counts (bullets, rows, items),
- length limits,
- allowed and forbidden elements,
- and whether extra text is allowed.

How to request structure (prompt snippets)

Format	Minimal structure request
Headings	Use headings in this exact order: H1, H2, H3. Do not add others.
Bullets	Write exactly 8 bullets. Each bullet 12-18 words. No sub-bullets.
Tables	Return a table with columns: A, B, C. Include at least 6 rows.
JSON	Output valid JSON only matching this schema. No extra keys or text.
Schemas	Validate: required fields, types, enums; fix errors then output final.

Tip: Put structure requirements near the end, right before "Output:".

The figure above shows structure request snippets. Minimal patterns for headings, bullets, tables, JSON, and schemas.

1) Requesting headings like a professional

When to use

- chapters, reports, documentation, lesson plans, SOPs,
- anything that must scan well.

The professional pattern

- Define the headings in the exact order.
- Specify what to do inside each section (bullets, paragraphs, tables).
- Add a stop condition: do not add extra headings.

Prompt snippet

"Use these headings in this exact order:

1. Overview
2. Key concepts
3. Examples
4. Common mistakes
5. Checklist

   Rules: Do not add or rename headings. Keep each section under 150 words."

Extra stability trick

Add counts per section:

- "Section 2 must contain exactly 5 bullets."
- "Section 3 must contain exactly 2 examples."

2) Requesting bullets without drift

When to use

- executive summaries, action lists, slide content, quick guides.

The professional pattern

- Specify the number of bullets.
- Specify bullet length or sentence count.
- Specify whether sub-bullets are allowed.
- Specify the content categories each bullet must cover.

Prompt snippet

"Write exactly 8 bullets. No sub-bullets.

Each bullet is 12–18 words.

Bullets must cover in order: goal, audience, context, constraints, example, risks, next steps, checklist reminder."

Common failure and fix

Failure: "Here are some bullets" but count varies.

Fix: "Exactly N bullets" plus "verify the count before output."

3) Requesting tables that are actually usable

When to use

- planning, tracking, comparisons, extraction tasks, analytics summaries.

The professional pattern

- Define columns explicitly.
- Define row count rules.
- Define how to handle missing values.
- Forbid extra columns and narrative text.

Prompt snippet

"Return a table with columns: Item, Owner role, Due date, Status, Risk, Notes.

Include at least 10 rows.

If a value is missing, write Unknown.

Do not add commentary before or after the table."

Table quality tips

- Keep each cell short: "one sentence max per cell."
- Use consistent units: "dates must be YYYY-MM-DD."

4) Requesting JSON the right way

When to use

- automation, integrations, structured extraction, downstream parsing.

The professional pattern

- Demand JSON only, no extra text.
- Provide a schema or at least an explicit key list.
- Specify types and allowed values.
- Add rules for missing data.
- Add validation instructions.

Prompt snippet

"Output valid JSON only. No markdown, no explanation.
Keys must be exactly: title, summary, risks, next_steps.
Types: title is string, summary is array of 3 strings, risks is array of objects, next_steps is array of objects.
If unknown, use null. Do not invent facts."

A simple schema-style example

```
{
  "title": "string",
  "summary": ["string", "string", "string"],
  "risks": [{"risk": "string", "impact": "low|medium|high", "mitigation":
"string"}],
  "next_steps": [{"action": "string", "owner_role": "string", "due_date":
"YYYY-MM-DD|null"}]
}
```

Common failure and fix

Failure: model wraps JSON in markdown or adds commentary.
Fix: "JSON only, no code fences, no extra text" plus "if you add any non-JSON text, revise."

5) Requesting schemas and strict validation

"Schema" means more than "some keys." It means the output must satisfy rules:

- required fields exist,
- types are correct,
- enums use only allowed values,

- no additional properties,
- formatting constraints (date format, email format).

The professional pattern

- Provide rules as a checklist.
- Require a validation pass before final output.
- Require correction if any rule fails.

Prompt snippet

"Validate the output against these rules before responding:

1. Required fields present: A, B, C
2. Types: A string, B integer, C array of objects
3. Enums: status ∈ [planned, in_progress, done]
4. No extra keys

If any rule fails, fix and output only the corrected final JSON."

The "Output:" anchor that improves compliance

Place your structure contract near the end of the prompt, right before the word **Output:**.

Example:

- Objective and context first
- Constraints and non-goals next
- Output requirements and schema last
- Then: "Output: …"

This ordering reduces the chance that format rules get buried.

Verification: the pro move that prevents format drift

Add a short verification step:

- "Before finalizing, verify structure, counts, and schema rules. Fix violations."

This single line prevents most issues:

- wrong bullet count,
- extra headings,
- extra text around JSON,
- missing table columns.

Guardrails

Format control is not only about asking for headings or JSON. It is also about preventing the three most common failures:

1. **Length drift**: too long, too short, or inconsistent across runs.
2. **Structure drift**: missing sections, reordered sections, extra sections.
3. **Content drift**: includes things you explicitly did not want, or invents things you did not provide.

Professional prompts handle this with **guardrails**, and they put guardrails near the end of the prompt so the model sees them as a final contract.

The three-rail model

Think of guardrails as three rails you can tighten:

- **Length rail**: how much the model is allowed to output.
- **Structure rail**: what shape the output must follow.
- **Content rail**: what must not appear.

When outputs drift, tighten one rail at a time, then add a verification step.

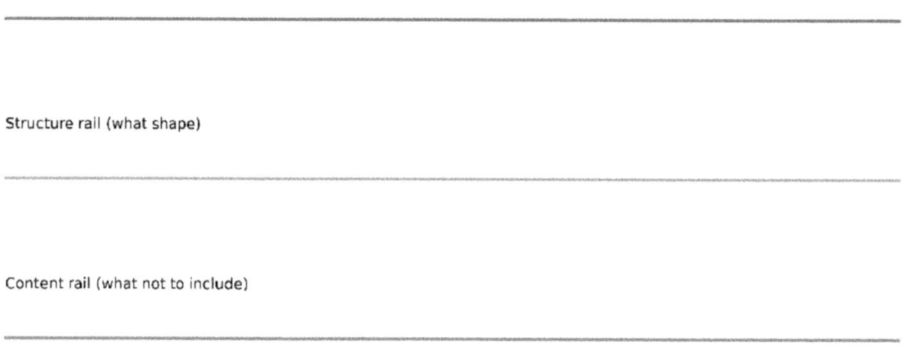

The figure above shows the three-rail model. Control length, structure, and forbidden content to prevent drift.

Guardrail 1: Length limits

What to specify

- **Word range**: "120–160 words"
- **Maximum words**: "Max 200 words"
- **Bullet count**: "Exactly 7 bullets"
- **Sentence count**: "Max 10 sentences"
- **Character limits** (for UI fields): "Max 280 characters"

Why "range" often works better than "exact"

Exact word counts can force unnatural writing. A range gives flexibility while still controlling length.

Strong prompt snippets

- "Length: 900–1,100 words."
- "Exactly 8 bullets, no sub-bullets."
- "Max 120 words, plain text."

Add the verification clause

"Verify the output meets the length and count constraints. If not, revise."

Guardrail 2: Required sections

What to specify

- Headings and order: "Use these headings in this exact order."
- Required elements inside each section: "Section 2 contains exactly 5 bullets."
- Required fields: "Include fields A, B, C."
- Required columns: "Return a table with columns X, Y, Z."

Strong prompt snippets

- "Use headings in this order: Overview, Key Points, Risks, Next Steps. Do not add headings."
- "Output a table with columns: Item, Owner role, Due date, Status. At least 8 rows."
- "Include exactly two examples labeled Example 1 and Example 2."

The most important structure guardrail

Add a stop condition:

- "Do not add extra sections beyond the required structure."

Guardrail 3: Forbidden content

Forbidden content guardrails prevent the model from "helpful additions" and reduce hallucination pressure.

Common forbidden content rules

- No extra sections, no appendix, no commentary.
- No invented facts, statistics, citations, or sources.
- No personal or sensitive data.
- No legal or medical advice (if that is not the task).
- No vendor names or competitor mentions (if requested).
- No policy-violating content.

Strong prompt snippets

- "Use only the provided input. Do not invent facts. If missing, write Unknown."
- "No citations, no links, no references."
- "Do not include private data or personal identifiers."

- "Do not add explanations outside the requested format."

The guardrails checklist (copy and paste)

Use this block near the end of your prompt:

- Length limits: word range, bullet count, sentence limits
- Required sections: headings in order, required fields
- Forbidden content: no extra sections, no invented facts, no sensitive data
- Stop condition: stop after final required section
- Verification: self-check and revise if needed

Format Guardrails Checklist (copy into your prompts)

```
GUARDRAILS

[ ] Length limits
    • word range or max words
    • exact bullet count or max sentences

[ ] Required sections
    • headings in exact order
    • required fields / columns

[ ] Forbidden content
    • no extra sections
    • no invented facts or citations
    • no sensitive data
    • no policy-violating content

[ ] Stop condition
    • stop after final required section

[ ] Verification
    • self-check: counts, order, forbidden content
    • revise if any check fails
```

The figure above shows Guardrails checklist. Copy-paste guardrails to enforce format compliance.

Best practice: place guardrails right before "Output:"

A reliable order:

1. Objective
2. Audience
3. Context
4. Guardrails (length, structure, forbidden content)
5. Output:

This keeps the "contract" close to the generation moment.

A complete guardrails example (short)

"Guardrails:

- Length: 120–160 words.
- Structure: Subject line, greeting, 3 bullets, call-to-action, sign-off.
- Forbidden: no apologies, no invented dates, no extra sections.
- Verification: confirm bullet count is exactly 3 and word count is in range. Revise if not.
  Output: …"

"Do not" instructions that actually work

"Do not" rules are essential for professional prompting, but many fail because they are vague. The model cannot reliably follow a prohibition unless you also tell it what to do instead, where to stop, and how to verify.

"Do not" instructions that actually work

Weak "do not"	Why it fails	Stronger replacement
Do not be verbose.	No measurable limit.	Max 120 words; 6 bullets; no paragraphs.
Do not include extra info.	"Extra" is subjective.	Only include A,B,C. Exclude everything else.
Do not invent facts.	Model may still guess.	Use only provided inputs. If missing, write Unknown.
Do not use jargon.	Jargon not defined.	Define any term on first use; grade 8 reading level.
Do not add anything else.	Often ignored without stop rule.	Stop after section 4. Output only the table.

The figure above shows Do-not rule formula. Pair prohibitions with measurable alternatives, a stop point, and a self-check.

A working "do not" rule has four parts:

1. **Forbidden behavior** (what must not happen)
2. **Measurable alternative** (what to do instead)

3. **Stop point** (where the output must end)
4. **Self-check** (verify and fix violations)

Why weak "do not" instructions get ignored

Weak "do not" rules fail for predictable reasons:

- They are subjective: "do not add extra info"
- They lack limits: "do not be verbose"
- They lack alternatives: "do not use jargon"
- They lack stop points: the model continues after it is done
- They lack verification: the model does not notice it broke the rule

The fix is to convert prohibitions into measurable constraints and pair them with a stop condition.

Weak vs strong "do not" rules

Key pattern:

- Replace vague prohibitions with concrete structure, counts, and boundaries.

Do-not rule formula:

Forbidden behavior + Measurable alternative + Stop point + Self-check

The figure above shows weak vs strong do-not rules. Make prohibitions measurable and enforce them with stop conditions.

The "Do not" patterns that work in practice

Pattern 1: Replace "do not be verbose" with a measurable cap

Instead of:

- "Do not be verbose."

Use:

- "Max 120 words. Exactly 6 bullets. No paragraphs. Stop after bullet 6."

Why it works:

- The model can measure length and count bullets.

Pattern 2: Replace "do not include extra info" with explicit inclusion rules

Instead of:

- "Do not include extra information."

Use:

- "Include only A, B, and C. Exclude everything else. If A, B, or C is missing, write Unknown. Stop after section C."

Why it works:

- The model knows what "in scope" means.

Pattern 3: "Do not invent facts" needs an input rule and unknown handling

Instead of:

- "Do not invent facts."

Use:

- "Use only the provided inputs. Do not add facts, numbers, dates, or citations not present in the inputs. If information is missing, write Unknown or ask up to 5 clarifying questions."

Why it works:

- It removes the pressure to fill gaps and tells the model what to do when it cannot know.

Pattern 4: "Do not use jargon" must define what counts as jargon

Instead of:

- "Do not use jargon."

Use:

- "Write at grade 8 reading level. If you must use a technical term, define it in one sentence the first time it appears. Avoid acronyms unless expanded on first use."

Why it works:

- It converts "jargon" into enforceable rules.

Pattern 5: "Do not add anything else" must include a stop condition

Instead of:

- "Do not add anything else."

Use:

- "Stop after the final required section. Output only the table. Do not include preface, commentary, or conclusion."

Why it works:

- A stop condition tells the model exactly where the output ends.

The professional "Do not" block (copy and paste)

- **Forbidden:**
  - Do not add extra sections beyond the required structure.
  - Do not exceed the word or bullet limits.
  - Do not invent facts, statistics, dates, or citations.
  - Do not include sensitive or personal data.

- **Instead do:**
  - Include only the specified fields or headings.
  - Mark missing values as Unknown or ask questions first.
- **Stop point:**
  - Stop after the final required section, no appendices.
- **Self-check:**
  - Verify structure, counts, and forbidden items. Revise if any violation exists.

Where "do not" rules belong in a prompt

Put them near the end, right before "Output:", along with length and structure requirements. This makes them part of the final contract.

Recommended ordering:

1. Objective and context
2. Output requirements
3. Do not rules + stop point
4. Verification
5. Output:

<u>Validation prompts, "Check your output against this schema"</u>

When your output must be machine-readable or consistently structured, you should not rely on a single instruction like "output JSON." Professional prompts add a validation step:

- generate a draft,
- validate against a schema and constraints,
- fix violations,
- output only the final validated result.

This reduces the most common format failures:

- missing required fields,
- extra keys,

- wrong types,
- invalid enums,
- broken date formats,
- extra commentary around JSON or tables.

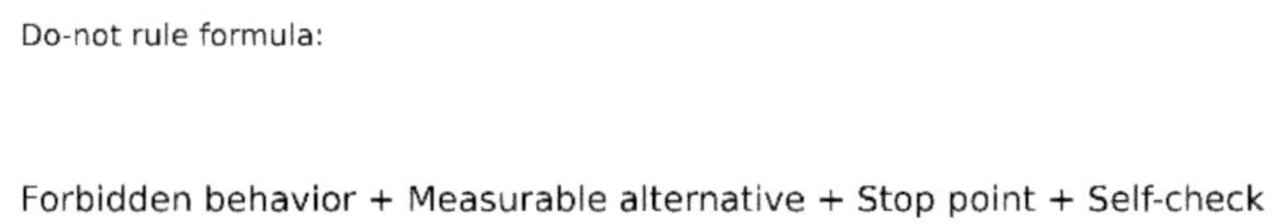

The figure above shows how to Validate → fix loop. Repeat until the output passes the schema checks.

What "schema validation" means in plain language

A schema is a set of rules the output must follow. It can be formal (JSON Schema) or simple (a checklist of required keys and types). Either way, validation means:

- check the output against rules,
- correct any violations,
- repeat until it passes.

You are not asking the model to "be careful." You are giving it a test and requiring it to pass.

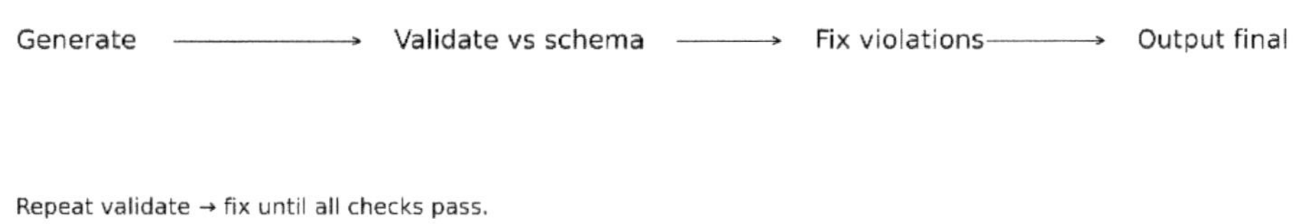

The figure above shows validation prompt template. A reusable block for schema-based output control.

The validation prompt template (copy and paste)

Use this pattern in your prompt, near the end:

1. Generate a draft output.
2. Check it against the schema and constraints.

3. If any rule fails, correct and re-check.
4. Return only the final validated output.

This creates a built-in quality gate.

What to validate (the practical checklist)

Even without formal JSON Schema, you can validate the rules that usually matter:

Structure checks

- required sections or fields exist
- no extra sections or fields
- order is correct (if order matters)

Type checks

- string vs number vs boolean
- arrays vs objects
- null allowed or not

Enum checks

- allowed values only (for example status must be planned, in_progress, done)

Format checks

- dates use one format (YYYY-MM-DD)
- IDs follow a pattern
- emails or URLs (if required)

Count checks

- exactly N bullets
- at least N rows
- max N items in an array

Forbidden content checks

- no invented facts
- no citations unless provided
- no extra commentary outside the required format

Strong prompt snippets you can reuse

JSON only, validated

"Output valid JSON only, no markdown and no extra text.
Validate against the schema below. If any check fails, fix and re-validate.
Return only the final JSON."

Table output, validated

"Return a table with columns A, B, C and at least 8 rows.
Validate: columns match exactly, no extra columns, missing values are 'Unknown.'
If validation fails, correct the table and output only the corrected table."

Mixed format with strict boundaries

"Output two sections only:

1. Summary (5 bullets)
2. JSON block matching schema
   Validate bullet count and JSON schema. If any violation exists, revise.
   Stop after the JSON."

Why validation prompts improve reliability

Validation prompts work because they force the model into a different mode:

- not only generating,
- but also checking constraints and correcting errors.

They also reduce "format drift" across reruns because the model is repeatedly steered back to the same structure until it passes.

<u>Practice, 12 format drills</u>

These drills build the muscle of format control. The goal is not creativity, it is **compliance**. You will practice writing prompts that consistently produce the same structure across multiple runs.

How to use the drills:

1. Pick one drill.
2. Run it 3 to 5 times with the same input.
3. Score compliance.
4. Tighten guardrails until you get consistent passes.

Rules for all drills

For every drill, include these three lines at the end of your prompt:

- "Verify the output matches the required format."
- "If any rule fails, fix the output and re-check."
- "Return only the final output and stop."

This turns each drill into a validation loop.

Practice: 12 format drills (track your consistency)

#	Drill type	Format rules (what to enforce)
1	JSON extraction	JSON only; required keys; null for unknown; no extra text
2	JSON with enums	Enums only; types correct; no extra keys; validate then output
3	Outline (H1/H2)	Headings in order; no extra headings; max 2 sentences per section
4	Outline + bullets	Each H2 has exactly 4 bullets; no sub-bullets; 12-18 words each
5	Rubric	0-2 scoring; 8 criteria; total and threshold included
6	Email	Subject; greeting; 3 bullets; CTA; sign-off; 120-160 words
7	SOP steps	Title; purpose; scope; 7 steps; prerequisites; risks; checklist
8	Table report	Table columns fixed; min 8 rows; Unknown for missing; no commentary
9	Comparison table	3 options; columns: pros/cons/risk/cost/time; recommend 1
10	Meeting notes	Agenda; decisions; action items table; owners; due dates
11	FAQ	10 Q/A pairs; each answer ≤ 60 words; consistent tone
12	Checklist	Exactly 12 items; grouped into 3 sections; stop after item 12

The figure above shows format drills overview. A quick index of drills and the format rules each one trains.

The 12 format drills

Drill 1: JSON extraction (simple)

Goal: extract facts into JSON.

Prompt requirements:

- JSON only, no extra text.
- Keys: title, summary, entities, dates.
- Unknown values must be null.

Input suggestion: a short news paragraph or a project note.

Drill 2: JSON with enums and types (strict)

Goal: enforce types and allowed values.

Prompt requirements:

- JSON only.
- status must be one of: planned, in_progress, done.
- due_date must be YYYY-MM-DD or null.
- No extra keys.

Drill 3: Outline using headings (H1 and H2)

Goal: stable hierarchical structure.

Prompt requirements:

- Headings in exact order.
- Only H1 and H2.
- Max 2 sentences per section.
- No extra headings.

Drill 4: Outline plus bullets (counts)

Goal: consistent content density.

Prompt requirements:

- Each H2 has exactly 4 bullets.
- No sub-bullets.
- Each bullet is 12–18 words.

Drill 5: Rubric output

Goal: produce an evaluation rubric.

Prompt requirements:

- 8 criteria, each scored 0–2.
- Define what 0, 1, 2 mean for each criterion.
- Provide total score and a threshold.

Drill 6: Professional email format

Goal: force email structure.

Prompt requirements:

- Subject line.
- Greeting.
- Exactly 3 bullets.
- Call-to-action.
- Sign-off.
- 120–160 words.

Drill 7: SOP (standard operating procedure)

Goal: structured operational instructions.

Prompt requirements:

- Title, purpose, scope, prerequisites.
- Exactly 7 steps (numbered).
- Risks and mitigations.
- End with a checklist.

Drill 8: Table report (fixed columns)

Goal: enforce tabular structure.

Prompt requirements:

- Table columns fixed in order.
- Minimum 8 rows.
- Missing values are "Unknown."
- No commentary outside the table.

Drill 9: Comparison table (3 options)

Goal: compare consistently.

Prompt requirements:

- 3 options only.
- Columns: pros, cons, risk, cost, time.
- Final line: recommend 1 option with one reason.

Drill 10: Meeting notes template

Goal: repeatable meeting capture.

Prompt requirements:

- Agenda (bullets).
- Decisions (numbered).
- Action items table: action, owner role, due date.
- Open questions (max 5).

Drill 11: FAQ format

Goal: consistent Q/A output.

Prompt requirements:

- Exactly 10 Q/A pairs.
- Each answer max 60 words.
- Tone consistent and beginner-friendly.
- No extra sections.

Drill 12: Checklist output (strict stop)

Goal: hard stop discipline.

Prompt requirements:

- Exactly 12 items.
- Group into 3 sections with headings.
- Stop after item 12, no conclusion.

Drill score tracker (repeat 5 runs and record compliance)

Drill #	Run 1	Run 2	Run 3	Run 4	Run 5	Notes

The figure above shows the score tracker. Repeat the same drill across multiple runs and record compliance.

Scoring and repetition

The fastest way to improve is to run the same drill multiple times and track pass rate.

Scoring options:

- **Pass/Fail**: did it meet all format rules?
- **0–2**: 0 failed, 1 partial, 2 fully compliant.

Target:

- reach **5 out of 5 compliant runs** before moving to the next drill.

Troubleshooting when a drill fails

If you get failures, tighten guardrails in this order:

1. Add exact counts (bullets, sections, rows).
2. Add “no extra sections” and a stop condition.
3. Add “output only” rules (especially for JSON).
4. Add a self-check and revision loop.

Part 2. Core prompting patterns (your toolbox)

Chapter 5. The 5 core patterns

Direct instruction prompts

A **direct instruction prompt** is the simplest and most powerful pattern in your toolbox. It is used when you already know what you want and you want the model to produce one best deliverable in a reliable format.

Direct instruction works because it reduces ambiguity. You specify the job, the context, the output shape, and the constraints. The model completes the work inside your boundaries.

This is the default pattern for professional use cases:

- emails, reports, summaries, lesson content, SOPs
- extraction into tables or JSON
- rewriting and editing
- planning drafts and checklists

Direct instruction prompt template (copy and fill)

```
DIRECT INSTRUCTION PROMPT

Objective:
- Produce: <deliverable>
- For: <audience/channel>
- Success: <what good looks like>

Context:
- Inputs: <paste or reference>
- Definitions: <key terms>

Output requirements:
- Structure: <headings/fields in order>
- Length: <word range or counts>
- Format: <markdown/table/JSON>

Constraints:
- Must include: <A, B, C>
- Must avoid: <X, Y, Z>
- Unknown handling: <ask questions or write Unknown>

Verification:
- Check output against requirements and fix violations.

Output:
<begin here>
```

The figure above shows when to use direct instruction prompts. Best for clear tasks with one target deliverable.

What a direct instruction prompt is

A direct instruction prompt is a structured brief that includes:

- **Objective:** what to produce and why
- **Audience:** who it is for and how it will be used
- **Context:** the inputs and definitions
- **Output requirements:** structure, length, format
- **Constraints:** must include, must avoid, non-goals, unknown handling
- **Verification:** check and fix before final output

It is "direct" because it does not ask the model to brainstorm first or explore options. It tells it to produce the deliverable.

When to use this pattern

Use direct instruction when:

- the task is clear,
- you want one best answer,
- consistency matters more than variety,
- format matters.

When not to use it:

- You do not know what you want yet. Use clarifying questions or option generation.
- You need multiple alternatives. Use option generation with a rubric.
- You need the model to follow a process across steps. Use a multi-step workflow prompt.

The professional template (copy and fill)

You can paste this template into your book as the standard pattern:

DIRECT INSTRUCTION PROMPT

Objective: produce <deliverable> for <audience/channel>, success = <definition of good>.

Context: inputs, definitions.

Output requirements: structure, length, format.

Constraints: must include, must avoid, unknown handling.

Verification: self-check and fix violations.

Output: begin.

Three examples (same pattern, different jobs)

Example 1: Executive summary

"Objective: Summarize the text below for a non-technical executive.
Output requirements: Exactly 7 bullets in this order: problem, approach, results, evidence, limitations, risks, next steps. Max 120 words.
Constraints: Use only the provided text. If missing, write Unknown. No extra sections.
Verification: Check bullet count and order, revise if needed.
Output: …"

Example 2: Table extraction

"Objective: Extract requirements from the meeting notes into a table.
Output requirements: Table columns must be Requirement, Owner role, Deadline, Risk. Minimum 8 rows.
Constraints: Use only provided notes. Unknown if missing. No commentary outside the table.
Verification: Ensure columns match exactly and row count is at least 8.
Output: …"

Example 3: Rewrite with boundaries

"Objective: Rewrite the paragraph for clarity for general readers.
Output requirements: One revised paragraph, then 5 bullets describing changes.
Constraints: Do not add new facts. Keep within ±10% length. Grade 8 reading level.
Verification: Check length and no-new-facts rule.
Output: …"

Common failure modes, and fixes

Failure: output drifts into extra content

Fix:

- add "Do not add extra sections"
- add "Stop after the final required section"

Failure: wrong format (bullets become paragraphs, JSON includes commentary)

Fix:

- state "Output only X, no extra text"
- add a validation line: "If you output anything else, revise"

Failure: invented facts when inputs are incomplete

Fix:

- "Use only provided inputs"

- "Unknown if missing" or "ask up to 5 clarifying questions first"

Role and persona prompts

Role and persona prompts tell the model to respond "as if" it were a particular kind of expert, worker, or communication style. This pattern is popular because it can quickly improve tone, structure, and relevance. It also has pitfalls, especially when users treat "role" as a guarantee of truth or authority.

Used correctly, role and persona prompts help you:

- align tone and vocabulary with an audience,
- choose the right depth and framing,
- adopt a consistent voice across outputs,
- produce domain-appropriate formats (briefs, memos, lesson plans, triage notes).

Used incorrectly, they can:

- increase overconfidence and hallucination risk,
- create bias, stereotyping, or inappropriate assumptions,
- conflict with your own instructions (format, scope),
- add fluff when you need precision.

Role vs persona (simple distinction)

- **Role**: functional expertise and task framing.
  Example: "Act as a cybersecurity analyst writing an incident summary."
- **Persona**: voice, tone, and communication style.
  Example: "Write in a calm, encouraging, beginner-friendly tone."

You often want role + persona together, but role should never override facts.

What role and persona prompts are good for

1) Audience alignment

If your audience is executives, customers, or beginners, the role prompt helps the model choose vocabulary and structure.

Example:

"Write as a technical writer for non-technical stakeholders."

2) Consistent voice at scale

Brand tone and internal style consistency are where persona prompts shine.

Example:

"Use a concise, friendly, no-hype tone. Avoid jargon. Use short paragraphs."

3) Domain-appropriate deliverables

Some roles come with standard formats.

Examples:

- Product manager: PRD sections
- Consultant: executive summary, findings, recommendations
- Teacher: lesson objectives, activities, assessment
- QA engineer: test cases, steps to reproduce, expected vs actual

Role prompts help the model choose the right "shape" of output faster.

The professional way to write role and persona prompts

The biggest mistake is to write a role prompt as a costume:

"Act as a world-class genius expert who always gives perfect answers."

That makes outputs sound confident, not correct.

Instead, specify:

- domain and task,
- audience and channel,
- boundaries and uncertainty rules,
- output requirements.

A safe, professional template

"Role: You are a <job role> performing <task>.

Persona: Write in a <tone> style for <audience>.

Boundaries: Use only provided inputs, label assumptions, ask questions if needed.

Output: <format requirements>."

Example prompts (usable patterns)

Example 1: Role improves structure

"Role: You are a policy analyst.

Task: Draft a one-page internal policy summary from the text below.

Persona: Neutral and clear.

Constraints: Use only the text provided. No legal advice. Unknown if missing.

Output: Headings in order: Purpose, Scope, Rules, Exceptions, Examples, Next steps."

Example 2: Persona improves readability

"Persona: You are a patient instructor.

Task: Explain these concepts to a beginner using simple language.

Constraints: Define jargon on first use, include one analogy and one

example.
Output: 5 short sections with headings and a 10-item checklist."

Example 3: Role plus evaluation

"Role: You are a QA engineer.
Task: Convert the requirements below into test cases.
Output: Table with columns: Test ID, Precondition, Steps, Expected result, Priority.
Constraints: No assumptions. If requirement is unclear, list questions first."

When to avoid role and persona prompts

There are situations where role prompts do more harm than good.

1) When factual accuracy is the priority

Role prompts can increase confidence and narrative coherence, which can mask uncertainty.

Avoid:
"Act like a doctor and diagnose me."
Prefer:
"Provide general information, list possibilities, and tell me what questions to ask a clinician."

2) When the task is already unambiguous and highly structured

If you have strict output requirements, the role prompt may add unnecessary flavor.

Avoid:
"Act like a charismatic marketing guru" for JSON extraction.
Prefer:
"Output valid JSON only matching this schema."

3) When role cues invite bias or stereotypes

Avoid personas tied to demographic traits or stereotypes. Keep personas professional and task-based.

Avoid:
"Write like a stereotypical X."
Prefer:
"Write in a direct, respectful tone for a busy executive."

4) When role conflicts with constraints

If you ask for "friendly conversational tone" but also demand strict legal compliance, you may get drift.

Fix:
Make the hierarchy explicit:
"Follow format and safety rules first. Persona is secondary."

5) When you are using the model for verification

If you want it to check structure or schema, roles can distract.
Prefer:
"Validate against this checklist and correct violations."

How to make role prompts safer and more reliable

Use these guardrails with roles:

1. **Grounding rule**
   "Use only the provided inputs. Do not invent facts. If missing, say Unknown."
2. **Uncertainty rule**
   "When uncertain, ask clarifying questions or label assumptions."
3. **No authority claim**
   Do not ask the model to claim credentials or imply real-world authority.
4. **Format contract**
   Role is not a substitute for structure. Still specify headings, counts, schema.
5. **Evaluation step**
   "Check the output against the rubric and revise if needed."

Quick checklist: should you use a role prompt here?

Use role/persona if you need:

- a specific voice, tone, or audience fit,
- domain-standard structure,
- consistent writing style across many outputs.

Skip role/persona if you need:

- strict schema compliance,
- high-stakes factual accuracy without sources,
- minimal wording and maximum precision,
- pure extraction or validation tasks.

Copy-paste mini blocks (ready to use)

Role block

"Role: You are a <role> completing <task>."

Persona block

"Persona: Tone is <tone>. Style is <rules>."

Safety and grounding block

"Use only provided inputs. No invented facts. Unknown if missing. Ask questions if needed."

Priority block

"Priority order: format and constraints first, then tone and persona."

If you use role and persona prompts this way, they become a controlled tool instead of a costume.

Step-by-step decomposition prompts

Step-by-step decomposition prompts are for tasks that are too big, too fuzzy, or too error-prone to do in one pass. Instead of asking for the final answer immediately, you ask the model to break the work into smaller steps, execute them in order, and produce a final deliverable.

This pattern improves:

- correctness (fewer skipped requirements),
- completeness (covers all parts of the task),
- consistency (repeatable workflow),
- debuggability (you can see where it went wrong).

It is especially useful for:

- planning and project work,
- complex writing (chapters, reports, lesson plans),
- analysis and decision support,
- transforming messy inputs into structured outputs,
- multi-constraint tasks (format + tone + content + risk).

What "decomposition" means

Decomposition means converting a task like:

"Write a chapter on prompt engineering for beginners"

into a sequence like:

1. define goal and audience,
2. choose outline and section objectives,
3. draft section by section,
4. check against requirements,
5. revise and finalize.

A model can do this internally, but when you explicitly ask for decomposition, you reduce the chance it will jump to an answer that is coherent but incomplete.

Two forms of decomposition prompts

1) Plan then execute (most common)

You ask for an explicit plan and then the final output.

Best when:

- you want transparency,
- you may want to edit the plan,
- the output is long.

2) Execute with internal steps, output only final

You ask the model to follow steps but not to reveal its internal reasoning.

Best when:

- you want a clean final deliverable,
- you still want the benefits of process control.

The professional decomposition template (copy and fill)

Step-by-step decomposition prompt

Objective: Produce <deliverable> for <audience/channel>.

Inputs: <paste or reference>.

Constraints: <must include, must avoid, non-goals>.

Output requirements: <structure, length, format>.

Process:

1. List up to <N> sub-tasks needed to complete the objective.
2. For each sub-task, state the output it should produce.
3. Execute sub-tasks in order using only the given inputs.
4. Assemble the final deliverable in the required format.
5. Verify against all constraints and revise if needed.

   Output: Return only the final deliverable.

This template forces the model to build a workflow and then comply with it.

Practical examples

Example 1: Turning notes into a report

"Objective: Write an executive report from the notes below.

Output requirements: Headings in this exact order: Summary, Key findings, Risks, Recommendations, Next steps. 900–1,100 words.

Constraints: Use only the notes. Unknown if missing. No invented numbers.

Process:

1. Extract facts and categorize them into the five headings.
2. Identify gaps and list up to 5 clarifying questions (if needed).
3. Draft each section with concise paragraphs.
4. Verify headings and length, then revise.
   Output: Return only the report."

Example 2: Complex planning with dependencies

"Create a 6-week launch plan for a beginner AI prompt engineering course.
Output: Table with columns Week, Milestone, Tasks, Owner role, Dependencies, Risks, Success metric.
Process:

1. Define milestones for each week.
2. List tasks under each milestone and link dependencies.
3. Add risks and mitigations for each week.
4. Add metrics per milestone.
5. Validate table format, then output final table only."

Example 3: Data analysis without invented causes

"Analyze the KPI table below.
Process:

1. Compute changes vs last period.
2. Summarize 3 key movements.
3. Propose 3 hypotheses labeled as hypotheses.
4. List what data would confirm each hypothesis.
5. Provide 5 actions ranked by impact and effort.
   Output: Use headings and a final action table."

How to stabilize step-by-step outputs

Use checkpoints

Insert explicit checkpoints between steps:

- "After step 2, confirm you have all required sections covered."
- "Before final output, run a compliance checklist."

Limit the number of steps

Too many steps create noise. Use 4–7 steps for most tasks.

Specify what each step produces

Instead of "think step-by-step," say:

- "Step 1 produces an outline with section objectives."
- "Step 2 produces extracted bullet facts."
- "Step 3 produces the final draft."

This prevents the model from doing vague planning.

Add validation

End with:

- "Verify the output meets all constraints. If any fail, revise."

Common failure modes and fixes

Failure: The plan is good but the final output ignores it

Fix:

- require assembly:
  "Use the plan headings exactly. Do not add new sections."

Failure: The model jumps straight to the answer

Fix:

- enforce sequencing:
  "Do steps 1–5 in order. Do not produce the final deliverable until step 4 is complete."

Failure: The model invents details to fill gaps

Fix:

- add unknown handling:
  "If needed information is missing, write Unknown or ask clarifying questions."

Failure: Outputs become too long

Fix:

- add length caps per step:
  "Step 1 outline max 8 bullets. Final output 900–1,100 words."

When to use decomposition prompts

Use this pattern when:

- the task has multiple constraints,
- the input is messy,
- you need high completeness,
- you will reuse the workflow.

Skip it when:

- the task is simple and short,
- you need a fast one-liner,
- strict schema output is the only goal (then use validation prompts).

Copy-paste micro patterns (fast versions)

Plan then write

"First write a 6-bullet plan. Then write the deliverable following the plan exactly."

Extract then draft

"First extract facts into bullets under the required headings. Then draft the final output using only those bullets."

Check then revise

"Before finalizing, run a checklist for structure, length, and forbidden content. Revise if any fail."

Step-by-step decomposition prompts turn complex tasks into controlled workflows. They do not just help the model think, they help you manage quality.

Example-driven prompts

Example-driven prompting, often called few-shot prompting, means you teach the model what you want by showing it examples of inputs and ideal outputs. Instead of describing the rules in abstract terms, you demonstrate the pattern.

This is one of the most reliable ways to control:

- formatting and structure,
- tone and style,
- decision criteria,
- classification labels,
- edge-case handling.

It works especially well when the task is hard to describe but easy to show.

What few-shot prompting is

A few-shot prompt includes:

1. a short instruction,
2. 1 to 5 examples (input → output),
3. the new input,
4. the request to produce output in the same style.

In plain language: "Here is how to do it. Now do it again with this new case."

When to use few-shot prompts

Use this pattern when:

- you need consistent formatting or labeling,
- you are extracting information into structured formats,
- you need a specific voice or style,

- you have tricky edge cases,
- you are mapping messy input into a clean template.

It is ideal for:

- customer support replies,
- rubric scoring and feedback,
- rewriting into a house style,
- tagging and categorization,
- converting notes into meeting minutes,
- information extraction into JSON or tables.

When to avoid few-shot prompts

Avoid or limit examples when:

- the examples contain sensitive data,
- the output must be grounded in new source text, and examples might "leak" content into outputs,
- you are tight on context window and the examples crowd out the real input,
- you need creativity and variety more than consistency.

In those cases, use direct instruction with clear constraints instead.

Why examples work better than rules (most of the time)

Rules can be interpreted in multiple ways. Examples reduce interpretation.

Examples show the model:

- the exact structure, order, and level of detail,
- what to include and exclude,
- how to handle unknowns,
- what "good" looks like.

Examples also teach boundaries indirectly. If your examples never include extra commentary, the model is less likely to add it.

The professional few-shot template (copy and fill)

Few-shot prompt

Instruction: Describe the task in one or two sentences.

Format rules:

- Output must match the examples.
- No extra text beyond the format.

Examples:

Example 1

Input: <...>
Output: <...>
Example 2
Input: <...>
Output: <...>
Now do this one:
Input: <new input>
Output:
Add a validation line if structure matters:
"Before finalizing, check that your output matches the pattern and constraints in the examples."

How many examples should you use?

- 1 example: simple formatting, tone, or a clear pattern.
- 2 to 3 examples: best balance for most professional tasks.
- 4 to 5 examples: only when edge cases matter.

More examples are not always better. Too many examples can:

- consume space,
- bias the output toward irrelevant details,
- reduce flexibility.

What makes a good example set

A strong example set is:

- short,
- representative,
- consistent in structure,
- includes at least one edge case if relevant,
- uses the same labels and formatting you want.

Include an edge case when

- there are missing values,
- ambiguous inputs,
- borderline classifications,
- conflicting constraints.

Edge cases teach the model how to behave when the input is imperfect.

Few-shot patterns you can reuse

Pattern 1: Format imitation (structure control)

Best for: outlines, templates, SOPs, meeting notes, emails.
Example:

- show a perfect output skeleton,
- then ask the model to fill a new input into it.

Key rule to add:
"Match headings, ordering, and brevity exactly."

Pattern 2: Classification and labeling

Best for: tagging, routing, triage.
Example:
Input: short item
Output: label + brief reason
Add rule:
"If uncertain, output label = Unknown and one question."

Pattern 3: Scoring with a rubric

Best for: evaluating writing, prompt quality, compliance.
Example:
Input: a prompt
Output: scores per criterion + one improvement tip
Add rule:
"Use the same criteria and scoring scale as the examples."

Pattern 4: Transformation style (rewrite into a house voice)

Best for: rewriting marketing copy, internal docs, support responses.
Example:
Input: messy text
Output: rewritten text + optional change notes
Add rule:
"Keep meaning, do not add new facts."

Practical examples (ready to paste)

Example A: Few-shot for extracting into JSON

Instruction: Extract key fields from text into JSON. Use null if missing. Output JSON only.
Example 1
Input: "Launch moved to March. Owner is Sam. Risk: supplier delay."
Output:

```
{
"owner": "Sam",
"date": "March",
"change": "Launch moved",
```

"risk": "supplier delay"
}
Example 2
Input: "Owner unknown. Deadline June 10. No risks listed."
Output:
{
"owner": null,
"date": "June 10",
"change": null,
"risk": null
}
Now do this one:
Input: <paste your text>
Output:
Add a validator:
"Ensure keys match exactly and no extra text appears."

Example B: Few-shot for an executive email

Instruction: Write a short executive email following the pattern. Keep 120–160 words. No extra sections.
Example 1
Input: "Need approval for training budget. Audience: CFO."
Output:
Subject: Training budget approval
Hi <Name>,
[short context]

- [bullet 1]
- [bullet 2]
- [bullet 3]

  Can you approve by <date>?
  Thanks,

<Name>
Now do this one:
Input: <paste scenario>
Output:

Example C: Few-shot for meeting action items

Instruction: Convert notes into action items table. Use Unknown for missing. Output only the table.
Example 1
Input: "Mo drafts slides by Friday. Sara reviews Monday. Risk: missing data."
Output:

Action	**Owner**	**Due date**	**Risk**
Draft slides	Mo	Friday	Missing data
Review slides	Sara	Monday	Unknown

Now do this one:
Input: <paste notes>
Output:

Common failure modes and fixes

Failure: The model changes the format

Fix:

- add "Output must match the examples exactly."
- provide a strict skeleton in the examples.

Failure: The model adds commentary

Fix:

- add "Output only X, no explanation."
- show examples that include no commentary.

Failure: The model copies example content into the new output

Fix:

- keep examples generic,
- explicitly instruct:
  "Do not reuse names or details from examples."

Failure: Examples contradict each other

Fix:

- make examples consistent in structure and rules,
- remove mixed styles.

Pro tips for few-shot prompts

Put rules above examples, not buried below

Models pay attention to early constraints, but examples also strongly influence. Combine both:

- rules for boundaries and forbidden content,
- examples for structure and style.

Use "good and bad" examples when you need stronger boundaries

Show one "bad" output and label it wrong, then show the corrected output. This helps when the model keeps making the same mistake.

Keep examples short and close to the real task

The closer your examples are to your real input type, the stronger the pattern transfer.

A mini checklist for example-driven prompts

- 1 to 3 examples for most tasks.
- At least one edge case if missing data is common.
- Explicitly forbid extra text when format matters.
- Add unknown handling: null or "Unknown."
- Add a verification line: "Check output matches the example pattern."

Few-shot prompts are your fastest path to consistent style and structure when rules alone are not enough.

Critique and revise prompts

Critique and revise prompts turn the model from a one-shot generator into a quality-improvement loop. Instead of asking for a single draft and hoping it is good, you ask for:

1. a draft,
2. a critique against explicit criteria,
3. a revision that fixes the critique,
4. a final check.

This pattern is one of the most practical for professional work because it reduces rework, improves consistency, and makes quality measurable.

Use it for:

- writing (chapters, emails, reports, proposals),
- formatting (tables, JSON, templates),
- clarity and tone alignment,
- compliance with constraints (length, required sections, forbidden content),
- improving prompts themselves.

What "critique and revise" actually means

A critique is not "be better." A critique is a structured evaluation against standards. The revision step then targets those gaps.

A professional critique includes:

- what passed,
- what failed,
- why it matters,
- what to change,
- and a revised version that implements changes.

Critique and revise works best when you provide a rubric or checklist, even a simple one.

When to use this pattern

Use critique and revise when:

- quality matters more than speed,
- your first draft is usually close but imperfect,
- you need strict compliance with format rules,
- you want consistent outputs across different topics.

Avoid it when:

- the task is trivial,
- you need many creative options quickly (use option generation instead),
- you are highly constrained by token budget or context length.

The professional template (copy and fill)

Critique and revise prompt

Objective: Produce <deliverable> for <audience>.

Inputs: <paste content or describe task>.

Output requirements: <structure, length, format>.

Constraints: <must include, must avoid, non-goals, unknown handling>.

Rubric (0–2 each, or pass/fail):

- Objective fit
- Completeness
- Accuracy and grounding
- Clarity
- Format compliance
- Tone and audience fit
- Risk handling

Process:

1. Draft the deliverable.
2. Critique the draft against the rubric. List violations and improvements.
3. Revise to fix every violation.
4. Re-check the revised output against the rubric.
   Output: Return only the final revised deliverable plus a short compliance summary (score or pass/fail).

You can shorten it further by removing the scoring and keeping a simple checklist.

Two variations you should know

Variation A: Visible critique (best for learning and debugging)

Output includes critique and revised version.

Use when:

- you are training yourself or a team,
- you need to see what went wrong.

Suggested output format:

- Critique (bullets)
- Revision plan (bullets)
- Revised output (final)

Variation B: Hidden critique, final-only (best for production)

The model critiques internally but returns only the final.

Use when:

- you want clean deliverables,
- you do not need the commentary.

Prompt line:

"Do a critique internally, revise, and return only the final output."

How to write critique criteria that produce better revisions

The critique becomes useful when criteria are specific and measurable.

Good criteria:

- "Exactly 7 bullets in a specific order."
- "120–160 words."
- "No invented facts. Unknown if missing."
- "Tone: neutral, confident, no hype."
- "Include 2 examples and 5 pitfalls."

Weak criteria:

- "Make it better."
- "Be more professional."
- "Improve the clarity."

Convert vague criteria into tests.

Example 1: Critique and revise an email

Prompt:

"Draft an email asking for a status update on my application.

Constraints: 120–160 words, includes exactly 3 bullets, one clear call-to-action, no apologies, no invented dates.

Process: draft, critique against constraints, revise, output final and pass/fail summary."

What happens:

- The model drafts an email.
- The critique detects missing bullets or wrong length.
- The revision produces a compliant email.

This pattern reduces trial-and-error.

Example 2: Critique and revise a chapter section

Prompt:

"Write a 900–1,100 word section on 'Clarity beats cleverness.'

Required: 4 headings, 2 examples, 1 checklist, no jargon without definitions.

Process: draft → critique against checklist → revise → output final."

The critique catches:

- missing examples,
- too much jargon,
- missing checklist,
- headings out of order.

Then revision fixes those systematically.

Example 3: Critique and revise JSON output (format compliance)

Prompt:

"Extract entities into JSON matching this schema.

Rules: JSON only, required keys, no extra keys, null for unknown, enum values restricted.

Process: draft JSON → validate → fix → re-validate → output final JSON only."

This is the same pattern applied to structure, not writing.

Common failure modes and fixes

Failure: Critique is generic

Fix:

- supply a rubric with measurable rules.
- require the critique to reference specific constraints.

Add:

"Critique must cite which rule failed and where."

Failure: Revision ignores critique

Fix:

- require a revision plan that maps critique items to changes.
- require a re-check after revision.

Add:

"After revision, re-check every rule and confirm pass/fail."

Failure: The model keeps adding extra commentary

Fix:

- define output boundaries:
  "Return only the final deliverable and a one-line compliance report."

Failure: The model invents facts during revision

Fix:

- add grounding constraints:
  "Use only provided inputs. Unknown if missing."

A compact "production" version (fast and effective)

Use this when you want final-only output:

"Create <deliverable> with the following requirements: <list>.

Before responding, check your output against the requirements. If any requirement fails, revise until all pass.

Return only the final output and stop."

This is short, but it creates a built-in improvement loop.

Why critique and revise is a professional pattern

Professionals do not judge quality by intuition. They judge it by standards:

- Does it meet requirements?
- Does it match the audience?
- Is it accurate and grounded?
- Does it comply with format?
- Is it actionable?

Critique and revise prompts encode those standards so the model can systematically improve its own draft.

Pattern selection guide: which to use for which task

You now have five core prompting patterns. The skill is not knowing them, it is choosing the right one quickly. This guide helps you map a task to the best pattern, with practical rules of thumb and explainable selection logic.

The five patterns:

1. Direct instruction
2. Role and persona
3. Step-by-step decomposition
4. Example-driven (few-shot)
5. Critique and revise

The fast selector (use this first)

Ask three questions:

1) Is the task clear and the deliverable obvious?

- Yes → **Direct instruction**
- No → **Step-by-step decomposition** (clarify, plan, then execute)

2) Does format consistency matter a lot?

- Yes, strict structure or labels → **Example-driven (few-shot)**
- Yes, and you must pass constraints → **Critique and revise** (with validation)

3) Is tone or audience fit the main challenge?

- Yes → **Role and persona** (but keep it secondary to constraints)

If you answer these three, you can pick a pattern in under 10 seconds.

A practical decision flow

Use this flow when you are unsure:

1. Need one best deliverable, task is clear → **Direct instruction**
2. Task is complex or multi-part → **Step-by-step decomposition**
3. Output must match a template exactly → **Example-driven**
4. First draft quality matters, you want improvement loop → **Critique and revise**
5. The output must sound like a specific professional voice → **Role and persona** (plus a structure contract)

Most real tasks use a hybrid:

- Direct instruction + role and persona (tone)
- Decomposition + critique and revise (quality)
- Few-shot + validation (structure)

Pattern-by-pattern: what it is best for

1) Direct instruction prompts

Best for:

- emails, summaries, reports, rewrites, basic planning
- extracting content into simple structures
- anything where you know what "done" looks like

Use when:

- you want one answer in one pass
- you can specify objective, format, constraints

Avoid when:

- task is ambiguous and needs discovery
- you want multiple options

2) Role and persona prompts

Best for:

- tone matching (executive, beginner, customer support)
- consistent house style
- domain standard writing forms (consulting memo, lesson plan, analyst brief)

Use when:

- audience alignment is the main challenge
- you want consistent voice across many outputs

Avoid when:

- strict schema output is the goal
- factual accuracy is high-stakes and sources are missing
- the role increases confidence without grounding

3) Step-by-step decomposition prompts

Best for:

- complex tasks with many constraints
- project planning and multi-step workflows
- converting messy inputs into structured outputs
- analysis tasks where completeness matters

Use when:

- the task has multiple parts that can be missed
- you want a controllable process

Avoid when:

- the task is simple and short

4) Example-driven prompts (few-shot)

Best for:

- consistent formatting and labeling
- classification and routing
- extraction into JSON and tables
- rewriting into a precise style
- edge-case handling (missing values, ambiguous inputs)

Use when:

- rules are hard to describe but easy to demonstrate
- you need the output to "look like this"

Avoid when:

- examples consume too much space
- examples contain sensitive details
- you need creativity more than consistency

5) Critique and revise prompts

Best for:

- quality-sensitive writing (chapters, proposals, policies)
- compliance with requirements (length, sections, forbidden content)
- improving prompts themselves
- upgrading a draft into a final deliverable

Use when:

- first drafts are rarely perfect
- you want systematic improvement

Avoid when:

- speed matters more than quality

- you only need a quick rough draft

Task-to-pattern map (quick reference)

Writing and editing

- Draft a clean email, memo, or summary → **Direct instruction**
- Match a brand voice or audience tone → **Role and persona + Direct instruction**
- Rewrite and ensure it meets constraints → **Critique and revise**

Structured output and formatting

- JSON/table must match a template exactly → **Example-driven**
- JSON/table must pass strict rules → **Critique and revise** (validation loop)
- Extract fields from messy notes → **Decomposition** (extract then format)

Planning and problem solving

- Build a project plan with dependencies → **Decomposition**
- Generate several options then pick one → **Decomposition + Critique and revise**
- Create SOPs and operational steps → **Direct instruction** or **Decomposition** if complex

Evaluation and decision support

- Score content with a rubric → **Example-driven** (if you have scoring examples)
- Improve quality until it meets a threshold → **Critique and revise**
- Compare options using a rubric → **Direct instruction** (with rubric) or **Critique and revise** (for better rigor)

Teaching and content creation

- Beginner explanations with consistent voice → **Role and persona + Direct instruction**
- Multi-section lessons with activities → **Decomposition**
- Ensure clarity and completeness → **Critique and revise**

Common pattern combinations (the "pro blends")

Blend 1: Direct instruction + Role and persona

Use when:

- structure is clear, but tone must match audience

Example:
"Role: product manager. Persona: concise and neutral. Output: PRD sections in this order…"

Blend 2: Decomposition + Few-shot

Use when:

- the task avoids missed steps and must match a template

Example:
"Step 1 extract facts, step 2 map facts into the example template."

Blend 3: Few-shot + Critique and revise

Use when:

- format must match examples and must pass validation

Example:
"Match the example outputs exactly. Then validate keys, types, and counts and fix any violations."

Blend 4: Decomposition + Critique and revise

Use when:

- the work is complex and quality must be high

Example:
"Plan, draft section by section, critique against rubric, revise, output final."

A simple cheat rule to remember

- Want one good answer now → **Direct instruction**
- Want the right voice → **Role and persona**
- Want completeness on complex tasks → **Decomposition**
- Want consistent structure → **Few-shot**
- Want a better second draft → **Critique and revise**

If you teach this as a chapter ending, readers will stop guessing and start selecting patterns intentionally.

Exercises: classify tasks and choose the right pattern

This exercise trains pattern selection, the skill that turns prompting into a repeatable professional workflow. You will read a task, identify what is hardest about it (clarity, format, tone, complexity, or quality), then choose the best core pattern.

The five patterns:

1. Direct instruction
2. Role and persona

3. Step-by-step decomposition
4. Example-driven (few-shot)
5. Critique and revise

How to do the exercise

For each task:

1. Circle the main challenge:
- Clarity (unclear goal),
- Complexity (multi-step),
- Format (must match a template),
- Tone (audience/voice),
- Quality (needs improvement loop).
2. Choose the primary pattern.
3. Optional: choose a secondary pattern if you would combine patterns in real work.

Task set A (beginner friendly)

Choose the best pattern for each task.

1. "Write an email to my manager asking for feedback on my performance."
2. "Convert this messy set of meeting notes into action items with owners and due dates."
3. "Explain 'prompt engineering' to complete beginners using a friendly tone."
4. "Extract product requirements from this document into JSON with fixed keys."
5. "Create a one-page SOP for onboarding a new employee."
6. "Rewrite this paragraph to be clearer without changing meaning."

Task set B (format-heavy)

7. "Output valid JSON only matching this schema. If a field is missing, use null."
8. "Create a comparison table of three options with columns pros, cons, risks, cost, time."
9. "Write a report with headings in this exact order and do not add any other sections."
10. "Classify these 30 customer messages into labels and provide a one-sentence reason per label."

Task set C (complex and quality-critical)

11. "Draft a chapter section, then improve it until it meets a checklist for clarity, structure, and length."
12. "Create a 6-week project plan with dependencies, risks, and success metrics."
13. "Generate five alternative taglines, then critique them and recommend the best one using a rubric."
14. "Summarize this report, but ask clarifying questions first if the audience and goal are unclear."

Answer key (recommended pattern choices)

A. Beginner friendly

1. **Direct instruction**
   Optional blend: Role/persona (tone respectful and confident)
2. **Step-by-step decomposition**
   Optional blend: Direct instruction for final table format
3. **Role and persona**
   Optional blend: Direct instruction for structure and length
4. **Example-driven (few-shot)** if you can show a sample JSON output
   If strict compliance is needed: Critique and revise with schema validation
5. **Direct instruction**
   If onboarding is complex: Decomposition
6. **Direct instruction**
   If you need improvement loop: Critique and revise

B. Format-heavy

7. **Critique and revise** (schema validation)
   Optional blend: Few-shot if you have a perfect example output
8. **Direct instruction**
   If the table must be consistent across many cases: Few-shot
9. **Direct instruction**
   Add stop conditions and verification for strict compliance
10. **Example-driven (few-shot)**
    Few-shot is ideal for classification labels and consistent reasoning style

C. Complex and quality-critical

11. **Critique and revise**
    Optional blend: Decomposition (outline then draft then revise)
12. **Step-by-step decomposition**
    Optional blend: Critique and revise (check plan completeness and constraints)
13. **Critique and revise**
    Optional blend: Decomposition (generate options then evaluate)
14. **Step-by-step decomposition**
    Because it requires clarifying questions and staged execution

Quick scoring rubric for learners

Give yourself 1 point each:

- You chose a pattern that fits the main challenge.
- You explained why in one sentence.
- You proposed a useful blend when appropriate.

Target score:

- 12 out of 14 indicates strong pattern selection skill.

Extension drill (advanced)

Rewrite 3 tasks from above into actual prompts using your chosen pattern.
Include:

- objective,
- output requirements,
- constraints,
- and verification.

This is how pattern selection becomes a real workflow.

Chapter 6. Asking better questions, elicitation and clarifying

How to make the AI ask you questions first

Most prompt failures come from missing information. Humans naturally ask follow-up questions when a request is unclear. A model will often guess instead, unless you explicitly instruct it to clarify first.

This section teaches a professional technique: **elicitation**. You design the prompt so the model asks you targeted questions before it produces the final deliverable. Done well, this prevents hallucination, reduces rework, and locks the output to your real intent.

Why you should force clarifying questions

Without clarification, the model must choose defaults:

- audience assumptions,
- tone assumptions,
- scope assumptions,
- format assumptions,
- success criteria assumptions.

Those defaults may be reasonable, but they are not yours.

If you add a clarification step, you replace guessing with a short interview that gathers:

- objective,
- audience,
- constraints,
- inputs,
- success conditions.

The two-phase approach (ask first, then deliver)

The most reliable way is to explicitly split the interaction into phases:

Phase 1: Questions only

Phase 2: Output only

This avoids a common problem where the model asks questions and also generates a draft, mixing both.

Copy-paste template (strict)

"Before you write anything, ask me up to 7 clarifying questions.

Do not generate the final output yet.

After I answer, produce the final deliverable in the required format."

This is the cleanest "questions first" control.

The "minimum necessary questions" rule

Professionally, you do not want 20 questions. You want the smallest set that changes the output.

Add constraints like:

- "Ask up to 5 questions only."
- "Ask only questions that materially change the result."
- "If you can safely assume, list the assumption and proceed."

This produces a fast, high-signal clarification pass.

What questions should the model ask?

Good clarifying questions cluster into five categories:

1) Objective and use case

- What are you trying to achieve?
- What decision will this output support?
- What is the deliverable used for?

2) Audience and tone

- Who is the reader and what is their level?
- What tone is appropriate?
- Where will this be delivered (email, slides, report)?

3) Inputs and constraints

- What source material should be used?
- What constraints must be respected (length, format, policy)?
- What must be avoided?

4) Scope and boundaries

- What is in scope vs out of scope?
- Do you want a high-level overview or deep detail?
- Any time period or region constraints?

5) Success and stop conditions

- What does "good" look like?
- What must the output include?
- When should it stop (no extra sections)?

If you want consistent clarifications, you can instruct the model to ask exactly one question from each category.

Three ways to make the AI ask questions first

Method A: "Questions only" gate (most reliable)

Use when you want a clean two-turn workflow.

Prompt:
"Ask me 5 clarifying questions first.
Only ask questions, no draft.
After I answer, you will produce: <deliverable format>."
Pros:

- no mixed output,
- you control inputs before writing.

Method B: Conditional questions (ask only if needed)
Use when tasks are usually clear, but sometimes ambiguous.
Prompt:
"If any required information is missing, ask up to 5 clarifying questions.
Otherwise proceed without questions."
Pros:

- faster when the request is complete.

Method C: Assumptions with confirmation (fastest)
Use when you want progress immediately but still reduce guessing.
Prompt:
"List the assumptions you must make.
Ask up to 3 questions only for the assumptions that would change the output.
Then draft using those assumptions, clearly labeled."
Pros:

- you get a draft quickly,
- assumptions are visible.

Professional question sets you can reuse

Universal question set (5 questions)

1. What is the objective and intended outcome?
2. Who is the audience and where will this be used?
3. What inputs should I use and what must I ignore?
4. What constraints matter most (format, length, tone, must include, must avoid)?
5. What does success look like and when should I stop?

Writing-specific question set

- What is the target reader and tone?
- What length and structure do you want?
- Any required points or forbidden content?

- Any example you want me to match?

Data/analysis question set

- What is the decision you will make from this analysis?
- What timeframe and baseline should I use?
- What metrics matter most?
- What assumptions are allowed?
- How should uncertainty be reported?

Add a "question quality" constraint

Not all questions are useful. You can require the model to ask high-quality questions.

Add:

- "Questions must be specific and actionable, no yes/no questions unless necessary."
- "Each question must explain why it matters in one short phrase."

Example:

"Ask 5 questions. After each question, add (why: …) in 5 words."

This produces questions that actually move the work forward.

A ready-to-use prompt block (drop into any prompt)

Paste this near the top of your prompt when you want questions first:

"Clarification first:

Ask me up to 6 questions before you start.

Ask only questions that materially affect the output.

Do not draft yet.

After I answer, produce the final output with the required format and constraints."

Common mistakes and fixes

Mistake 1: The model asks questions and drafts anyway

Fix:

- enforce "questions only":
  "Only ask questions. Do not draft until I respond."

Mistake 2: Too many questions

Fix:

- cap and prioritize:
  "Ask at most 5. Prioritize objective, audience, constraints."

Mistake 3: Questions are too generic

Fix:

- require specificity:
  "Questions must be specific enough that my answers can be pasted into the prompt."

Mistake 4: The model guesses instead of asking

Fix:

- forbid guessing:
  "If information is missing, do not guess. Ask."

Mini lab (quick practice)

Take a vague task like:
"Write a professional email."
Rewrite it into an elicitation prompt:
"Before drafting, ask 5 questions about audience, purpose, tone, constraints, and call-to-action. Ask questions only. Then draft the email in 120–160 words with exactly 3 bullets."
Run it once. Answer the questions. Compare the final output quality to a one-shot prompt. You will usually see a major improvement because you removed hidden assumptions.

Using intake forms and requirements gathering

When prompting becomes professional work, the biggest upgrade is moving from "one-off chat requests" to a repeatable process. The simplest professional process is an intake form.

An intake form is a structured set of questions the model uses to gather requirements before it produces the deliverable. It prevents guessing, reduces revisions, and makes outputs consistent across projects and team members. Think of it as turning prompting into a lightweight specification workflow.

Why intake forms work

Intake forms solve three recurring problems:

1. **Hidden assumptions**
   People forget to mention audience, constraints, success criteria, or what to avoid.
2. **Inconsistent outputs**
   Two people ask "write a report" and get two completely different reports.

3. **Rework loops**
   You spend time correcting structure and scope instead of improving content.

An intake form forces the minimum information needed for predictable results.

The intake form mindset: requirements, not requests

A request is: "Write a professional email."

A requirement is:

- objective,
- audience,
- context inputs,
- output format,
- constraints and non-goals,
- success and stop conditions,
- verification criteria.

The model performs better when you give it requirements, or when you make it collect them.

When to use intake forms

Use an intake form when:

- tasks repeat (emails, briefs, SOPs, summaries, social posts),
- multiple people use the same workflow,
- format compliance matters (tables, JSON, templates),
- you want fewer revisions,
- your inputs are often incomplete.

Skip the form when:

- the task is trivial,
- you only need a quick idea,
- you already have a complete specification.

Two ways to use intake forms

Approach A: Human fills the form first (fastest output)

You provide a form, fill it, and paste the answers into the prompt.

Best for:

- production work,
- teams and repeatable processes.

Approach B: The AI runs the form as a mini interview

You instruct the AI to ask the form questions first, then produce the deliverable.

Best for:

- interactive work,
- when you do not know what details are missing.

Both approaches are professional. The difference is whether the "form completion" happens before the prompt or within the prompt.

A universal intake form (copy and reuse)

Use this as a general requirements gatherer for most deliverables.

Universal Intake Form (10 fields)

1. Deliverable type: email, report, SOP, outline, table, JSON, script, etc.
2. Objective: what outcome should this support?
3. Audience: who will read it, and what is their level?
4. Channel: where will it be used (email, doc, slide, chat, web)?
5. Inputs: paste source text, notes, data, links, or "none."
6. Scope: what topics must be included?
7. Non-goals: what must be excluded or avoided?
8. Output requirements: structure, headings, format, length.
9. Constraints: tone rules, allowed claims, compliance limits, deadlines.
10. Success criteria: what does "good" look like, and when should it stop?

If you get these 10 fields, you can produce stable prompts for almost anything.

Specialized intake forms (by common deliverable)

1) Email intake form

- Purpose: inform, request, persuade, apologize, follow up
- Recipient role and relationship
- Tone: friendly, neutral, formal, urgent
- Must include: key points, dates, links, attachments
- Call-to-action: what should they do next, by when
- Length and structure: word range, bullets, subject line rules

2) Report or chapter section intake form

- Target reader (executive vs technical)
- Required sections and order
- Depth level and length range
- Required examples, visuals, or checklists

- Sources allowed: provided text only or general knowledge
- Risk and limitations section required or not

3) SOP intake form

- Process name and goal
- Who performs it and what tools they have
- Preconditions and prerequisites
- Step count and level of detail
- Safety and compliance constraints
- Common failure modes and escalation path
- Acceptance checklist at the end

4) JSON or data extraction intake form

- Schema: required keys, types, allowed values
- Unknown handling: null vs "Unknown"
- Output only rule: JSON only, no extra text
- Validation: check keys, types, enums, formats
- Examples: at least one perfect sample output if possible

5) Rubric or evaluation intake form

- What is being evaluated and for what purpose
- Criteria list and scoring scale
- What a high score looks like
- Threshold for pass/fail
- Output format: table or bullets
- Required recommendations

How to run the intake form inside a prompt

If you want the AI to gather requirements first, add a strict two-phase instruction:

"Phase 1: Ask the intake form questions only.

Phase 2: After I answer, produce the deliverable."

Copy-paste prompt for AI-led intake

"Before writing, run this intake form. Ask one question at a time, maximum 8 questions.

Do not draft until I answer.

After I answer all questions, produce the deliverable using the stated output requirements."

This prevents mixed outputs and keeps the process clean.

How to keep intake forms short and high-signal

A professional intake form is not long. It is targeted.

Use these techniques:

- **Cap the number of questions**: "Ask up to 6 questions."
- **Ask only decision-changing questions**: "Only ask what materially affects output."
- **Use multiple choice** where possible: reduce ambiguity and speed responses.
- **Default options**: "If not specified, assume X and state the assumption."

Example:

"Choose tone: (A) neutral professional, (B) warm and friendly, (C) formal."

Turning intake answers into a reusable prompt

Once you collect answers, convert them into a prompt block:

- Objective:
- Audience:
- Inputs:
- Output requirements:
- Constraints and non-goals:
- Success and stop conditions:
- Verification:

This becomes a reusable template your team can run repeatedly.

Mini lab: build an intake form for your book workflows

Pick one recurring task for your book project, for example:

- "Generate chapter outlines,"
- "Write exercises,"
- "Create a one-page cheat sheet,"
- "Rewrite content for beginners."

Create a 6-question intake form for it using:

- objective, audience, scope, constraints, format, success criteria.

Then test it:

- run the same intake form twice with different answers,
- compare how much cleaner and more relevant the outputs become.

Common mistakes and fixes

Mistake 1: Intake form collects opinions, not requirements

Fix:

Ask for measurable items:

- length, structure, required points, forbidden content.

Mistake 2: Too many open-ended questions

Fix:

Use bounded options and checklists.

Mistake 3: The AI drafts before gathering requirements

Fix:

Add a hard gate:

"Ask questions only. Do not draft yet."

Mistake 4: Missing success and stop conditions

Fix:

Include one question:

"What does success look like, and what should I not include?"

Intake forms make prompting scalable. They turn "talking to AI" into a repeatable requirements workflow that produces consistent, professional outputs.

Progressive refinement, draft, questions, refine, final

Progressive refinement is a professional workflow for getting high-quality outputs when requirements are incomplete or evolving. Instead of forcing a perfect prompt up front, you run a controlled loop:

1. produce a draft based on stated assumptions,
2. ask targeted questions to remove the biggest uncertainties,
3. refine the draft using the answers,
4. deliver a final version that matches the clarified requirements.

This approach is faster than endless upfront clarification, and safer than letting the model guess silently.

Why progressive refinement works

Many real-world tasks start fuzzy:

- "Write a chapter section,"
- "Create a plan,"
- "Draft an email,"
- "Summarize this report."

At the start, you often do not know:

- the right tone,
- the audience level,
- the structure,

- the desired depth,
- the success criteria.

Progressive refinement handles that uncertainty explicitly. The draft gives you something concrete, and the questions eliminate the highest-impact unknowns before finalizing.

The four-phase loop

Think of it as a controlled collaboration:

Phase 1: Draft (with explicit assumptions)

The model produces a first-pass output using reasonable defaults, but it must label assumptions.

Key instruction:

"Draft using stated assumptions. Do not invent facts. Mark unknowns as Unknown."

Phase 2: Questions (targeted, minimal)

The model asks only the questions that change the output materially.

Key instruction:

"Ask up to 5 questions that would change the draft most."

Phase 3: Refine (apply answers, not new creativity)

The model updates the draft using the new requirements and fixes any constraint violations.

Key instruction:

"Revise the draft to incorporate answers. Keep the same structure unless requested otherwise."

Phase 4: Final (clean deliverable + compliance check)

The model outputs a final version that follows format rules and stops.

Key instruction:

"Return only the final deliverable. Verify it meets constraints."

The professional template (copy and fill)

Progressive refinement prompt

Objective: Produce <deliverable> for <audience/channel>.

Inputs: <paste or reference>.

Constraints: <must include, must avoid, non-goals>.

Output requirements: <structure, length, format>.

Workflow:

1. Draft a v1 based on reasonable assumptions. List assumptions explicitly at the top.

2. Ask up to 5 clarifying questions that would most improve v1.
3. After I answer, revise to v2 incorporating all answers and removing assumption text from the final.
4. Verify v2 meets all constraints and output only the final deliverable.

This template creates a disciplined loop without wasting time.

How to control the questions in Phase 2

Without control, the model might ask too many or ask low-value questions.

Use these rules:

- Cap the questions: "Ask up to 5."
- Make them decision-driven: "Only questions that materially change output."
- Require coverage of essentials: objective, audience, constraints, format, success criteria.
- Allow safe defaults: "If a question is minor, assume a default and state it."

Example instruction:

"Ask 5 questions total. At least one each for audience, tone, format, and success criteria. No redundant questions."

What to include in the assumptions list (Phase 1)

Assumptions are a feature, not a flaw, if they are visible.

A good assumptions list includes:

- audience level assumption,
- tone assumption,
- length assumption,
- structure assumption,
- scope boundaries,
- unknown data policy (Unknown vs questions).

Example:

"Assumptions: audience is beginner, tone is neutral, target length 900–1,100 words, include 2 examples, avoid vendor-specific references."

This keeps the draft usable while clearly marking what might change.

Two output formats for progressive refinement

Option A: Separate sections (best for learning)

- Assumptions
- Draft v1
- Clarifying questions

This is ideal for book instruction because readers can see the mechanics.

Option B: Minimal output (best for production)

- Draft v1
- Questions

Assumptions are embedded as short notes inside the questions, or listed as one compact line.

Practical example (book writing context)

Prompt:

"Objective: Write a chapter subsection on 'prompt guardrails.'

Inputs: none.

Constraints: beginner-friendly, no jargon without definitions, include 1 checklist, include 1 example prompt.

Workflow: Draft v1 with assumptions, then ask 5 questions, then revise after answers."

What happens:

- v1 gives you a usable draft.
- questions clarify tone, length, examples, formatting preferences.
- final version becomes tightly aligned to your book style.

Common failure modes and fixes

Failure 1: The draft is too confident despite missing inputs

Fix:

Add:

"Do not invent facts. Use placeholders or write Unknown."

Failure 2: The model asks generic questions

Fix:

Require specificity:

"Each question must reference a draft section it affects."

Failure 3: The model keeps assumptions in the final

Fix:

Add:

"Final output must not contain the assumptions list."

Failure 4: The model changes structure dramatically during refine

Fix:

Add:

"Keep structure stable unless my answers require changes."

Failure 5: The loop becomes endless

Fix:
Limit iterations:
"Only one refinement cycle: v1 → questions → v2 final."

Mini lab: run one refinement cycle

Pick one task and run the loop once.
Task:
"Write a one-page cheat sheet for prompt engineering beginners."
Use progressive refinement:

1. Draft v1 with assumptions (length, sections, tone).
2. Ask 5 questions (audience, format, must include, must avoid, success criteria).
3. Answer the questions in one message.
4. Produce v2 final with a compliance check.

Compare v1 to v2. The improvement is usually clear: fewer missing requirements, tighter structure, better audience fit, less drift.

Why this belongs in your toolbox

Progressive refinement is how professionals handle uncertainty. It combines:

- direct instruction (deliverable),
- elicitation (questions),
- decomposition (staged work),
- critique and revise (improve before final).

Once readers master this loop, they stop fighting the model and start steering it with a repeatable process.

Prompts for uncertainty, "If you lack info, list assumptions"

A professional prompt does not pretend uncertainty does not exist. It handles it deliberately.
When information is missing, models often fill gaps to keep the answer coherent. That can produce confident, readable output that is wrong or misaligned with what you meant. The solution is to add an uncertainty protocol to your prompt:

- identify missing information,
- list assumptions explicitly,
- label uncertainty,
- ask clarifying questions when necessary,
- and avoid inventing facts.

This section gives you reusable prompt patterns that make uncertainty visible and safe.

Why "list assumptions" works

If you do not tell the model how to behave under uncertainty, it will default to "complete the task anyway." Listing assumptions changes the default behavior from guessing silently to:

- showing what it is assuming,
- making uncertainty inspectable,
- giving you a chance to correct direction before finalizing.

Assumptions also make outputs easier to audit and reuse.

Assumptions, unknowns, and questions (the difference)

Treat these as three separate tools:

- **Unknowns**: facts that cannot be derived from inputs.
  Output should say "Unknown" or use null.
- **Assumptions**: choices the model must make to proceed, where multiple valid defaults exist.
  Output should state the chosen default.
- **Clarifying questions**: when an assumption would materially change the output.
  The model should ask you instead of choosing.

A good uncertainty prompt tells the model which tool to use in which situation.

The uncertainty protocol (simple and effective)

Add this block to your prompts when inputs are incomplete:

1. Do not invent facts.
2. If a required fact is missing, write Unknown.
3. If a choice is needed, list assumptions explicitly.
4. Ask clarifying questions for assumptions that would change the outcome.
5. Proceed only after uncertainty is handled (or proceed with labeled assumptions if allowed).

Copy-paste prompt blocks (ready to use)

Block A: Assumptions + unknown handling (fast)

"Uncertainty rules:

- Use only the provided inputs. Do not invent facts.
- If a required detail is missing, write Unknown.

- If you must choose defaults to proceed, list your assumptions first, then produce the output."

Use when:

- you want progress now,
- you can tolerate reasonable defaults.

Block B: Assumptions + questions first (safer)

"Uncertainty rules:

- Do not guess missing facts.
- List assumptions you would need to make.
- Ask up to 5 clarifying questions for the assumptions that most affect the output.
- Do not produce the final deliverable until I answer."

Use when:

- correctness and alignment matter,
- you want a clean two-phase workflow.

Block C: Conditional questions (hybrid)

"If the task can be completed using the provided inputs, proceed.
If any information is missing or ambiguous, do not guess. Ask up to 5 clarifying questions.
If you can proceed with safe defaults, list assumptions explicitly and continue."

Use when:

- many tasks are complete, but some are not,
- you want speed without risky guessing.

Block D: Assumptions embedded inside the output (production friendly)

"Proceed with the deliverable. If any critical assumptions are required, include a short 'Assumptions' section with max 5 bullets. Do not include any other commentary."

Use when:

- you want the final to include assumptions for audit,
- you cannot do multiple turns.

How to write good assumptions (not generic)

Weak assumptions are vague:

- "Assume typical context."

Strong assumptions are specific and testable:

- "Assume audience is beginner."
- "Assume tone is neutral and instructional."
- "Assume output length is 900–1,100 words."
- "Assume no vendor names are allowed."
- "Assume examples should be non-technical."

A good assumption is something you could accept or reject quickly.

The "assumption ladder" (prioritize what matters)

Not all uncertainty matters equally. Teach the model to prioritize assumptions that most change the output:

High-impact assumptions:

- objective and success criteria,
- target audience level,
- required format and length,
- allowed sources (provided text only vs general knowledge),
- constraints and forbidden content.

Low-impact assumptions:

- minor wording preferences,
- optional stylistic choices that do not affect correctness.

Add a line:

"Prioritize assumptions about objective, audience, format, and constraints."

Examples (plug into your book workflows)

Example 1: Writing a section with missing requirements

"Write a beginner-friendly subsection on 'validation prompts.'

Uncertainty rules: If you lack info, list assumptions (max 5 bullets).

Do not invent facts. If you need audience level, length, or tone, ask 3 clarifying questions first."

Example 2: Data extraction where fields might be missing

"Extract fields into JSON: title, owner, deadline, risks.

Uncertainty rules: Use null for missing facts. Do not infer dates.

If you must assume a deadline format, list the assumption, then output JSON only."

Example 3: Planning without constraints

"Create a 4-week plan.

If constraints are missing, list assumptions about scope, resources, and time budget.

Ask 5 questions if those assumptions would change milestones."

Common mistakes and fixes

Mistake 1: "List assumptions" but the model still invents details

Fix:

Add a hard rule:

"Do not invent facts, numbers, names, dates, or citations not in the input."

Mistake 2: Assumptions are too many

Fix:

Cap them:

"List at most 5 assumptions, prioritize the highest impact."

Mistake 3: Assumptions leak into the final when you do not want them

Fix:

Specify where assumptions belong:

- "Assumptions section only," or
- "Assumptions are internal, final output must not include them."

Mistake 4: The model asks too many questions

Fix:

Cap and prioritize:

"Ask up to 3 questions only, focused on objective, audience, and format."

A strong, compact "uncertainty clause" (best default)

If you want one reusable line, use this:

"Uncertainty: If any required info is missing, do not guess. Either ask up to 5 clarifying questions or list up to 5 explicit assumptions, then proceed without inventing facts."

This single clause can dramatically improve reliability and reduce hallucinations, especially in early drafts and complex tasks.

Practice, convert 8 tasks into "question-first" workflows

This practice set trains a professional habit: when a task has missing requirements, you do not guess. You run a short intake, then produce the deliverable.

For each task below you will produce a "question-first workflow" prompt. The workflow has two phases:

- **Phase 1: Questions only**
- **Phase 2: Final output only**

Your goal is to write prompts that force the model to ask only the questions that materially change the output.

The question-first workflow template (copy and reuse)

Use this structure for every exercise:

Question-first workflow

Objective: <deliverable>

Format target: <headings/table/JSON/word range>

Constraints: <must include, must avoid, unknown handling>

Phase 1 (questions only):

- Ask up to 5 clarifying questions.
- Ask only questions that materially affect the output.
- Do not draft yet.

Phase 2 (final output):

- After I answer, produce the deliverable in the required format.
- Verify structure and constraints, then output final only and stop.

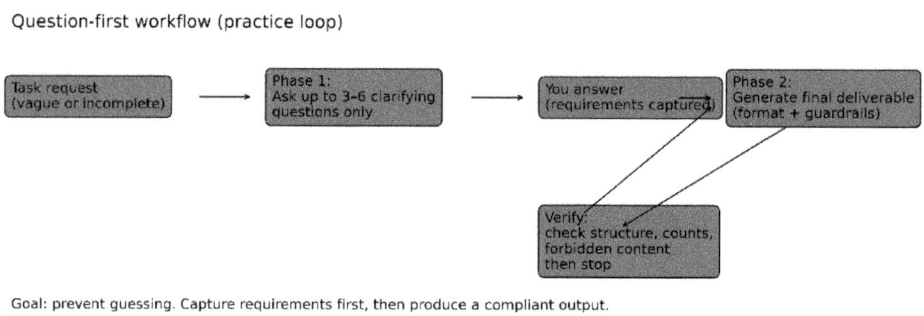

The figure above shows Question-first workflow. Ask clarifying questions first, capture requirements, then generate and verify the final deliverable.

Exercise set: 8 tasks

Task 1: Professional email request

Task statement:

"Write an email requesting a meeting with a potential client."

Convert to question-first workflow prompt:

"Before drafting, ask up to 5 questions about: who the client is, meeting purpose, desired outcome, tone, and scheduling constraints. Ask questions only. After I answer, write an email with subject line, greeting, 3 bullets, clear CTA, 120–160 words. Stop after the sign-off."

Task 2: Executive summary of a document

Task statement:

"Summarize this document for leadership."

Question-first workflow prompt:

"Ask up to 5 questions first: audience level (executive vs senior manager), purpose (inform vs decision), desired length, must-include points, and confidentiality constraints. Do not summarize yet. After I answer, produce a summary with exactly 7 bullets in the required order and max 140 words. Unknown if missing. Output only bullets."

Task 3: SOP creation

Task statement:

"Create an SOP for onboarding new employees."

Question-first workflow prompt:

"Ask 5 questions only: role being onboarded, tools and systems involved, time window, compliance requirements, and success criteria. Do not write the SOP yet. After I answer, produce an SOP with sections: Purpose, Scope, Prerequisites, Steps (exactly 7), Risks, Checklist. Keep it beginner-friendly. Stop after checklist."

Task 4: JSON extraction from notes

Task statement:

"Extract key details into JSON."

Question-first workflow prompt:

"Ask up to 4 questions: which schema keys, allowed values for enums, unknown handling (null vs 'Unknown'), and whether to include source quotes. Ask questions only. After I answer, output valid JSON only matching the schema, no extra text. Validate keys and types, then output final JSON."

Task 5: Build a 4-week project plan

Task statement:

"Make a 4-week plan to launch an online course."

Question-first workflow prompt:

"Ask up to 5 questions first: target audience, scope of course, available resources, timeline constraints, and success metrics. Do not draft the plan yet. After I answer, output a table with columns Week, Milestone, Tasks, Owner role, Dependencies, Risks, Success metric. Exactly 4 rows. No commentary outside the table."

Task 6: Compare tools and recommend one

Task statement:

"Compare three tools and tell me which is best."

Question-first workflow prompt:

"Ask up to 5 questions first: what goal matters most, budget range, must-have features, constraints (privacy, platform), and evaluation criteria. Do not recommend yet. After I answer, compare 3 options using a rubric (0–2 across 8 criteria), show tradeoffs, recommend one, and stop."

Task 7: Rewrite content for a new audience

Task statement:

"Rewrite this text to be more engaging."

Question-first workflow prompt:

"Ask up to 5 questions first: target audience, desired tone, length limit, channel (blog, email, landing page), and any forbidden claims. Ask questions only. After I answer, rewrite the text. Constraints: do not add new facts, keep within ±10% length, include one clear CTA if appropriate. Output final only."

Task 8: Diagnose why a metric changed

Task statement:

"Explain why our conversion rate dropped."

Question-first workflow prompt:

"Ask up to 5 questions first: timeframe, baseline comparison, related changes (pricing, traffic, product), data available, and what actions you want from the analysis. Do not explain yet. After I answer, produce: (1) summary of change, (2) 3 hypotheses labeled as hypotheses, (3) data needed to confirm, (4) 5 actions ranked by impact and effort. No invented causes."

Self-check: did you write a real question-first workflow?

For each prompt you write, confirm it includes:

- a question cap (3–6 questions),
- "questions only, no draft" instruction,
- output format requirements for phase 2,
- unknown handling (Unknown or questions),
- a stop condition ("stop after final output").

Extension challenge (optional)

Pick any two tasks above and rewrite the prompt using two variations:

1. Strict two-phase: questions only, then final only.

2. Hybrid: list assumptions + ask only the top 3 questions, then draft with assumptions labeled.

Compare which workflow gives you faster alignment with fewer revisions.

Chapter 7. Few-shot prompting, teaching by examples

What makes a good example (variety, edge cases, counterexamples)

Few-shot prompting works when your examples teach the model three things at once:

1. the output shape,
2. the decision logic,
3. the boundaries.

Many few-shot prompts fail because the examples are too similar, too clean, or missing the "what not to do" cases. A professional example set behaves like a tiny training dataset: it covers normal cases, edge cases, and common failure modes.

This section shows how to design examples that reliably transfer the behavior you want.

The goal of a good example set

A good example set should make the model able to answer:

- What does a correct output look like?
- What should I do when input is messy or incomplete?
- Where is the boundary between categories?
- What should I avoid doing, even if it sounds plausible?

If your examples answer those questions, your outputs will become consistent.

1) Variety: cover the real range of inputs

Variety means your examples are not duplicates. They should represent the diversity the model will see.

What variety should cover

- different lengths of input (short, medium, long)
- different input styles (formal notes, chat messages, bullet lists, paragraphs)
- different topics (so the pattern does not become topic-specific)
- different difficulty levels (easy and moderately hard)
- different outcomes (not all "positive" cases)

Why variety matters

If all examples look the same, the model learns superficial patterns:

- similar wording,

- same content structure,
- same "happy path" assumptions.

Then when the real input changes, output quality collapses.

Practical rule

Use 2 to 4 examples that differ in input style and content, while keeping output format identical.

2) Edge cases: teach the model what to do when reality is messy

Edge cases are where most failures happen. If your example set includes at least one edge case, you teach the model how to behave when:

- information is missing,
- the input is ambiguous,
- values conflict,
- the input contains noise,
- the request asks for too much.

The most valuable edge cases to include

Missing values

- Show how to output Unknown or null.

Ambiguity

- Show how to ask a clarifying question or choose a labeled assumption.

Conflicting information

- Show how to flag conflict instead of choosing one.

Out-of-scope input

- Show how to refuse, redirect, or omit content.

Boundary cases

- Show what happens when the input is close to a threshold.

Example (classification task)

If you are labeling customer messages as "Bug" vs "Feature request," include an example that is borderline and show the correct label plus the reason.

3) Counterexamples: show "wrong" and why it is wrong

Counterexamples are the fastest way to enforce boundaries, especially when the model keeps making the same mistake.

A counterexample is a pair:

- Bad output (explicitly labeled wrong)
- Corrected output (explicitly labeled correct)

This teaches:

- what not to do,
- how to fix it,
- which rule matters.

When to use counterexamples

- the model repeatedly adds extra sections,
- it keeps inventing facts,
- it mislabels categories,
- it drifts into the wrong tone,
- it breaks strict JSON or schema rules.

How to write counterexamples safely

Keep them short and explicit:

- "Bad output: … (wrong because …)"
- "Correct output: … (follows rule …)"

This reduces the chance the model imitates the bad output.

Building a "gold standard" few-shot set (step-by-step)

Step 1: Lock the output format

Before you choose examples, decide the exact output shape:

- headings and order,
- JSON schema,
- table columns,
- rubric format,
- bullet count.

Your examples should match this format exactly, every time.

Step 2: Choose 2 to 3 representative examples

Include:

- one normal case,
- one different-style case,
- one slightly more complex case.

Step 3: Add 1 edge case

Pick the most common failure you expect:

- missing values, ambiguous input, conflicting info.

Step 4: Add 1 counterexample (optional but powerful)

Use it only if you need strict boundary training:

- show the common wrong output, then corrected.

You now have a professional-quality example set without wasting context window.

Example design patterns you can reuse

Pattern A: Normal + missing data (best default)

- Example 1: full information
- Example 2: missing key field, demonstrate Unknown/null handling

Pattern B: Easy + hard + borderline (classification)

- Example 1: obvious label A
- Example 2: obvious label B
- Example 3: borderline case with explanation

Pattern C: Bad vs good (format compliance)

- Counterexample: wrong because it adds text around JSON
- Correct example: JSON only, schema keys only

Pattern D: Conflict handling (analysis)

- Example shows conflicting inputs
- Correct output flags conflict and lists what is needed to resolve it

Quality checklist for your examples

Before using your examples, verify:

- Output format is identical across examples
- Labels and terminology are consistent
- Edge case shows how to handle missing or messy inputs
- Counterexample is clearly marked wrong and followed by corrected output
- Examples are short and do not include irrelevant detail
- No sensitive or private data is included
- Examples represent the real inputs you expect

If you pass this checklist, your few-shot prompts will behave like a controlled template rather than a guess.

Pro tips that improve transfer

Keep the examples closer to your real inputs than to your ideal world

If real inputs are messy, include mess.

Keep rules above examples and keep examples above the new input

Order matters:

- rules,
- examples,
- new input,

- output.

Use the same "unknown policy" everywhere

Pick one:

- Unknown, null, N/A, or questions first.
  Do not mix policies across examples.

Do not overload examples with style flourishes

Examples are for teaching the pattern, not showing off writing.

Mini lab: upgrade a weak example set

If your current few-shot prompt uses 1 perfect example only, upgrade it by adding:

- one example with missing values,
- one borderline classification, or
- one counterexample showing the common mistake.

This small change often doubles consistency without adding many tokens.
A good few-shot prompt does not just show what you want. It shows what to do when things go wrong, and what not to do at the boundary.

<u>Positive vs negative examples</u>

Few-shot prompting teaches by demonstration. The most common approach is to show only "good" examples, also called **positive examples**. That works for many tasks. But when you need strict boundaries, you should also use **negative examples**, also called counterexamples, which show what not to do.

Used correctly, positive and negative examples together create a powerful teaching set:

- positives define the target pattern,
- negatives define the boundaries and common failure modes.

Definitions (simple and practical)

Positive examples

Examples of correct behavior:

- Input → ideal output
- consistent formatting
- correct labels
- correct tone and structure

Purpose:

- teach the pattern you want repeated.

Negative examples

Examples of incorrect behavior, clearly labeled as wrong:

- Bad output → explanation of why wrong
- followed by corrected output

Purpose:

- prevent predictable errors,
- teach boundaries,
- reduce format drift and hallucination pressure.

Important: never include negative examples without clearly marking them as incorrect and providing a corrected version.

When positive examples are enough

Use only positive examples when:

- the task is mostly formatting and imitation,
- mistakes are rare or low cost,
- the output is flexible (creative writing, brainstorming),
- you are short on prompt space.

Typical cases:

- outlines that just need structure,
- rewriting into a consistent voice,
- extracting a few fields from clean inputs.

Positive-only example sets work well when the main challenge is "show me the shape."

When you should add negative examples

Use negative examples when:

- the model repeatedly makes the same mistake,
- your task has strict compliance rules,
- you need sharp boundaries between categories,
- you must prevent unsafe or forbidden content,
- you must stop extra commentary.

High-value situations:

- JSON only output, no extra text,
- schemas with no extra keys,
- strict label classification (spam vs not spam),
- compliance writing (no invented facts, no claims),
- sensitive tone requirements (no blame, no apology, no hype).

Negative examples teach the model "what failure looks like," which is often the missing piece.

The biggest mistake with negative examples

If you show a bad example without clear labeling, the model may imitate it.

Avoid this:

- showing "bad output" as a normal example.

Do this instead:

- label it loudly as wrong,
- explain the failure rule in one line,
- show the corrected output right away,
- then proceed with positive examples.

The recommended structure: sandwich method

A reliable ordering is:

1. Rules (short)
2. Positive example
3. Negative example (wrong + why)
4. Corrected example
5. New input to solve

This "sandwich" reinforces correct behavior and prevents the model from ending on the wrong pattern.

How to write negative examples safely (professional format)

A good negative example includes four parts:

1. **Bad output** (short)
2. **Why wrong** (reference a rule)
3. **Correct output** (what it should be)
4. **Rule reminder** (one sentence)

Keep negative examples short, otherwise you waste context and increase risk of imitation.

Examples (ready to reuse)

Example 1: JSON-only task (classic failure)

Rule:

"Output valid JSON only. No markdown. No commentary. Keys must match schema."

Positive example:

Input: "Owner is Sam. Deadline June 10. Risk: delay."

Output:

```
{
"owner": "Sam",
"deadline": "2025-06-10",
"risk": "delay"
}
```

Negative example (wrong):
Bad output:
"Here's the JSON you asked for:

```
{
"owner": "Sam",
"deadline": "2025-06-10",
"risk": "delay"
}"
```

Why wrong:
It includes extra text before JSON.
Correct output:

```
{
"owner": "Sam",
"deadline": "2025-06-10",
"risk": "delay"
}
```

Rule reminder:
Return JSON only, nothing else.
This single negative example often stops the most frequent JSON formatting error.

Example 2: Classification boundary (borderline cases)

Task:
Label messages as Bug, Feature request, Billing, or Other.
Positive example:
Input: "App crashes when I click Save."
Output: Bug, reason: crash on action.
Negative example (wrong):
Input: "Can you add dark mode?"
Bad output: Bug
Why wrong: This is not a defect; it is a requested capability.

Correct output:
Feature request, reason: asks to add functionality.
Negative examples sharpen category boundaries.

Example 3: Avoiding invented facts (hallucination control)

Rule:
"Use only provided inputs. If missing, write Unknown."
Positive example:
Input: "Project starts Monday. Owner: Lina."
Output:
Start date: Monday
Owner: Lina
Budget: Unknown
Negative example (wrong):
Bad output:
Budget: $50,000
Why wrong:
Budget was not provided, so it must not be invented.
Correct output:
Budget: Unknown

How many negative examples should you include?

Most prompts need only:

- 1 negative example for the most common failure mode.

Add more only if:

- you see repeated failures across different types,
- you have enough context budget.

A practical rule:

- 2 to 3 positive examples,
- 1 negative example for the top mistake,
- optional second negative example for a second recurring mistake.

Choosing what your negative example should target

Pick the failure that costs you the most time.
Common targets:

- extra sections or commentary,
- wrong label categories,
- invented facts,
- ignoring stop conditions,

- wrong formatting (tables vs bullets),
- wrong key names or extra keys in JSON.

One well-chosen negative example often fixes more than adding multiple new rules.

Where negative examples can backfire

Avoid negative examples when:

- the content is sensitive or unsafe, even as a "bad example,"
- you fear the model may echo the bad content,
- the task is creative and you do not want hard constraints.

In those cases, use "do not" rules and validation check instead.

Mini checklist for balanced few-shot sets

- 2–3 positive examples define structure and tone.
- 1 negative example blocks the most common error.
- Negative example is clearly labeled wrong and immediately corrected.
- Examples are short and consistent.
- The new task input appears after examples.

Positive examples show the path. Negative examples build the guardrails. Together they create few-shot prompts that behave predictably under real-world messiness.

How many examples to use and how to compress them

Few-shot prompting is powerful, but examples cost space. Too few examples and the model may not learn the pattern. Too many and you crowd out the real input, increase noise, and risk overfitting to irrelevant details.

This section gives practical rules for:

- how many examples to use,
- how to pick the right ones,
- how to compress examples without losing training signal.

How many examples to use (practical guidance)

0 examples (zero-shot)

Use when:

- the task is straightforward and easy to describe,
- format is not strict,
- you have strong direct constraints.

Best for:

- simple summaries,
- basic rewrites,
- direct instruction tasks with clear output rules.

1 example (one-shot)

Use when:

- the main goal is "match this shape,"
- the task is simple but formatting matters,
- tone imitation is important.

Best for:

- email template imitation,
- consistent outline structure,
- a fixed table layout,
- a single transformation style.

Risk:

- one example can be too narrow. If the new input differs, performance may degrade.

2 to 3 examples (sweet spot)

This is the best default for professional use.

Use when:

- you want stable behavior across topics and input styles,
- you have labels or structured outputs,
- you want to reduce "format drift."

Best for:

- classification and routing,
- extraction into JSON and tables,
- consistent meeting notes format,
- rubric scoring.

Why it works:

- enough variety to generalize,
- still compact enough to leave room for real input.

4 to 5 examples (edge-case coverage)

Use when:

- edge cases matter,
- the task has tricky boundaries,

- you want very consistent labeling or strict handling of missing/conflicting data.

Best for:

- compliance-sensitive templates,
- complex classification,
- messy data extraction,
- multi-field schemas with common missing values.

Caution:

- beyond 5 examples you often get diminishing returns unless you are extremely careful with compression.

More than 5 examples (only for special cases)

Use when:

- you are effectively building a mini dataset,
- you have enough context budget,
- the task is highly sensitive to subtle differences.

If you go beyond 5:

- compress aggressively,
- remove narrative,
- keep examples uniform.

A simple decision rule

Choose example count by asking:

1. Is the output format strict?
- No → 0 to 1 example
- Yes → 2 to 3 examples
2. Are there important edge cases?
- No → keep 2 to 3
- Yes → add 1 edge-case example (3 to 4)
3. Is the model repeatedly failing in the same way?
- Yes → add 1 negative example (wrong + corrected)

Most professional prompts settle at:

- 2 positives + 1 edge case + optional 1 negative.

What to compress first (when you need space)

To compress examples, remove what does not teach the pattern.

Compress in this order:

1. remove storytelling and filler words,
2. shorten inputs, keep only the relevant parts,

3. shorten outputs, keep only structural essentials,
4. convert prose outputs into skeletons,
5. replace repeated text with placeholders.

Your goal is to keep the "training signal":

- structure,
- labels,
- boundary behavior,
- unknown handling,
- stop conditions.

Compression techniques that actually work

Technique 1: Use skeleton outputs instead of full outputs

Instead of long examples, show a structural skeleton.

Example:

Output format:

- Subject:
- Greeting:
- 3 bullets:
- CTA:
- Sign-off:

Then one short example shows how it fills in.

This compresses dramatically while preserving structure.

Technique 2: Replace repeated details with placeholders

Use consistent placeholders:

- <NAME>, <DATE>, <AMOUNT>, <PRODUCT>, <ROLE>.

This prevents the model from copying irrelevant specifics and saves space.

Technique 3: Make inputs shorter but keep the decision cues

If you are labeling messages, keep only the line that contains the classification signal.

Do not include extra background that does not affect the label.

Technique 4: Use "micro-examples"

A micro-example is 1 to 2 lines:

Input: "App crashes on save."

Output: Bug

This is extremely effective for classification tasks and routing.

Technique 5: Compress multiple examples into a table

For label tasks, tables are compact and clear:

Input Label Reason

This can fit many examples in little space while keeping consistency.

Technique 6: Use one edge-case example instead of many

Edge cases should be representative, not exhaustive.

Pick the most frequent failure:

- missing values,
- ambiguity,
- conflict.

One strong edge case often improves reliability more than three weak ones.

Technique 7: Add a single negative example for the main failure

Instead of adding many positives, add one "wrong vs correct" pair for the top mistake.

This is high impact and compact.

Example: Compressing a few-shot set (before vs after)

Before (too long)

- 4 examples with long paragraphs,
- each output includes extra commentary,
- inconsistent naming and formatting.

Result:

- inconsistent output,
- wasted context space.

After (compressed and stronger)

Rules:

- Output must match format exactly.
- Unknown values must be null.
- No extra text.

Examples (micro + one edge case):

1. Input: "Owner Sam. Deadline June 10."
   Output: {"owner":"Sam","deadline":"2025-06-10","risk":null}
2. Input: "Owner unknown. Risk: delay."
   Output: {"owner":null,"deadline":null,"risk":"delay"}

Negative (top failure):

Bad: "Here is JSON: {…}"

Correct: {…}

Now do this:
Input: <text>
Output:

This compressed set often outperforms the long one because it is consistent and teaches boundaries.

Preventing overfitting to your examples

Too many examples can cause the model to:

- mimic irrelevant details,
- reuse names or topics,
- ignore new input.

Avoid overfitting by:

- using placeholders,
- varying topics while keeping format identical,
- avoiding distinctive phrasing in examples,
- adding an instruction:
  "Do not reuse names or details from examples."

Checklist: your examples are compact and effective

- Example count matches task complexity (usually 2–3).
- Examples cover at least one edge case if needed.
- Outputs are consistent in shape and labels.
- Examples are short, without filler.
- Placeholders replace irrelevant details.
- One negative example exists if a failure repeats.
- Enough context remains for the actual input.

Few-shot prompting is not about piling on examples. It is about selecting a small set that teaches the full behavior: the normal pattern, the messy case, and the boundary.

Style transfer vs content transfer

Few-shot prompting is great at teaching patterns, but it also creates a risk: the model may copy content from your examples instead of transferring only the style. Professionals separate these two goals:

- **Style transfer**: copy the voice, structure, formatting, level of detail.
- **Content transfer**: copy facts, claims, names, numbers, or ideas.

In most professional scenarios, you want strong style transfer and near-zero content transfer.

This section shows how to get the benefits of few-shot without "example leakage."

What style transfer is (what you want)

Style transfer is the model learning:

- the structure (headings, bullet count, order),
- tone (formal, friendly, neutral),
- brevity level (short bullets vs long paragraphs),
- vocabulary level (beginner vs expert),
- formatting (tables, JSON, checklists),
- reasoning shape (label + one-sentence reason).

Style transfer is desirable because it makes outputs consistent.

Examples:

- your support replies all sound like one brand,
- your JSON outputs always match the same schema,
- your outlines always follow the same chapter pattern.

What content transfer is (usually what you do not want)

Content transfer is the model reusing:

- names, dates, places,
- specific phrases that carry meaning (not just tone),
- unique details or claims,
- the example's argument or storyline,
- example-specific numbers and metrics.

This becomes a problem when:

- the output includes details not in the new input,
- the output "hallucinates" by borrowing plausible content from examples,
- sensitive data in examples leaks into new outputs.

Why models mix style and content

Few-shot examples are powerful conditioning. The model does not "understand" your intent to transfer only style unless you constrain it. It learns from everything in the examples:

- structure and tone,
- but also topical details and phrasing.

If your examples are vivid or specific, you increase content leakage risk.

How to decide what you want transferred

Before writing examples, decide which category you are teaching:

If your goal is style transfer

You want:

- formatting consistency,
- tone consistency,
- structure consistency,
- minimal example specificity.

If your goal is content transfer

This is rarer but valid in some cases, for example:

- training a consistent reasoning framework,
- teaching a specific policy rule interpretation,
- mapping a domain definition to outputs.

Even then, you should transfer content only when it is intended and safe.

The "anti-leak" rules for style transfer (copy-paste block)

Add this block directly above your examples:

"Examples are for style and structure only.

Do not reuse names, numbers, facts, or unique phrases from the examples.

Use only the new input for content.

If a required detail is missing from the new input, write Unknown or ask a question."

This one block prevents many example-driven hallucinations.

How to design examples for style transfer (safe examples)

1) Use placeholders, not real specifics

Replace details with tokens like:

- <NAME>, <DATE>, <COMPANY>, <AMOUNT>, <PRODUCT>.

This teaches structure without teaching facts.

2) Keep examples generic and interchangeable

Avoid distinctive narratives.

Avoid unique events.

Avoid unusual numbers.

3) Use multiple topics if the task is general

If you always use marketing examples, outputs may drift toward marketing.

4) Keep outputs consistent but not verbose

Short outputs reduce the chance of the model copying content.

5) Include one "missing data" example

Teach "Unknown" behavior so the model does not fill gaps by borrowing example facts.

How to design examples when you need content transfer (controlled content)

Sometimes you do want the model to transfer content rules. For instance:

- "Use these criteria to label requests."
- "Follow this policy decision logic."
- "Use this formatting and this vocabulary list."

In that case:

- keep the transferable content explicit and bounded,
- isolate it as a list of rules rather than burying it in example narratives,
- include a reminder:
  "Do not introduce facts not present in the new input."

Common failure modes and fixes

Failure 1: Example names appear in new output

Fix:

- use placeholders,
- add "do not reuse names from examples."

Failure 2: Example numbers and metrics appear in new output

Fix:

- remove numbers from examples,
- or replace with <NUMBER>.

Failure 3: Example arguments or storyline gets copied

Fix:

- shorten examples to structural skeletons,
- vary topics across examples.

Failure 4: The model blends example facts with new input

Fix:

- force grounding:
  "Use only the new input for factual content."

Failure 5: The model paraphrases unique phrases from examples

Fix:

- avoid distinctive phrasing,
- or add:
  "Do not reuse any full sentence from examples."

Practical patterns you can use

Pattern A: Skeleton-only few-shot (best for style transfer)

Instead of full examples, provide a skeleton that the model must fill.

Example skeleton:

- Heading 1:
- Heading 2:
- Checklist:
- Example:
- Stop.

This teaches pure structure with minimal content leakage risk.

Pattern B: Table examples for labeling

Use micro-examples in a table:

Input | Label | Reason

Short, generic, consistent.

Pattern C: Output-only examples

If input is long and variable, you can show only output shape:

"This is what the final should look like."

Then provide new input.

This works well for reports and checklists.

A clear way to phrase your intent (recommended wording)

If you want style transfer:

"Match the structure and tone of the examples. Do not reuse their content."

If you want controlled content transfer:

"Follow the same decision rules as the examples, but use only the new input's facts."

These lines prevent confusion between "sound like this" and "say this."

Mini lab: turn unsafe examples into safe style transfer examples

Take one of your few-shot prompts and check:

- does it include real names, numbers, or proprietary details?
- are the examples too story-like?

Rewrite:

- replace specifics with placeholders,
- shorten outputs to only what teaches structure,
- add an "anti-leak" block.

Then run the prompt twice and verify:

- the structure stays consistent,

- no example details appear in new outputs.

Style transfer is a superpower when controlled. Content transfer is a liability unless intentionally bounded. The difference is not the model, it is your example design and your rules.

Lab, build a mini style guide with 5 examples and tests

This lab turns few-shot prompting into a reusable asset: a mini style guide that consistently produces the same voice and structure across many topics.

You will build:

- a one-page style guide (rules + do and do not),
- 5 curated examples (the "training set"),
- a set of tests that verify the model follows the style.

Outcome: you will have a copy-paste prompt block you can reuse for emails, chapters, summaries, and internal docs.

Lab overview

You will complete three deliverables:

1. **Style guide rules**: tone, structure, clarity rules, formatting constraints.
2. **Five examples**: designed for variety and edge cases.
3. **Five tests**: short inputs that measure whether the style transfers correctly.

Keep everything short. Your goal is consistency, not length.

Step 1: Choose your target style (name it)

Give the style a short label. Examples:

- "Clean professional"
- "Beginner-friendly instructor"
- "Executive concise"
- "Support agent calm"
- "Technical writer neutral"

Naming the style prevents drift because you are anchoring a specific identity and expectations.

Step 2: Write the mini style guide (rules that are testable)

A good style guide is not vague. It is measurable.

Mini style guide template (copy and fill)

Style name: <name>

Audience: <who>

Tone: <3 adjectives, for example: calm, clear, confident>
Reading level: <beginner, general, expert>
Structure defaults: <headings, bullets, sections>
Length defaults: <word range or bullet counts>
Clarity rules: define terms, avoid ambiguity, no fluff
Forbidden: hype, invented facts, moralizing, long disclaimers
Unknown handling: Unknown or ask up to N questions
Stop condition: stop after final required section
Example rules that work well:

- "Use short paragraphs, max 3 sentences each."
- "Prefer bullets over long prose."
- "Define technical terms on first use."
- "No invented facts. Unknown if missing."
- "No extra sections beyond the template."

Step 3: Build 5 examples (your few-shot training set)

Your examples must teach the style under realistic variation. Each example should include:

- a short input,
- an ideal output in your style,
- consistent structure.

What the five examples should cover

1. Normal case (easy)
2. Different topic, same structure (variety)
3. Input with missing info (edge case)
4. Slightly complex case (multi-step reasoning, still short)
5. A counterexample pair (optional but powerful): wrong vs corrected

If you include a counterexample, keep it short and clearly labeled as wrong.

Keep examples safe and reusable

- Use placeholders: <NAME>, <DATE>, <TEAM>
- Avoid real company details or personal data
- Avoid distinctive numbers unless your style requires them

Step 4: Add tests (style compliance checks)

Tests are short prompts you run after your examples to see if the style transfers.

A test includes:

- a new input,

- and a requirement:
  "Output must match the style guide rules exactly."

What to test

- structure stays the same across different topics,
- tone stays consistent,
- forbidden items do not appear,
- unknown handling is correct,
- stop condition is respected.

A strong test suite includes:

- one very short input,
- one long or messy input,
- one with missing key info,
- one that tempts the model to be verbose,
- one that tempts it to invent facts.

Step 5: Assemble the final "style guide prompt block"

This is what you will actually reuse.

Reusable prompt block structure

1. Style guide rules
2. "Examples are for style only" anti-leak rule
3. Five examples
4. New input
5. Verification instructions

Add:

"Before finalizing, verify compliance with the style guide. Fix violations. Output final only."

A complete lab artifact (example you can adapt)

Mini style guide (example)

Style name: Clean professional
Audience: busy professionals
Tone: clear, direct, respectful
Reading level: general
Structure default: short heading + bullets + next step
Length: 120–180 words unless specified
Clarity: define uncommon terms, avoid vague adjectives
Forbidden: hype, emojis, filler, invented facts

Unknown handling: write Unknown or ask up to 3 questions
Stop: stop after "Next step"
Anti-leak:
"Use examples for structure and tone only. Do not reuse names, dates, or details from examples."

Five examples (example set)

Example 1 (normal)
Input: "Summarize this meeting: we agreed to ship feature A next week. <NAME> owns testing."
Output:
Heading: Summary

- Decision: ship feature A next week
- Owner: <NAME> for testing
  Next step: confirm test plan by <DATE>

Example 2 (different topic)
Input: "Write a short update on project status: on track, risk is vendor delay."
Output:
Heading: Status update

- Status: on track
- Risk: vendor delay
  Next step: request updated vendor timeline by <DATE>

Example 3 (missing info edge case)
Input: "Create an email asking for approval."
Output:
Heading: Approval request

- Request: approval for <ITEM>
- Reason: <REASON>
- Deadline: Unknown
  Next step: confirm item and deadline

Example 4 (slightly complex)
Input: "Summarize tradeoffs between option A and B for leadership."
Output:
Heading: Tradeoff summary

- Option A: <PRO> / <CON>
- Option B: <PRO> / <CON>

- Recommendation: <RECOMMENDATION>
  Next step: validate assumption about <KEY RISK>

Example 5 (counterexample)
Input: "Write a concise update."
Bad output (wrong): long paragraph, multiple extra sections
Why wrong: violates length and structure rules
Correct output:
Heading: Update

- Key point: <POINT>
  Next step: <ACTION>

Five tests (run after building your own set)

Test 1: "Write an update about a policy change for staff."
Test 2: "Summarize these messy notes: <paste notes>"
Test 3: "Draft a request but do not invent missing dates."
Test 4: "Explain a technical concept to a general reader in the style."
Test 5: "Generate a response that must stop after the final section."
Scoring:

- Pass if structure, tone, and stop condition match.
- Fail if it adds extra sections, becomes verbose, or invents facts.

Common mistakes in this lab, and fixes

Mistake: examples too similar

Fix: vary topics and input shape while keeping output structure identical.

Mistake: examples contain real facts you do not want repeated

Fix: use placeholders and generic inputs.

Mistake: style guide rules are vague

Fix: convert into counts, limits, and explicit forbidden items.

Mistake: no tests for missing info

Fix: include at least one missing-data test and enforce Unknown handling.

What "good" looks like at the end

You know your mini style guide works when:

- you can paste any new input and get the same structure and tone,
- outputs do not copy example details,
- missing information is handled consistently,
- your tests pass across multiple runs.

This lab produces a reusable asset: a small, high-quality example set plus tests that keep your outputs stable as tasks change.

Chapter 8. Multi-step prompting and chaining

Why multi-step is more reliable than one giant prompt

A single giant prompt asks the model to do everything at once: understand the goal, interpret the inputs, decide what matters, choose a structure, write the output, and self-correct. It can work, but it fails in predictable ways. Multi-step prompting, also called chaining, breaks the work into smaller controlled steps with intermediate checkpoints. Each step has a clear purpose, a tighter scope, and simpler success criteria. This usually produces outputs that are more accurate, complete, and consistent.

The core idea: reduce cognitive load and ambiguity

When you ask for too much in one prompt, several things happen:

- requirements compete for attention,
- the model may satisfy some constraints and ignore others,
- it may jump to a coherent answer before it has fully analyzed the input,
- it may fill missing pieces with guesses to keep the narrative smooth.

Multi-step prompts reduce these failure modes because each step focuses on one job.

What "multi-step" actually means

A multi-step workflow might look like this:

1. Clarify requirements and missing info
2. Extract facts from the source text
3. Organize facts into a structure
4. Draft the deliverable
5. Validate against constraints and revise

Each step produces a small intermediate output that you can inspect and correct before moving on.

Why multi-step is more reliable (the practical reasons)

1) You prevent skipped requirements

In long prompts, it is common for the model to miss one rule, like:

- "exactly 7 bullets,"
- "no extra sections,"
- "use only provided inputs,"
- "stop after JSON."

Multi-step workflows let you enforce requirements at the right moment:

- define format before drafting,
- validate after drafting,
- correct before final output.

2) You separate "thinking tasks" from "writing tasks"

Many tasks contain two different jobs:

- reasoning and selection (what matters, what to include),
- communication (how to present it).

If you merge them, the writing often "wins" and the model produces fluent text that hides reasoning gaps.

Multi-step splits them:

- Step: extract facts
- Step: organize
- Step: write

This produces clearer, more grounded outputs.

3) You reduce hallucination pressure

Hallucinations often happen when the model feels it must complete a narrative without enough input.

Multi-step reduces that pressure by adding an explicit stage for:

- identifying missing info,
- listing Unknown values,
- asking clarifying questions.

If the model can pause and say "missing," it is less likely to invent.

4) You gain checkpoints and early error detection

With a giant prompt, you only see the failure at the end. Then you have to re-run the whole thing.

With multi-step, you catch errors early:

- Did it extract the right facts?
- Did it choose the correct structure?
- Are constraints feasible?

Fixing a step is faster than rewriting the entire prompt.

5) You can reuse steps as modular tools

Once you have a reliable chain, you can reuse components:

- a robust extraction step,
- a formatting step,
- a validation step,

- a critique step.

This is how teams build stable internal prompting workflows.

6) Multi-step improves consistency across runs

One-shot prompts are more sensitive to randomness and minor phrasing changes.

When you constrain steps, you narrow the space of possible outputs:

- extraction step produces a consistent "facts list,"
- formatting step produces a consistent template,
- validation step enforces compliance.

That reduces drift.

Common failure modes of "one giant prompt"

A single prompt often fails in these patterns:

- **Overly long output** because you asked for too many things at once.
- **Missing sections** because the model prioritizes narrative flow.
- **Wrong structure** because the model defaults to generic formatting.
- **Invented details** because it tries to be helpful and complete.
- **Contradictory outputs** because constraints compete (short + detailed + comprehensive).

Multi-step prompting is essentially a way to avoid these conflicts by sequencing decisions.

When a giant prompt can still be fine

One prompt works well when:

- the task is short and unambiguous,
- you have complete inputs,
- structure is simple,
- you do not need strict validation.

Example:

"Rewrite this paragraph for clarity, keep meaning, 120–150 words."

But as soon as tasks become multi-constraint, multi-step wins.

The professional rule of thumb

Use multi-step prompting when at least two of these are true:

- multiple inputs (notes + data + constraints),
- strict output format (schema, fixed headings),
- high completeness requirement,
- high risk of hallucination,
- high quality expectations,

- you will reuse the workflow.

A simple multi-step chain you can reuse

If you want one universal chain, this is a strong default:

1. Clarify and gather requirements
2. Extract facts or key points from inputs
3. Create an outline or structure
4. Draft the output
5. Validate against constraints and revise
6. Return final only

This chain is short, modular, and reliable.

Mini lab: transform a giant prompt into a chain

Take a giant prompt like:

"Write a full chapter section with examples, checklist, and JSON schema for outputs, keep it short but detailed."

Convert it into steps:

1. Ask 5 questions about audience, length, required sections, forbidden content, success criteria.
2. Propose an outline with headings and exact counts.
3. Draft each section.
4. Validate counts and forbidden items.
5. Output final.

The result is usually more compliant and easier to refine.

Multi-step prompting is more reliable because it turns one complex problem into a sequence of simpler, testable problems. Instead of hoping the model satisfies every requirement simultaneously, you guide it through a controlled workflow where each step can be checked and corrected.

<u>Stages, plan, generate, verify, polish</u>

Multi-step prompting becomes reliable when it follows a consistent pipeline. The most practical pipeline for professional work has four stages:

1. **Plan**: decide what to produce and how it will be structured.
2. **Generate**: create the draft output according to the plan.
3. **Verify**: check the draft against requirements, constraints, and facts.
4. **Polish**: improve readability and tone without changing meaning or violating constraints.

This section shows what each stage does, what to ask for, and how to write prompts that keep the stages clean.

Stage 1: Plan

The planning stage reduces ambiguity before you start writing. It produces a structure the model can follow.

What "plan" should include

- the objective in one sentence,
- the audience and tone,
- the output format (headings, JSON schema, table columns),
- section order and counts (how many bullets, examples, steps),
- any assumptions and unknown handling,
- a stop condition.

What to ask for in the plan stage

Ask for a compact plan, not an essay.

Good plan outputs:

- a 6 to 10 bullet outline,
- headings with one-line purpose each,
- a table of sections with length targets,
- a schema summary.

Example plan prompt (copy and adapt)

"Plan only. Do not write the final content yet.

Create an outline for <deliverable> for <audience>.

Include required headings in exact order, and specify counts for examples and checklists.

List any missing information as questions.

Output: outline only."

Stage 2: Generate

Generation is where the model writes the deliverable using the plan.

Rules for the generation stage

- follow the plan exactly,
- do not add extra sections,
- use only allowed inputs,
- respect length and format contracts,
- mark missing facts as Unknown.

Example generate prompt (copy and adapt)

"Generate the deliverable using the approved outline.
Follow section order exactly.
Constraints: <must include, must avoid>.
Output requirements: <format, length>.
Stop after the final required section."

Tip: if you want stability, provide a skeleton and tell the model to fill it.

Stage 3: Verify

Verification is the reliability engine of the chain. It detects the common problems before you accept the output.

What verification should check

Format compliance

- required headings present and ordered correctly,
- bullet and section counts,
- length limits,
- JSON validity and schema compliance.

Constraint compliance

- forbidden content not present,
- non-goals not violated,
- no extra commentary.

Grounding and accuracy

- no invented facts beyond the input,
- assumptions clearly labeled or removed from final if required,
- ambiguous statements flagged.

Two verification modes

Mode A: Visible verification (learning and debugging)

The model returns:

- a checklist of pass/fail items,
- a list of violations,
- corrected output.

Mode B: Silent verification (production)

The model verifies internally and returns only the corrected final output.

Example verify prompt (copy and adapt)

"Verify the draft against this checklist: <list>.
If any item fails, revise the draft until all items pass.
Return only the corrected final output."
For structured outputs:
"Validate against this JSON schema. If invalid or extra keys exist, fix and re-validate. Return JSON only."

Stage 4: Polish

Polish makes the output easier to read and more audience-appropriate, without changing the substance.

What polish should do

- improve clarity and flow,
- reduce redundancy,
- tighten wording,
- align tone to audience,
- standardize terminology.

What polish must not do

- add new facts,
- change numbers or claims,
- introduce new sections unless allowed,
- violate length or format constraints.

Example polish prompt (copy and adapt)

"Polish the verified output for clarity and tone.
Do not add new facts or sections.
Keep within the same structure and length limits.
Return the polished final only."

Putting the four stages together (a complete chain)

Here is a reusable chain you can teach readers:

1. **Plan**
   "Draft an outline with headings and counts. Ask questions for missing info."
2. **Generate**
   "Write the deliverable following the outline. Use only allowed inputs. Respect format."

3. **Verify**
   "Check compliance with format, constraints, and grounding. Fix violations."
4. **Polish**
   "Improve readability and tone without changing content. Preserve structure."

This pipeline is stable across many tasks.

Example: applying the stages to one task (email)

Plan

- subject line goal,
- 3 bullet points,
- CTA,
- word range.

Generate

- write email with fixed structure.

Verify

- word count range, bullet count, CTA included, no forbidden phrases.

Polish

- tighten wording and tone, keep structure.

Common mistakes and fixes

Mistake 1: Stages blur together

Fix:

Add gates:

- "Plan only, do not draft yet."
- "Verify only, do not rewrite unless a rule fails."
- "Polish only, do not add facts."

Mistake 2: Verification is vague

Fix:

Use a checklist with measurable criteria:

- counts, headings, keys, types, forbidden items.

Mistake 3: Polish introduces new content

Fix:

Add:

"Do not add facts. Do not add sections. Only improve wording."

Mini checklist for readers

If you want reliability:

- plan defines structure,
- generate follows structure,
- verify enforces rules,
- polish improves readability only.

This four-stage chain is a professional default because it makes quality controllable and repeatable.

Using intermediate representations, outlines, tables, checklists

Multi-step prompting becomes significantly more reliable when you insert intermediate representations between the raw input and the final output. An intermediate representation is a structured artifact the model produces in the middle of a workflow so you can:

- reduce ambiguity,
- catch errors early,
- enforce completeness,
- and make the final output easier to generate consistently.

The three most useful intermediate representations are:

- **outlines** (structure and coverage),
- **tables** (extraction and alignment),
- **checklists** (verification and stop conditions).

Why intermediate representations improve reliability

When you ask for a final deliverable immediately, the model must:

- interpret requirements,
- decide what matters,
- choose a structure,
- draft content,
- and self-correct.

That is a lot of "competing objectives" at once. Intermediate representations split the work so each step has one clear job:

- Outline step: decide structure and coverage
- Table step: capture facts and map them to fields
- Checklist step: verify compliance and completeness

This reduces missed requirements, hallucinations, and format drift.

Intermediate representation 1: Outlines

What outlines are best for

Outlines are best when you need:

- a stable structure for long outputs,
- guaranteed coverage of required topics,
- consistent section ordering,
- predictable length and pacing.

They are ideal for:

- chapter sections,
- reports,
- proposals,
- lesson plans,
- SOPs.

What a "professional outline" should contain

A useful outline is not just headings. It includes:

- headings in required order,
- the purpose of each section in one line,
- required elements per section (examples, bullets, tables),
- optional notes on length targets,
- questions for missing requirements.

Example outline prompt (copy and adapt)

"Create an outline only.
Use headings in this exact order: <list>.
For each heading, provide: purpose, key points (3 bullets), and required elements (examples/checklists).
Do not write full paragraphs yet."

How outlines reduce drift

Once you approve an outline, the generation step becomes simpler:
"Write section-by-section following this outline exactly."
This prevents:

- missing sections,
- random extra sections,
- wrong ordering.

Intermediate representation 2: Tables

What tables are best for

Tables are best when you must:

- extract information from messy inputs,
- map facts to consistent fields,
- compare options,
- ensure completeness and traceability.

They are ideal for:

- requirements extraction,
- meeting action items,
- test cases,
- risk registers,
- comparison matrices,
- project plans.

The table-first workflow (high reliability)

A strong chain is:

1. extract facts into a table,
2. generate the narrative using only the table.

This prevents invented details because the table becomes the "source of truth."

Example table prompt (copy and adapt)

"Extract information from the text into a table with columns: <A,B,C>.
Use 'Unknown' for missing values.
Do not add commentary outside the table."

Then generate from the table

"Using only the table above, write the final report.
Do not introduce facts not present in the table."

Why tables reduce hallucinations

Because you force a step where the model must say:

- "I do not have this field" → Unknown

Instead of guessing to keep a narrative smooth.

Intermediate representation 3: Checklists

What checklists are best for

Checklists are best when you need:

- format compliance,
- constraint compliance,

- completeness verification,
- repeatability across runs.

They are ideal for:

- strict format outputs (JSON, tables, schemas),
- multi-constraint writing (length, sections, forbidden content),
- team workflows.

The checklist-first verification loop

A professional chain often ends with:

1. generate draft,
2. check against checklist,
3. fix violations,
4. output final only.

Example checklist prompt (copy and adapt)

"Before finalizing, check the output against this checklist:

- Required headings present and ordered correctly
- Exactly 7 bullets in section 2
- Word count 900–1,100
- No invented facts, Unknown if missing
- No extra sections

  If any item fails, revise until all pass. Return only the final output."

Why checklists improve consistency

They turn vague "be careful" instructions into a test.

If the model fails a test, it revises. That is how professionals reduce rework.

How to choose the right intermediate representation

Use this simple mapping:

- Need structure and coverage → **Outline**
- Need extraction and alignment → **Table**
- Need compliance and quality gate → **Checklist**

Most high-quality workflows use two or three:

- Outline → Draft → Checklist
- Table → Draft → Checklist
- Outline → Table → Draft → Checklist (for complex work)

Example chains you can reuse

Chain A: Writing a chapter section

1. Outline with headings and required elements
2. Draft section-by-section

3. Checklist verification for structure, examples, length
4. Polish (optional)

Chain B: Turning notes into an SOP

1. Table: extract steps, prerequisites, risks
2. Outline: SOP sections
3. Draft SOP using extracted table
4. Checklist verification

Chain C: JSON extraction with strict schema

1. Table: raw extraction of fields
2. Convert table to JSON
3. Validate JSON against schema checklist
4. Output JSON only

Best practices (the small rules that make it work)

Make intermediate outputs "clean and reusable"

- no extra commentary,
- consistent formatting,
- clear Unknown handling.

Keep intermediate outputs shorter than the final

Intermediate steps should simplify, not expand.

Use strict boundaries between steps

Write prompts that separate phases:

- "Outline only, do not draft."
- "Table only, no explanation."
- "Final output only, no checklist text."

Use "source of truth" language

- "Use only the table to write the report."
- "Do not add facts beyond the extracted fields."

This dramatically reduces drift and hallucination.

Mini lab: build a chain using all three

Pick a messy input, like meeting notes.

1. Table: extract action items (Action, Owner role, Due date, Risk).
2. Outline: sections for a follow-up email (Summary, Actions, Risks, Next steps).
3. Draft: write the email using only the table.
4. Checklist: verify bullet count, length, and no invented dates.

You will see the difference immediately: the final output becomes more consistent, more grounded, and easier to control.

Keeping context clean, what to carry forward

Multi-step prompting becomes unreliable when context becomes messy. As you chain steps, you accumulate drafts, notes, partial conclusions, and repeated instructions. If you carry everything forward, two things happen:

- the model starts following outdated or conflicting instructions,
- the model spends attention on irrelevant text instead of the current task.

Professional chaining relies on **clean context discipline**: carry forward only what the next step needs, in a compact, structured form.

The principle: each step gets only the inputs it needs

Treat each step like a function:

- it should have a small, explicit input,
- produce a clean output,
- and avoid inheriting unrelated baggage.

You want the next step to see:

- the final requirements,
- the chosen plan or schema,
- the minimal source facts,
- and the current draft if revision is required.

You do not want the next step to see:

- old prompts,
- earlier incorrect drafts,
- brainstorming options you rejected,
- long conversations that contain conflicting preferences.

What to carry forward (the "carry set")

In most chains, the next step needs only five things:

1. **Objective**
   One sentence: what are we producing and for whom?
2. **Constraints and non-goals**
   Must include, must avoid, unknown handling, stop condition.
3. **Output requirements**
   Structure, ordering, length, and format contract.

4. **Source of truth**
   The authoritative input: extracted facts table, approved outline, or provided data.
5. **Current artifact** (only if revising)
   The latest draft, not older versions.

If you carry these five, the chain stays stable.

What not to carry forward (common context pollution)

Avoid carrying:

- multiple versions of the draft,
- the entire conversation history,
- raw brainstorming lists,
- contradictory requirements ("short but very detailed"),
- repeated copies of the same rules,
- irrelevant examples from other tasks.

If a detail is not used by the next step, remove it.

Use "context packets" to keep chains clean

A context packet is a compact block you paste into the next step. It summarizes the current truth without noise.

Context packet template (copy and reuse)

Context packet

Objective: <one sentence>
Audience: <who>
Source of truth: <text/table/outline>
Output requirements: <format, structure, length>
Constraints: <must include, must avoid, unknown handling>
Stop condition: <where to end>
Instruction:
"Use only this context packet. Ignore earlier drafts and instructions."

This creates a clean handoff between steps.

The golden rule: keep one "source of truth"

Chaining fails when the model has multiple competing sources:

- raw notes,
- extracted table,
- a draft that includes invented details,
- plus new user updates.

Pick one authoritative source for the next step.

Examples:

- For a report, the source of truth might be the extracted facts table.
- For a chapter, the source of truth might be the approved outline.
- For JSON, the source of truth is the schema and the extracted fields.

Then state it explicitly:

"Use only the table below as the source of truth."

How to handle revisions without dragging old mistakes forward

When revising, include:

- the latest draft only,
- the critique checklist or violations list,
- the requirements.

Do not include:

- earlier drafts,
- earlier critiques that were already fixed.

Revision packet template

Objective: <one line>

Requirements: <structure, length, constraints>

Draft to revise: <latest version>

Violations to fix: <bullet list>

Output: return revised draft only.

This prevents regression.

Keep instructions non-duplicative

Repeated instructions often create contradictions by accident. Instead of restating everything every step, carry a single "contract" section.

Prompt contract (compact)

- Format: <JSON/table/headings>
- Counts: <exact bullets/sections>
- Forbidden: <list>
- Unknown handling: <Unknown/null/questions>
- Stop: <where to end>

Reuse the same contract in each step. Do not rewrite it.

How to compress context without losing signal

Professional compression strategies:

1) Convert raw text into structured notes

Instead of pasting 2 pages of meeting notes, extract:

- decisions,

- action items,
- risks,
- owners,
- dates.

2) Replace long examples with templates

If examples are needed, use one skeleton and one short example.

3) Use labels and identifiers

- "Section A, Section B"
- "Requirement R1, R2"
- "Constraint C1, C2"

This reduces repeated prose.

4) Remove "why" commentary unless it affects decisions

Keep:

- decisions and rules,
- drop:
- discussion that does not affect output.

What to do when new information arrives mid-chain

When requirements change, update the context packet and restate the source of truth.

Example:

"Update: audience is executives, max 150 words, include ROI. Replace previous assumptions."

Then proceed with the updated packet only.

This prevents the model from blending old and new requirements.

A practical workflow: clean carry-forward in 4 steps

Here is a clean chaining loop you can teach:

1. Step output: outline/table/checklist
2. Create a context packet summarizing the approved result
3. Run the next step using only the packet + any new input
4. Discard older materials and keep only the latest packet

Over time you have one living specification, not a growing pile.

Common failure modes and fixes

Failure: model follows old instructions

Fix:

- "Ignore all prior instructions. Use only the context packet below."

Failure: output includes rejected ideas from brainstorming

Fix:

- do not carry brainstorming forward,
- carry only the final selected option.

Failure: model invents facts by blending drafts and notes

Fix:

- declare a single source of truth,
- forbid facts outside that source.

Failure: chain gets longer and quality drops

Fix:

- stop carrying everything,
- compress into packets every step.

Mini checklist: clean context in chaining

Before you run the next step, ask:

- Did I include only one source of truth?
- Did I remove older drafts and rejected options?
- Are constraints and output requirements explicit and compact?
- Is unknown handling defined?
- Is there a clear stop condition?

If yes, your chain will stay reliable and easy to control.

Keeping context clean is how multi-step prompting scales. You are not just asking the model to do steps. You are managing information flow so each step receives a clear, minimal, conflict-free specification.

Exercises, design a 4-stage workflow for a report

This exercise teaches you to build a reliable report pipeline using a four-stage chain:

1. Plan
2. Generate
3. Verify
4. Polish

You will design the workflow, then write prompts for each stage so the model produces consistent, auditable reports.

The scenario

You have messy inputs such as:

- meeting notes,
- interview transcripts,

- research snippets,
- metrics tables,
- stakeholder emails.

You need a professional report that is:

- structured,
- grounded in the provided inputs,
- consistent in tone and format,
- and compliant with constraints (length, sections, forbidden content).

Exercise instructions

You will produce two deliverables:

1. A 4-stage workflow definition (what each stage does).
2. A set of 4 prompts, one per stage, that you can copy and reuse.

Step 1: Define the report contract (before the chain)

Before writing prompts, define the "contract" that stays constant across all four stages.

Report contract (fill in)

- Audience: <executive, manager, technical, general>
- Objective: <inform, recommend, decide>
- Allowed sources: <only provided inputs, or general knowledge allowed>
- Length: <word range or page limit>
- Required sections (in order):
    1. <Section A>
    2. <Section B>
    3. <Section C>
    4. <Section D>
- Must include: <key items, data points, risks, recommendations>
- Must avoid: <forbidden content, speculation, sensitive items>
- Unknown handling: Unknown or questions
- Stop condition: stop after final section

This contract becomes the anchor for every stage.

Stage 1 prompt: Plan

Goal: produce a stable outline and identify gaps before writing.

What the Plan stage must output

- headings in the required order,
- 2 to 4 bullet points per section,

- what evidence from inputs supports each section,
- a short list of missing information as questions,
- a proposed length budget per section.

Plan prompt template (copy and fill)

"Plan only, do not write the report yet.

Using the inputs below, create an outline for a report.

Report contract:

- Audience: <...>
- Objective: <...>
- Sections (in order): <...>
- Length: <...>
- Constraints: <must include, must avoid, unknown handling>

Output:

1. Outline with headings in exact order
2. Under each heading: 3 bullets of key points + which input lines support them
3. Up to 5 clarifying questions for missing information
   No prose paragraphs. No final report."

What you should look for:

- correct section order,
- no invented facts,
- evidence mapping to inputs.

Stage 2 prompt: Generate

Goal: draft the report strictly following the approved plan.

What the Generate stage must do

- follow outline order exactly,
- use only allowed sources,
- include required elements (tables, bullets, recommendations),
- mark missing facts as Unknown.

Generate prompt template

"Write the report using the approved outline below.

Follow section order exactly and include all required elements.

Constraints:

- Use only the provided inputs and the outline evidence references.
- Do not invent facts, numbers, or dates. Use Unknown if missing.
- Keep length within <range>.

- Do not add extra sections.
  Stop after the final required section.

Outline:

<paste approved outline>

Inputs:

<paste source text or extracted table>"

Tip:

If your inputs are long, first extract facts into a table and use the table as the source of truth.

Stage 3 prompt: Verify

Goal: check compliance and fix issues before polishing.

What the Verify stage must check

- required sections present and ordered correctly,
- length limits met,
- required items included,
- forbidden content absent,
- no invented facts beyond inputs,
- consistent tone and clarity.

Verify prompt template (self-correcting)

"Verify the draft report against this checklist.

If any item fails, revise the report and re-check until all items pass.

Return only the corrected report.

Checklist:

- Sections match required order exactly
- Length within <range>
- Must include: <list>
- Must avoid: <list>
- Unknown used for missing facts
- No extra sections, no filler conclusion
- Claims grounded in provided inputs

Draft report:

<paste draft>"

This stage is where reliability is enforced.

Stage 4 prompt: Polish

Goal: improve readability and tone without changing meaning or violating constraints.

What the Polish stage must do

- tighten wording,
- remove redundancy,
- improve clarity and flow,
- keep structure unchanged,
- do not add facts or new sections.

Polish prompt template

"Polish the verified report for clarity and tone for <audience>.
Do not add new facts, numbers, or claims.
Do not change section order or add sections.
Keep within the same length range.
Return the polished report only.
Verified report:
<paste verified report>"

What to submit (exercise output)

At the end, the learner should have:

- a completed report contract,
- a Plan prompt,
- a Generate prompt,
- a Verify prompt,
- a Polish prompt.

This becomes a reusable workflow for any report.

Bonus challenge (optional)

Add an intermediate representation:

- Stage 1 produces an outline plus a facts table,
- Stage 2 generates the report using only the table,
- Stage 3 validates against constraints,
- Stage 4 polishes.

This version is even more grounded and consistent.

Scoring rubric (quick)

Score 0–2 for each:

- Contract completeness
- Plan quality (coverage + no invention)
- Generate compliance (structure + constraints)
- Verify effectiveness (catches issues + fixes)

- Polish discipline (improves clarity without adding content)

A perfect workflow is not the one with the longest prompts. It is the one that produces consistent, constraint-compliant reports with minimal rework.

Chapter 9. Self-critique and iterative improvement

Prompting the model to find its own errors

A professional prompt does not assume the first output is correct. It builds in an error-finding step.

Self-critique prompting means you ask the model to:

- check its output against explicit requirements,
- find violations, gaps, or inconsistencies,
- correct them,
- and re-check before returning the final.

This is not about "being humble." It is about turning quality into a repeatable process.

Why self-critique works

Models are good at generating text quickly, but they can:

- miss constraints (counts, ordering, forbidden content),
- drift from format (JSON, tables, headings),
- overstate uncertainty or understate it,
- invent details to fill gaps,
- overlook contradictions between inputs.

Self-critique works because it shifts the model from "produce" mode to "evaluate" mode. When you give it a checklist or rubric, it has something concrete to test.

Two kinds of self-critique

You can use self-critique in two ways depending on your needs.

1) Visible self-critique (learning and debugging)

The model returns:

- its critique,
- its fixes,
- and the improved output.

Best for:

- training yourself or a team,
- diagnosing recurring errors,
- building prompt templates.

2) Hidden self-critique (production)

The model critiques internally and returns only:

- the corrected final output.

Best for:

- clean deliverables,
- repeated workflows,
- strict formatting tasks.

Both use the same technique. Only the output differs.

What the model should critique (the professional checklist)

A strong self-critique checks four layers:

Layer A: Objective fit

- Did it answer the actual task?
- Did it match the audience?

Layer B: Completeness

- Are required sections included?
- Are key points missing?

Layer C: Constraint compliance

- Length limits, counts, ordering
- Required sections and forbidden content
- "Use only provided inputs" rules
- Stop conditions

Layer D: Reliability and grounding

- Are any facts invented?
- Are assumptions labeled?
- Are ambiguous claims clearly flagged?

If you do not specify these layers, the model will critique vague things like "tone could be improved" and miss real failures like "wrong number of bullets."

The simplest self-critique pattern (copy and paste)

Use this when you want quick improvement without long commentary:

"Before finalizing, check your output against these requirements:

<list requirements as bullets>.

If any requirement is not met, revise until all are met.

Return only the final revised output."

This one block alone improves compliance dramatically.

A stronger pattern: draft → critique → revise → re-check

Use this when quality matters and you want transparency.

Template (visible critique)

"Step 1: Produce a draft.
Step 2: Critique the draft against the checklist below. Mark each item Pass/Fail and explain failures briefly.
Step 3: Revise to fix every failure.
Step 4: Re-check and confirm all items Pass.
Output: show (a) critique table and (b) final revised output."

Template (final-only)

"Draft internally. Critique internally against the checklist. Revise until all items pass.
Return only the final output."

How to write critique criteria that catch real errors

Self-critique is only as good as the tests you give it.

Convert vague goals into testable rules

Instead of:

- "make it detailed,"

Use:

- "include exactly 2 examples and 1 checklist."

Instead of:

- "be professional,"

Use:

- "tone: neutral, concise, no hype, no emojis."

Instead of:

- "output JSON,"

Use:

- "valid JSON only, keys must match schema exactly, no extra keys."

The model can reliably critique measurable rules.

Prompts that make the model find specific error types

1) Constraint violation finder

"List every constraint from my prompt. For each, cite where in your output it is satisfied. If any are missing, revise."

This is excellent for:

- missed sections,
- wrong counts,
- ordering mistakes.

2) Missing information and assumption finder

"Identify any claims that rely on assumptions or missing inputs. Label each as Fact (from input), Assumption, or Unknown. Revise to remove unjustified assumptions."

This reduces:

- hidden guessing,
- invented details.

3) Consistency checker

"Check for internal contradictions, duplicated points, or inconsistent terminology. List issues and revise."

Useful for:

- long reports,
- multi-section chapters.

4) Format validator

"Validate output against this format contract: <schema/heading order/table columns>. If invalid, fix and re-validate. Return final only."

Best for:

- JSON, tables, schemas, structured deliverables.

Example: self-critique applied to a writing task

Prompt:

"Write a 900–1,100 word section for beginners.
Required: 4 headings, 2 examples, 1 checklist, define key terms, no fluff.
Before finalizing, run a pass/fail checklist and fix failures."

What self-critique catches:

- missing checklist,
- too many headings,
- examples not clearly labeled,
- jargon not defined,
- word count out of range.

The revision step becomes targeted instead of subjective.

Example: self-critique applied to JSON output

Prompt:

"Extract into JSON with keys: owner, due_date, risk.
Rules: JSON only, no extra keys, due_date must be YYYY-MM-DD or null.
Validate against schema and fix violations."

What self-critique catches:

- extra commentary around JSON,
- due_date in wrong format,
- missing key,
- extra fields.

This is one of the highest ROI uses of self-critique.

Common failure modes and fixes

Failure 1: The critique is too polite and not specific

Fix:

Require pass/fail per rule and require quoting the rule.

Add:

"Critique must be pass/fail for each requirement."

Failure 2: The model identifies issues but does not fix them

Fix:

Force mapping:

"For every failed item, describe the change you will make, then apply it."

Failure 3: The model introduces new errors while fixing

Fix:

Add a re-check loop:

"After revision, re-check all rules again."

Failure 4: The model adds the critique to the final when you want clean output

Fix:

Specify output boundaries:

"Return only the final revised output, no critique text."

A practical "error budget" rule (prevents endless loops)

Sometimes the model can loop. Put a cap on iterations:

"Do at most 2 revise cycles. If still failing, return the best attempt and list remaining failures."

This keeps the workflow predictable.

Mini lab: build a self-critique harness for your prompts

Take any prompt you use often, and add a critique harness:

1. Write a checklist of 6 to 10 measurable requirements.
2. Add a line: "Check each requirement pass/fail and revise until all pass."
3. Run the prompt twice and compare results.

Once you have a stable checklist, you can reuse it as a "quality gate" across many tasks.

Rubrics and scoring

Rubrics turn "make it better" into measurable quality. When you add scoring to a self-critique loop, you get three professional benefits:

- **Consistency**: the model evaluates outputs the same way every time.
- **Control**: you can set thresholds like "must score 14/16."
- **Repeatability**: teams can use the same rubric to produce comparable work.

A rubric is simply a list of criteria with a scoring scale. Your prompt then asks the model to score its output, explain weak points, revise, and re-score.

Why rubrics outperform vague feedback

Without a rubric, critique tends to be generic:

- "Could be clearer,"
- "Add more detail,"
- "Improve structure."

With a rubric, critique becomes actionable:

- "Missing required section,"
- "Exceeds word limit,"
- "Uses undefined jargon,"
- "Adds claims not in sources."

Rubrics force the model to check for objective issues first, before polishing style.

Choose a scoring scale that matches the task

Keep scales simple. Complex scoring encourages noisy justifications.

Pass/Fail (binary)

Best for:

- strict formatting,
- compliance rules,
- schemas and templates.

Example criteria:

- "Valid JSON only,"
- "Exactly 7 bullets,"
- "No extra sections."

0–2 scale (recommended default)

Best for most professional work because it is simple but not blunt.

- 0 = fails the criterion
- 1 = partially meets
- 2 = fully meets

1–5 scale (use sparingly)

Best when nuance matters, but it can increase inconsistency if criteria are not very clear.

Professional tip: if you are teaching beginners, 0–2 is easiest to understand and apply.

What makes a good rubric criterion

A good criterion is:

- specific,
- testable,
- tied to the deliverable's purpose.

Bad criteria are vague:

- "Good quality,"
- "More professional."

Better criteria:

- "Matches audience level,"
- "Includes required sections in order,"
- "Uses only provided inputs,"
- "Provides 2 examples and 1 checklist,"
- "Meets length range."

The more measurable the criteria, the more reliable the scoring.

The standard professional rubric (reusable)

This rubric works for many writing and analysis tasks. Use 6–10 criteria to keep it focused.

General-purpose rubric (0–2 each)

1. Objective fit (does it answer the task?)
2. Audience fit (tone and level appropriate)
3. Completeness (all required parts included)
4. Structure and format compliance (headings, order, schema)
5. Clarity (no ambiguity, defined terms)
6. Grounding (no invented facts, assumptions labeled)
7. Actionability (clear next steps, decisions, or outputs)

8. Concision (no filler, within length limits)

Total possible score: 16 (if 8 criteria).

How to embed a rubric into a prompt

There are two strong patterns.

Pattern A: Score then revise until threshold

Use when you want the model to self-improve.

Template

"Create <deliverable>.

Then score it using this rubric (0–2 each): <criteria list>.

If total score is below <threshold>, revise to improve the lowest-scoring criteria.

Re-score after revision.

Return: (1) score table and (2) final revised output."

Recommended threshold:

- 85 to 90 percent of maximum score.

Example:

- 14/16 or higher.

Pattern B: Score internally, return final only

Use when you want clean deliverables but still want rubric discipline.

Template

"Use the rubric below to evaluate your draft and revise until you reach at least <threshold>.

Do the scoring internally.

Return only the final output."

This works well for production workflows.

Make scoring reliable: define what 0, 1, 2 means

If you do not define the scale per criterion, scoring can become arbitrary.

Example definitions for one criterion:

Criterion: Structure compliance

- 0: missing sections or wrong order
- 1: sections present but formatting inconsistent
- 2: sections complete and in exact order, formatting correct

Do this for your most important criteria:

- format compliance,
- grounding,
- completeness.

You do not need full definitions for every criterion if your prompt is already strict, but adding them improves consistency.

Two common rubric styles

1) Compliance-first rubric (best for strict outputs)

Prioritizes:

- format and constraints,
- no invented facts,
- stop conditions.

Use for:

- JSON, tables, structured reports,
- regulated or sensitive content.

2) Communication-first rubric (best for writing and teaching)

Prioritizes:

- clarity,
- audience fit,
- structure,
- examples and pedagogy.

Use for:

- chapters, tutorials, emails, guides.

Example rubric prompt (writing)

"Write a beginner-friendly section on <topic>, 900–1,100 words, 4 headings, 2 examples, 1 checklist.

Then score the result using this rubric (0–2 each): Objective fit, Audience fit, Completeness, Structure compliance, Clarity, Grounding, Actionability, Concision.

If score < 14/16, revise once focusing on the lowest two criteria.

Return score table and final output."

Example rubric prompt (structured output)

"Extract requirements into JSON matching this schema exactly. JSON only.

Rubric (pass/fail): valid JSON, required keys present, no extra keys, types correct, null for unknown, no commentary.

If any fail, fix and re-check. Return final JSON only."

Here rubric scoring is binary because it is compliance-based.

Using rubrics for iterative improvement

A rubric becomes powerful when you use it across iterations:

1. Run the prompt and record scores.

2. Identify the lowest-scoring criterion.
3. Tighten prompt instructions specifically for that criterion.
4. Re-run and compare scores.

This is how you "debug" a prompt systematically.

Example:

- If "Grounding" scores low, add stronger "use only provided inputs" rules.
- If "Structure compliance" scores low, add a fixed skeleton and stop conditions.
- If "Concision" scores low, add word caps per section.

Common mistakes and fixes

Mistake 1: Too many criteria

Fix:

Use 6–10 criteria. Too many makes scoring noisy and slow.

Mistake 2: Criteria are not measurable

Fix:

Replace adjectives with tests: counts, sections, formats, forbidden items.

Mistake 3: The model inflates its own score

Fix:

- require evidence:
  "For each criterion, cite where it is satisfied."
- or force a stricter scale:
  "2 only if fully meets every requirement, otherwise 1 or 0."

Mistake 4: Revision makes one criterion better but breaks another

Fix:

- re-score after revision,
- require preservation rules:
  "Do not break format compliance while improving clarity."

Mistake 5: Endless loops

Fix:

Cap revisions:

"Revise at most twice. If still below threshold, return best attempt and list remaining gaps."

A reusable rubric block (drop into any prompt)

Paste this at the end of your prompt:

"Rubric (0–2 each): Objective fit, Audience fit, Completeness, Structure compliance, Clarity, Grounding, Actionability, Concision.
Threshold: at least 14/16.
If below threshold, revise focusing on the lowest-scoring criteria, then re-check."
This block upgrades most prompts into a controlled quality workflow.

Red-team prompts, "Find weaknesses, missing cases"

Red-teaming is a deliberate stress test. Instead of asking the model to improve the output directly, you ask it to act like a critical reviewer whose job is to find:

- weaknesses and blind spots,
- missing cases and edge conditions,
- ambiguous assumptions,
- failure modes and risks,
- and places where the output could mislead a reader.

In professional prompt engineering, red-team prompts are how you turn "seems fine" into "robust under pressure."

What red-team prompts are (and what they are not)

A red-team prompt is:

- a structured critique focused on failure, not polish,
- a search for what could go wrong, not what sounds good,
- a gap analysis that produces test cases and fixes.

A red-team prompt is not:

- adversarial content generation,
- instructions to break rules or create harmful outcomes,
- a justification for unsafe or deceptive behavior.

You are red-teaming the prompt or the output's reliability, clarity, and completeness.

When to use red-teaming

Use red-team prompts when:

- outputs will be reused widely (templates, SOPs, style guides),
- the task is high-stakes (policy, compliance, customer comms),
- the prompt will be used by a team,
- you are building a chained workflow and need stability,
- the model has been "mostly right" but fails on edge cases.

Skip red-teaming when:

- the task is one-off and low impact,
- you only need a quick draft.

What to red-team (targets)

You can red-team three things:

1. **The prompt** (will it produce reliable outputs?)
2. **The output** (what is missing or risky?)
3. **The workflow** (where will the chain fail?)

A good red-team prompt makes the target explicit:
"Red-team this prompt" or "Red-team this output."

The red-team checklist (what to look for)

Ask the model to search for these categories:

1) Missing requirements

- Are required sections missing?
- Are constraints underspecified?
- Are success and stop conditions absent?

2) Ambiguity and undefined terms

- Words like "best," "optimize," "detailed," "quick," "professional"
- Missing scope boundaries (what is included vs excluded)

3) Edge cases and missing scenarios

- missing data fields, conflicting inputs
- unusual but realistic inputs
- "none of the above" cases

4) Failure modes in formatting

- JSON validity, schema compliance
- headings and ordering drift
- extra commentary or trailing text

5) Grounding and hallucination risks

- where the model might guess facts
- where it might borrow from examples
- where it might overstate certainty

6) Safety, compliance, and reputational risk

- overly strong claims
- sensitive tone issues
- privacy leakage or inappropriate assumptions

Red-team prompt templates (copy and reuse)

Template A: Red-team a prompt (gap finder)

"Act as a strict reviewer. Red-team the prompt below.
Find: (1) ambiguities, (2) missing requirements, (3) likely failure modes, (4) missing edge cases.
Then propose fixes as concrete prompt edits.
Finally, generate 8 test inputs designed to break the prompt.
Prompt to red-team:
<paste prompt>"

Output you want:

- a list of weaknesses,
- a revised prompt,
- a test suite.

Template B: Red-team an output (weakness and risk scan)

"Red-team the output below.
Identify: missing cases, unsupported claims, ambiguous statements, and format violations.
For each issue, propose the smallest edit to fix it.
Then provide 5 adversarial test questions that would expose these weaknesses.
Output to red-team:
<paste output>"

Template C: Red-team a workflow (chain failure points)

"Red-team this multi-step workflow.
For each stage, identify: what could go wrong, what inputs might cause failure, and what validation should be added.
Propose improvements: revised stage prompts and a checklist per stage."

"Find missing cases" done right: require a test suite

Red-teaming is most valuable when it produces a test set you can actually run.

Ask for tests like:

- messy inputs,
- incomplete inputs,
- conflicting inputs,
- extreme length inputs (very short, very long),
- inputs that tempt hallucination,

- boundary cases for classification labels.

Example test suite request

"Generate 10 test inputs. Include:

- 2 missing-data cases
- 2 conflicting-data cases
- 2 unusually short cases
- 2 unusually long cases
- 2 borderline classification cases

  Label each test with what it is designed to break."

This turns red-teaming into a repeatable QA process.

How to turn red-team findings into a stronger prompt

When the model identifies weaknesses, your fixes should follow a consistent pattern:

Fix type 1: Replace vague words with measurable rules

- "detailed" → "include 2 examples, 1 checklist, 6 bullets"
- "best" → "rank top 3 using this rubric"

Fix type 2: Add unknown handling

- "Unknown if missing"
- "Ask up to 5 clarifying questions if critical info is missing"

Fix type 3: Add stop conditions

- "Stop after section X"
- "Return JSON only, no extra text"

Fix type 4: Add validation loops

- "Check output against schema and fix violations"
- "Re-check headings, counts, and forbidden content"

Fix type 5: Add edge-case examples (few-shot)

- add 1 missing-data example,
- add 1 borderline example,
- add 1 negative example for top failure mode.

Common red-team failure modes and how to avoid them

Failure: The critique is generic and polite

Fix:

Require concrete deliverables:

- "Provide exact edits to the prompt"
- "Provide a test suite"
- "Provide a checklist"

Failure: Too many issues with no prioritization

Fix:

Ask for ranking:

"Rank issues by impact and likelihood, top 5 only."

Failure: Suggested fixes make the prompt longer but not clearer

Fix:

Ask for minimal edits:

"Propose the smallest changes that address the top failures."

Failure: Red-team creates unrealistic tests

Fix:

Require realism:

"Test inputs must be plausible in real work scenarios."

Mini lab: red-team your own prompt template

1. Take a prompt you use often (email, SOP, JSON extraction, chapter writing).
2. Run Template A to identify weaknesses.
3. Apply the top 3 fixes only.
4. Run the proposed test suite and see what still breaks.
5. Add one more fix: either an edge-case example or a validation checklist.

After two cycles, you usually get a prompt that works reliably across messy inputs.

A compact "red-team block" you can append to any workflow

If you want a small reusable block:

"Before finalizing, red-team your output: identify missing cases, ambiguity, unsupported claims, and format violations.

List top 5 issues and fix them.

Then re-check compliance and return the final."

This is a lightweight red-team step that fits inside most chains.

Red-team prompts make your prompting robust. They force the model to hunt for failure modes and missing cases, then convert those findings into concrete prompt improvements and test inputs. That is how you move from prompts that work sometimes to prompts that work reliably.

Controlled revision, "Revise without changing meaning"

Controlled revision is the skill of improving writing while preserving the original meaning. In professional settings, this matters because you often need to:

- improve clarity without changing facts,
- tighten language without changing commitments,
- adjust tone without changing intent,
- fix structure without altering content,
- reduce risk without rewriting the message.

Models are good at rewriting, but they can accidentally drift, add new claims, or change emphasis. Controlled revision prompts prevent that by defining what must stay invariant and what is allowed to change.

The key idea: define invariants and allowed edits

A controlled revision prompt should specify two lists:

Invariants (must not change)

- factual claims and numbers
- meaning and intent
- commitments, deadlines, responsibilities
- named entities (people, products, policies)
- citations or source references
- scope boundaries

Allowed changes (can change)

- sentence structure
- word choice for clarity
- order of sentences for flow
- tone adjustments
- formatting (headings, bullets)
- removing redundancy
- fixing grammar

When you define both lists, you reduce "rewrite drift."

When to use controlled revision

Use it when:

- you are rewriting business communications,
- you are editing book chapters to be clearer,
- you are standardizing documents into a house style,

- you are reducing legal or reputational risk,
- you are converting long text into structured bullets,
- you are polishing a draft while preserving accuracy.

Avoid it when:

- you actually want new content or new ideas,
- you want a different argument or different strategy,
- you need creative rewriting where meaning can shift.

The controlled revision protocol (professional workflow)

A reliable controlled revision happens in three moves:

1. **Extract meaning anchors** (what must remain true)
2. **Revise within boundaries** (apply allowed edits only)
3. **Verify no meaning change** (diff-style check)

You can request all three in one prompt, or split into steps for strict control.

Meaning anchors: what the model should preserve

Meaning anchors are short bullets that capture the core intent and facts. They act like a "contract" for the rewrite.

Examples of anchors:

- "We are requesting approval for X by Friday."
- "The project timeline moved from May to June."
- "Owner is <NAME>, risk is vendor delay."
- "No budget amount is stated."

When anchors exist, the model is less likely to introduce new claims.

Copy-paste templates (ready to use)

Template A: Simple controlled revision (fast)

"Revise the text for clarity and professionalism without changing meaning.
Do not add new facts, numbers, names, or commitments.
Keep all key claims intact.
Output only the revised version."

Use when:

- the stakes are moderate,
- you trust the text is already accurate.

Template B: Anchors + revision + verification (high reliability)

"Controlled revision task.

Step 1: Extract meaning anchors from the original (5–10 bullets).
Step 2: Rewrite the text to improve clarity and flow, but do not change any anchors.
Allowed: grammar, wording, sentence order, formatting.
Not allowed: new facts, new claims, new commitments, changed emphasis.
Step 3: Verify anchor preservation: for each anchor, state Preserved/Not preserved. If any not preserved, revise again.
Return:

- Meaning anchors
- Revised text
- Anchor preservation check"

Use when:

- accuracy and intent must be preserved.

Template C: "Diff report" controlled revision (best for auditing)

"Rewrite without changing meaning.
After rewriting, produce a change log with two columns:

- Change made (wording/structure only)
- Why it does not change meaning

Do not add facts. Do not remove key details."

Use when:

- you need traceability,
- multiple stakeholders review changes.

Controlled revision knobs (what you can tune)

You can control revision behavior by specifying one or more knobs:

1) Tightness level

- Light edit: grammar and small clarity fixes only
- Medium edit: restructure sentences, improve flow
- Heavy edit: reformat into bullets, reorganize sections, but preserve meaning

2) Length constraint

- "Keep within ±10% length"
- "Reduce to 150 words" (compression but meaning preserved)
- "Expand to 300 words" (clarify but do not add new facts)

3) Tone constraint

- neutral and professional
- friendly and supportive

- firm and direct
- executive concise

4) Structure constraint

- preserve paragraph boundaries
- convert to bullets
- add headings but do not add new content

These knobs make controlled revision predictable.

Common risks and how to prevent them

Risk 1: The model adds "helpful" new details

Fix:

- "Do not add facts. If unclear, keep wording close to original."

Risk 2: The model changes meaning by changing modality

Subtle words matter:

- "will" vs "may"
- "must" vs "should"
- "confirmed" vs "expected"

Fix:

- "Preserve strength of claims and modality words."

Risk 3: The model removes an important caveat

Fix:

- "Do not remove limitations, exceptions, or conditions."

Risk 4: The model changes responsibility or ownership

Fix:

- "Do not change who is responsible for what."

Risk 5: The model makes the message sound more certain than the original

Fix:

- "Do not increase certainty. Preserve hedging where present."

A professional controlled revision checklist (use as a guardrail)

Add this checklist to your prompt when accuracy is critical:

- All names, dates, numbers unchanged
- No new facts introduced
- No commitments added or removed
- Modality preserved (must/should/may)
- Limitations and caveats preserved

- Tone improved without changing intent
- Output meets length and structure requirements

You can ask the model to check these before finalizing.

Practice exercises (for readers)

Use these prompts as drills:

1. Rewrite an email to be more direct without sounding rude. Preserve meaning.
2. Convert a paragraph into 5 bullets without adding facts.
3. Shorten a 300-word explanation to 150 words without losing key points.
4. Rewrite a policy summary to be clearer, preserving all caveats.
5. Rewrite a chapter section to be beginner-friendly without changing technical accuracy.

For each, require:

- meaning anchors,
- revised output,
- anchor preservation check.

A compact "Revise without changing meaning" block (best default)

If you want one reusable line to drop into any prompt:

"Revise for clarity and structure without changing meaning. Preserve all facts, names, numbers, modality, and commitments. Do not add new information. If something is unclear, keep it as-is rather than guessing."

That one block turns rewriting into controlled revision, which is the professional standard for safe, reliable editing.

<u>Practice, take messy outputs and improve them in 3 iterations</u>

This practice is designed to build a repeatable improvement loop. You will start with a messy or imperfect output and run three controlled iterations:

- **Iteration 1: Make it correct** (requirements and grounding)
- **Iteration 2: Make it clear** (structure and readability)
- **Iteration 3: Make it polished** (tone and concision)

The goal is not endless rewriting. The goal is predictable improvement with a fixed number of cycles.

The 3-iteration improvement protocol

Each iteration has:

1. a focus,

2. a checklist,
3. a revision action,
4. a short verification.

You will get better results if you force the model to:

- identify problems first,
- then revise,
- then re-check.

Before you start: set the output contract

Every improvement loop needs a target.

Define these before Iteration 1:

- Objective: what the output must accomplish
- Audience: who will read it
- Format: headings, bullets, JSON, table, length
- Constraints: must include, must avoid
- Grounding: allowed sources, Unknown policy
- Stop condition: where it ends

Even a short contract makes the loop much more effective.

Iteration 1: Make it correct

This iteration is about correctness and compliance, not style.

What "correct" means here

- meets required structure and constraints,
- does not invent facts,
- handles missing info as Unknown,
- removes forbidden content,
- fixes internal contradictions.

Iteration 1 prompt (copy and use)

"Iteration 1, correctness pass.

Task: Improve the output to meet the contract.

Do not focus on tone or elegance yet.

Contract:

- Objective: <...>
- Audience: <...>
- Format: <...>
- Constraints: <...>
- Grounding rules: <...>
- Unknown handling: <...>

Step A: List violations and risks (max 8 bullets).
Step B: Revise to fix all violations.
Step C: Re-check each contract item as Pass/Fail.
Return:

1. Violations list
2. Revised output v1
3. Pass/Fail check"

What to look for:

- constraints satisfied,
- no extra sections,
- no invented facts.

Iteration 2: Make it clear

Now that it is correct, you improve clarity and structure.

What "clear" means

- logical ordering,
- no redundancy,
- defined terms,
- specific instructions instead of vague language,
- better formatting (headings, bullets, tables).

Iteration 2 prompt

"Iteration 2, clarity pass.
Goal: Improve clarity and structure without changing meaning.
Do not add new facts. Preserve all key claims.
Step A: Identify the top 5 clarity issues.
Step B: Rewrite to fix them using these tools:

- tighter sentences
- headings and bullets
- consistent terminology
- remove fluff

Step C: Confirm: 'No meaning changes, no new facts.'
Return:

1. Clarity issues list
2. Revised output v2
3. Confirmation statement"

What to look for:

- easier to skim,

- fewer ambiguous phrases,
- better organization.

Iteration 3: Make it polished

This iteration is about audience fit, tone, and concision.

What "polished" means

- tone matches the audience,
- consistent voice,
- concise but complete,
- professional wording,
- clean formatting.

Iteration 3 prompt

"Iteration 3, polish pass.

Goal: Polish the text for <audience> while preserving meaning and the approved structure.

Constraints:

- keep within <length range>
- no new facts
- no new sections

Step A: Identify 5 micro-edits that improve tone and concision.

Step B: Apply them.

Step C: Final compliance check: format, length, forbidden items.

Return:

1. Micro-edits list
2. Final output v3
3. Final compliance check (Pass/Fail)"

What to look for:

- professional tone,
- tighter wording,
- no constraint regressions.

Practice set: 6 "messy outputs" to improve (use any 3)

Pick three examples and run the three-iteration protocol on each.

Messy output 1 (format drift)

Output problem:

- mixes bullets and paragraphs, adds extra sections, no clear structure.

Task:

- convert into a report with headings: Summary, Findings, Risks, Recommendations.

Messy output 2 (hallucination risk)

Output problem:

- includes numbers or claims not in the input.

Task:

- remove invented facts, mark Unknown, ask clarifying questions if needed.

Messy output 3 (too long and repetitive)

Output problem:

- verbose, repeats the same idea, weak structure.

Task:

- reduce to 180–220 words, keep all key points.

Messy output 4 (wrong tone)

Output problem:

- sounds rude, too casual, or too salesy.

Task:

- rewrite in neutral professional tone, keep meaning unchanged.

Messy output 5 (unclear requirements)

Output problem:

- output is generic because the prompt was vague.

Task:

- add an assumptions section or ask 5 questions first, then refine.

Messy output 6 (schema failure)

Output problem:

- JSON output contains extra commentary, wrong key names, wrong types.

Task:

- enforce JSON-only output and validate schema.

Scoring rubric for each iteration (quick)

Score each version 0–2:

1. Contract compliance
2. Grounding and no invention

3. Clarity and structure
4. Tone and audience fit
5. Concision

Target progression:

- v1 improves compliance and grounding,
- v2 improves clarity,
- v3 improves polish.

If v2 or v3 reduces compliance, your loop is not controlled. Add a stronger verification step.

Common mistakes and how to fix them

Mistake: Each iteration introduces new facts

Fix:

Add a strict rule:

"Do not add facts. If missing, write Unknown."

Mistake: Polish changes meaning

Fix:

Use meaning anchors:

"List 5 meaning anchors first and preserve them."

Mistake: Iterations become repetitive

Fix:

Change focus per iteration and cap outputs:

- "max 8 violations"
- "top 5 clarity issues"
- "5 micro-edits"

Mistake: Model keeps failing format rules

Fix:

Insert a validation step after each iteration:

"Check headings, counts, length, and forbidden items."

A single "3-iteration" prompt (compact version)

If you want one reusable block:

"Improve this output in exactly 3 iterations.

Contract: <objective, audience, format, constraints, grounding>.

Iteration 1: fix correctness and constraint violations.

Iteration 2: improve clarity and structure without changing meaning.

Iteration 3: polish tone and concision without changing meaning.

After each iteration, include a short Pass/Fail check against the contract. Return v1, v2, v3."

This practice builds real professional skill because it forces controlled progress. After doing a few runs, you will start writing better initial prompts and you will know exactly how to recover when outputs are messy.

Part 3. Practical skills, from novice to expert

Chapter 10. Prompt debugging, why it failed and how to fix it

Failure mode

wrong goal

A "wrong goal" failure happens when the model successfully produces an output, but it is solving a different problem than you intended. This is one of the most common prompt debugging issues because the output can look polished and confident while still being misaligned.

Wrong-goal failures are not mainly about model capability. They are about specification. Your prompt did not clearly define what "done" means, so the model picked a plausible goal and executed it well.

What "wrong goal" looks like in practice

Typical symptoms:

- You asked for a plan but got a tutorial.
- You asked for a summary but got an opinionated critique.
- You asked for options but got one recommendation.
- You asked for a beginner explanation but got advanced jargon.
- You asked for "best" and it optimized for popularity, not your constraints.
- You asked for "a prompt" and it produced a generic prompt instead of a reusable template.

A key sign is this sentence in your head:

"This is good, but it is not what I asked for."

Why the wrong goal happens

Wrong goal usually comes from one of these causes:

1) The objective is vague

Words like:

- "help," "best," "optimize," "detailed," "professional," "improve," "explain"

They do not specify a deliverable or success criteria.

2) The deliverable type is not specified

If you do not say whether you want:

- an outline, a table, a checklist, a JSON schema, an email, a report

The model guesses.

3) The audience and use case are missing

"Explain X" could mean:

- teach a beginner,
- brief an executive,
- persuade a customer,
- write documentation.

The model chooses a default.

4) Constraints and non-goals are absent

If you do not tell it what not to do, it may produce:

- extra sections,
- overly broad coverage,
- recommendations when you wanted neutral analysis.

5) The prompt mixes multiple goals

"Make it short but detailed and comprehensive" is a goal conflict. The model will prioritize one goal, and you may not like its choice.

The debugging method: identify the goal the model actually used

Before you fix the prompt, diagnose it.

Ask:

1. What goal did I intend?
2. What goal did the model pursue instead?
3. Which missing requirement caused the goal swap?

A quick diagnostic prompt (use as a tool)

"Restate my objective in one sentence. Then restate what you think success looks like. If there are multiple possible goals, list them and ask me to choose one before proceeding."

This forces goal alignment before work begins.

How to fix wrong-goal prompts (the professional playbook)

Fix 1: Replace vague objective with a concrete deliverable

Instead of:

"Help me with prompt engineering."

Use:

"Create a 1-page cheat sheet for beginners on prompt engineering, with 5 rules, 3 examples, and a checklist."

Deliverables eliminate goal confusion.

Fix 2: Add a success definition

Add a line like:

"Success is achieved when: <tests>."

Examples:

- "Success is: exactly 4 sections in this order, 900–1,100 words, includes 2 examples and 1 checklist."
- "Success is: valid JSON only matching this schema, no extra keys, null for unknown."
- "Success is: a decision memo with recommendation and risks."

Fix 3: Add non-goals (what to avoid)

Non-goals prevent the model from choosing the wrong "helpful" direction.

Examples:

- "Non-goals: do not give general background, do not recommend tools, do not add unrelated best practices."
- "Do not include step-by-step chain-of-thought. Output only final."
- "Do not assume facts not provided."

Fix 4: Specify the audience and intended use

Add:

- "Audience: beginner readers of my book."
- "Use: included as a chapter subsection."
- "Tone: neutral, instructional."

This prevents the model from aiming at the wrong reader.

Fix 5: Use a format contract

A format contract locks output shape.

Example:

"Output format must be:

1. Summary (max 80 words)
2. Key steps (exactly 6 bullets)
3. Example prompt (one block)
4. Checklist (exactly 8 items)
   Stop after checklist."

This prevents the model from redefining the goal mid-output.

Fix 6: Make the model confirm the goal before generating

This is a powerful guardrail.

Add:
"Before writing, restate the goal, deliverable type, audience, and success criteria in 2 lines. If any are unclear, ask up to 3 questions. Then proceed."
This catches wrong-goal failures early.

Before and after transformations

Transformation 1: "Explain" becomes a targeted deliverable

Weak prompt:
"Explain prompt engineering to me."
Why it fails:

- No audience, depth, structure, or use-case. The model chooses a goal.

Stronger prompt:
"Write a beginner-friendly subsection for a book titled 'AI Prompt Engineering.'
Objective: teach the core idea in 600–750 words.
Audience: novices.
Required: 2 simple examples, 1 common mistake list (5 bullets), and a short checklist (6 items).
Non-goals: no vendor names, no history of AI.
Stop after the checklist."
Now the goal is unambiguous.

Transformation 2: "Best" becomes a rubric-based decision

Weak prompt:
"What is the best way to write prompts?"
Why it fails:

- "Best" is undefined and the model chooses a generic goal.

Stronger prompt:
"Give 3 prompt-writing approaches for beginners.
Then evaluate them using this rubric (0–2 each): clarity, reliability, ease of use, repeatability.
Recommend one for a beginner writing business emails and explain why in 5 bullets.
Length: under 250 words."
Now "best" is defined by the rubric and use case.

A reusable "wrong goal prevention" header (paste into prompts)

Use this at the top of important prompts:

"Goal alignment:

- Deliverable: <what you want produced>
- Audience: <who it's for>
- Use case: <where it will be used>
- Success criteria: <measurable tests>
- Non-goals: <what to avoid>

  If any item is unclear, ask up to 3 questions before starting."

This small header prevents many wrong-goal failures.

Mini lab: debug a wrong-goal failure

1. Take a prompt that produced an output you disliked.
2. Write one sentence: "I wanted X, but got Y."
3. Rewrite the prompt using:
- deliverable type,
- audience,
- success criteria,
- non-goals,
- format contract.
4. Run again and compare.

You will usually see the model become dramatically more aligned because you replaced an implied goal with an explicit one.

Wrong-goal failures are the easiest to fix and the most valuable to learn from. The model is rarely "wrong" in a technical sense. It is doing exactly what your prompt allowed. Your job as a professional prompt engineer is to define the goal so clearly that there is no other reasonable goal to pursue.

Missing Context

A "missing context" failure happens when the model gives an answer that is generic, misaligned, or partially wrong because it did not receive the information it needed. The model is not refusing. It is guessing. The output may still sound confident because fluency is easy, but correctness and usefulness depend on context.

This is one of the highest impact debugging skills: learning to recognize missing context quickly and supplying it in the smallest, most structured way.

What missing context looks like

Common symptoms:

The answer is too general, like a textbook overview.

It focuses on the wrong audience or tone.
It assumes the wrong scope, region, timeframe, or industry.
It invents details to fill gaps.
It gives a solution that does not fit your constraints.
It misses key requirements you thought were obvious.
Typical "tell" phrases from the model:
"Generally," "Typically," "In most cases,"
lots of caveats or broad best practices,
recommendations that do not reference your specific situation.
If you read the output and think "It did not use my situation," you likely did not provide enough context.

Why missing context causes failure

Models generate the next likely tokens based on the input. If you do not provide crucial details, the model chooses defaults. Defaults are often reasonable, but they are still guesses.

Missing context usually falls into one of these buckets:

1) Missing objective and use case

Are you informing, persuading, deciding, teaching, or documenting?

2) Missing audience

Beginner vs expert, internal vs external, executive vs technical.

3) Missing source material

The model cannot summarize, extract, or analyze what it has not seen.

4) Missing constraints

Word limits, format requirements, forbidden content, compliance rules.

5) Missing scope boundaries

What is in scope and what is out of scope, and how deep to go.

6) Missing environment or tooling details

For technical tasks:
language, platform, versions, data format, APIs, libraries.

The core debugging move: identify what context is missing

Before rewriting the whole prompt, diagnose the gap.
Ask:
What would a competent human need to do this well?
Which of those inputs did I not provide?
Which missing input changes the output the most?
High-impact missing context is usually:

audience, objective, constraints, and the source of truth.

The "minimum context set" (carry this into most prompts)

If you provide these six items, most missing-context failures disappear:

Objective: what you want and why

Audience: who it is for

Inputs: source material to use

Output format: headings, bullets, JSON, table, length

Constraints: must include, must avoid, non-goals

Success criteria: what "good" means, and stop condition

If any of these are missing, the model will fill the gap with defaults.

Two strategies to fix missing context

Strategy A: Add context up front (best when you know what is missing)

You rewrite the prompt with a context packet.

Context packet template

Objective: <one sentence>

Audience: <who, level>

Context: <background facts and constraints>

Inputs: <paste text/data>

Output requirements: <format, length>

Constraints: <must include, must avoid>

Success: <tests and stop condition>

This is the most reliable method.

Strategy B: Make the model ask for context (best when you are unsure)

You use a question-first workflow.

Add:

"Before answering, ask up to 5 clarifying questions about audience, objective, constraints, and inputs. Do not draft until I answer."

This prevents the model from guessing and makes missing context visible.

Common missing-context patterns and how to patch them

Pattern 1: "Write a report" with no report definition

Fix:

Specify the report template:

required sections in order,

word count range,

audience and purpose.

Example patch:
"Report sections: Summary, Findings, Risks, Recommendations. 900–1,100 words. Audience: executives."

Pattern 2: "Summarize this" without the actual text

Fix:
Paste the text or provide a link plus key excerpts. If you cannot paste it, give a structured outline of the content.
Minimal patch:
"Here is the source text: <paste>. Use only this text."

Pattern 3: "Make it better" without success criteria

Fix:
Define what "better" means:
shorter, clearer, more formal, more persuasive,
include examples, remove jargon, improve structure.
Patch:
"Improve clarity and concision. Keep meaning unchanged. Reduce to 150–180 words."

Pattern 4: Wrong audience assumptions

Fix:
Add audience card:
role, knowledge level, and what they care about.
Patch:
"Audience: beginner readers, no jargon, define terms."

Pattern 5: Technical debugging without environment details

Fix:
Provide the "tech context pack":
language and version,
runtime environment,
error message,
minimal reproducible input,
expected vs actual.
Patch:
"Python 3.11, pandas 2.x, error stack trace: <paste>, input sample: <paste>."

A simple way to compress context (without bloating prompts)

Many people over-correct by pasting everything. Better is to compress context into structured fields.

Compression tools

bullets instead of paragraphs
short tables for facts
explicit Unknown values
"Assumptions" section
a single "source of truth" block

Professional rule:
Carry forward the smallest set that changes decisions.

Before and after transformations

Transformation 1: Generic output becomes specific

Weak prompt:
"Write a professional introduction for my chapter."
Missing context:
audience, tone, length, what the chapter covers, required structure.
Stronger prompt:
"Objective: Write a 180–220 word chapter introduction.
Audience: beginners.
Chapter topic: AI Prompt Engineering, focus on practical prompting patterns and debugging.
Tone: clear, confident, not hype.
Must include: what readers will learn, how the chapter is structured, one motivating example.
Must avoid: vendor names, exaggerated claims.
Output: 2 short paragraphs."

Transformation 2: Summary becomes usable

Weak prompt:
"Summarize this report for leadership."
Missing context:
leadership style, length, purpose, what to emphasize.
Stronger prompt:
"Summarize the report below for executives.
Purpose: decision support.
Length: max 120 words.
Format: 5 bullets in order: context, key finding, risk, recommendation, next

step.
Must include: the top metric change and its likely driver from the report.
Use only the report text."

The "missing context repair" prompt block (drop-in)

Paste this at the top when you suspect missing context:
"If any required context is missing, do not guess.
First, list the missing information you need in 3–6 bullet questions.
Then offer a best-effort draft using clearly labeled assumptions and Unknown for missing facts.
After I confirm or correct, produce the final."
This gives you progress without silent guessing.

Mini lab: diagnose and fix a missing context failure

Take an output you dislike.
Write: "This is wrong because it assumed ____."
Identify the missing context type:
objective, audience, inputs, constraints, scope, success criteria.
Add the minimum context set to the prompt.
Re-run and compare.
You will notice the model becomes:
less generic,
more aligned,
less likely to invent,
more consistent in format.
Missing context is not a model problem. It is an information flow problem. The professional fix is to supply a compact context packet, define a source of truth, and either provide constraints up front or force clarifying questions before drafting.

Conflicting Constraints

A "conflicting constraints" failure happens when your prompt asks for requirements that cannot all be satisfied at the same time, or that strongly compete. The model will usually do one of three things:
satisfy some constraints and quietly ignore others,
produce a messy compromise that pleases none of them,
or oscillate, for example short in one section and overly long in another.

Because the output can still read smoothly, this failure is easy to miss until you compare it to your requirements.

What conflicting constraints looks like

Common symptoms:

Output is too long despite a strict length limit.

It is short but shallow despite asking for "deep detail."

It follows the structure but ignores the "no repetition" rule.

It provides a final answer but also keeps asking questions.

It outputs JSON but includes commentary or headings too.

It claims to use "only the provided text" but adds background knowledge.

You often see phrases like:

"Here is a brief but comprehensive..." followed by a long answer,

or a short answer that is missing required sections.

Why conflicting constraints cause failure

A model is trying to satisfy your instructions, but it cannot solve an impossible set perfectly. When constraints conflict, it must choose priorities. If you do not specify the priority order, it will pick one implicitly based on patterns, or it will attempt a compromise.

Conflicts arise from:

unclear tradeoffs (short vs comprehensive),

mixed output formats (table and narrative and JSON),

incompatible process requirements (ask questions first and deliver final now),

insufficient budget (word count too low for number of required elements),

competing tone demands (formal but playful but extremely concise).

The most common constraint conflicts (and how to spot them)

1) Length vs depth

"Keep it under 150 words" + "cover everything in detail"

"One page" + "include 10 examples and a full checklist"

Spot it:

Count required components and estimate space.

Fix:

Choose one:

increase length,

reduce required components,

or move detail into an appendix.

2) Format purity vs explanation

"JSON only" + "explain your reasoning"

"Table only" + "include commentary and recommendations"

Fix:

Split into stages:

Stage 1: reasoning and explanation,

Stage 2: JSON/table only.

3) Questions-first vs immediate delivery

"Ask me questions first" + "give me the final answer now"

Fix:

Decide the workflow:

two-turn process (questions then final),

or assumptions-first (draft with assumptions + 3 questions).

4) Use only provided sources vs "add research"

"Use only this text" + "include the latest stats and citations"

Fix:

Pick the source policy:

either grounded-only,

or allow external info and specify how it should be cited.

5) Multiple audiences at once

"Write for beginners and experts"

"Executive summary and full technical deep dive" in one output

Fix:

Split deliverables:

Executive summary section, then technical appendix,

or produce two versions.

The debugging method: turn constraints into a contract and check feasibility

When you suspect a conflict, do this:

Step 1: List every constraint explicitly

Turn your prompt into a checklist:

length,

sections,

style,

format,

forbidden items,

source policy,
process steps.

Step 2: Identify direct contradictions

Look for pairs like:
"only X" vs "also Y,"
"ask first" vs "deliver now,"
"no extra text" vs "include explanation."

Step 3: Check budget feasibility

If you require:
6 headings,
12 bullets,
3 examples,
a checklist,
within 200 words, it will fail.

Step 4: Declare priority order

You must tell the model which constraints win if a conflict remains.

Example priority statement:

"Priority order: (1) JSON validity, (2) schema keys, (3) no extra text, (4) completeness."

How to fix conflicting constraints (professional solutions)

Fix 1: Add a priority ladder

Add one line:

"If constraints conflict, follow this priority order: <list>."

Example:

"Priority: (1) use only provided inputs, (2) required structure, (3) length, (4) style."

This single line often prevents silent rule-breaking.

Fix 2: Convert "soft" constraints into measurable targets

Instead of:
"short but detailed,"
Use:
"600–750 words, include 2 examples and 1 checklist."
Instead of:
"quick and comprehensive,"
Use:
"summary + appendix: 120-word summary, then 6 bullets for details."

Fix 3: Split into stages (best fix for format conflicts)

If you need reasoning and a strict output format, chain it:

Stage 1: analysis and explanation

Stage 2: final output only (JSON/table)

This removes the conflict instead of trying to "have both."

Fix 4: Split into multiple deliverables

If you need two audiences or two depth levels:

Deliverable A: executive summary

Deliverable B: technical deep dive

This is cleaner and more realistic than forcing one output to serve both.

Fix 5: Use "stop conditions" to prevent extra content

Add:

"Stop after section X."

"Do not add any other sections."

"Return only the final answer, no notes."

This prevents the model from trying to satisfy extra goals by adding extra text.

Before and after transformations

Transformation 1: Length vs depth

Weak prompt:

"Explain prompt engineering in 150 words with detailed examples and a checklist."

Conflict:

150 words cannot support detail + examples + checklist.

Fixed prompt:

"Explain prompt engineering for beginners.

Output:

120-word summary

2 mini examples (2 lines each)

6-item checklist

Total length: 300–380 words."

Now it is feasible.

Transformation 2: JSON-only vs explanation

Weak prompt:

"Extract the data into JSON and explain why you chose each field."

Conflict:
JSON-only and explanation cannot coexist.
Fixed workflow prompt:
"Step 1: Explain field mapping in 5 bullets.
Step 2: Output JSON only matching this schema.
No extra text in step 2."
This removes the conflict.

A reusable "conflict-safe" prompt header

Paste this at the top of complex prompts:
"Constraint handling:
If any requirements conflict, do not guess.
First, list the conflicts in bullets and propose a resolution.
Use this priority order if I do not respond: (1) source policy, (2) format, (3) required sections, (4) forbidden content, (5) length, (6) style.
Then proceed with the resolved requirements."
This forces conflicts into the open and prevents silent failure.

Mini lab: detect and repair conflicts

Take a prompt you have used that produced inconsistent results. Do this:
Extract all constraints into a checklist.
Mark any contradictions.
Choose one fix:
add priority ladder,
split into stages,
split deliverables,
adjust length or required components.
Re-run and verify each constraint pass/fail.
With a few cycles, you will start writing prompts that are feasible by design, and the model will stop "randomly ignoring" requirements because you removed the conflicts or told it exactly which constraints win.

Overly Broad Scope

An "overly broad scope" failure happens when the prompt asks for too much, covers too many topics, or lacks clear boundaries. The model responds with one of these predictable outcomes:
a shallow overview that misses what you actually care about,
a long answer that still feels incomplete,

a wandering answer that drifts into irrelevant areas,
or a confident answer that fills gaps with generic content.
This failure mode is not about intelligence. It is about scoping. Professionals treat scope as a design decision, not an afterthought.

What overly broad scope looks like

Symptoms you can spot quickly:
The answer starts broad and never gets specific.
It covers many topics but none in a usable way.
It feels like a blog post instead of a tool you can apply.
It includes sections you did not ask for.
It misses your real priorities because they were never stated.
You keep saying, "Focus on X," after the fact.
Common prompt patterns that trigger it:
"Tell me everything about…"
"Write a complete guide to…"
"Cover all aspects of…"
"Give me the best practices for…" with no constraints
"Create a comprehensive chapter…" without word limits or required sections

Why broad scope causes failure

Broad prompts force the model to choose:
what to include,
what to omit,
how deep to go,
and what order to present it.
If you do not decide these, the model will. It will default to general patterns like:
definitions, benefits, steps, tips, conclusion.
Those defaults may be reasonable, but they are rarely optimized for your exact use case.

The scoping triad: breadth, depth, and constraints

You cannot maximize all three at once:
breadth (cover many topics),
depth (go detailed),
tight constraints (short length, strict format).
If you demand all three, you get shallow content or constraint violations.

Professional scoping means selecting a balance:
narrow breadth + high depth, or
broad breadth + shallow depth, or
staged outputs (broad overview first, deep dive later).

The debugging method: find the hidden scope decisions

When an output feels too broad, ask:
What is the real outcome I need?
Who is the audience and what decisions will they make with this?
What is in scope, and what is explicitly out of scope?
What depth level is required?
What constraints define "done" (length, format, count)?
Then rewrite the prompt to encode those decisions.

How to fix overly broad scope (professional playbook)

Fix 1: State the objective as a specific deliverable

Instead of:
"Write about prompt engineering."
Use:
"Create a 1-page cheat sheet on prompt engineering for beginners with 5 rules, 3 examples, and a checklist."
Deliverables naturally narrow scope.

Fix 2: Define boundaries (in scope vs out of scope)

Add a "scope box":
In scope:
prompt structure, examples, constraints, validation
Out of scope:
model training history, vendor comparisons, advanced tooling
This prevents drift.

Fix 3: Limit breadth by choosing a single use case

Broad topic, narrow use case is powerful.
Example:
Instead of "prompt engineering," choose:
"prompt engineering for summarizing documents," or
"prompt engineering for writing business emails."
One use case gives the model a lens that filters content.

Fix 4: Use a depth level and section budget

Tell the model how deep to go and how much space each part gets.

Example:

"Write 900–1,100 words total.

Allocate: 150 words concept, 300 words method, 300 words examples, 200 words checklist."

This forces prioritization.

Fix 5: Ask for options then select (progressive scoping)

If you are not sure what to include, do not start with full writing.

Use a two-step workflow:

outline with 3 scope options,

choose one, then draft.

Prompt:

"Propose 3 outline options with different scope. Label each with what is included and excluded. I will choose one."

This prevents wasted drafts.

Fix 6: Use "top N" and "must include" lists

"Cover the top 5 most common mistakes" is better than "cover everything."

Add:

"include exactly N items,"

"prioritize by impact,"

"exclude anything not required."

Strong scoping patterns you can reuse

Pattern A: One-page output constraint

"Create a one-page guide. Must include: X. Must exclude: Y. Max 400 words."

Pattern B: Narrow lens

"Focus only on prompt engineering for customer support replies. Ignore other applications."

Pattern C: Layered output (overview then deep dive)

"Part 1: 120-word overview. Part 2: deep dive into one technique with examples."

Pattern D: Q-first scoping

"Ask 5 questions to narrow scope, then produce the deliverable."

Before and after transformations

Transformation 1: From "everything" to a bounded chapter section

Weak prompt:

"Write a complete chapter on prompt engineering."

Why it fails:
No boundaries, no audience, no length, no required structure.
Stronger prompt:
"Write a 1,000–1,200 word chapter section for beginners on 'Prompt debugging: missing context.'
In scope: symptoms, causes, fix patterns, 2 examples, 1 checklist.
Out of scope: model training, vendor tools, advanced automation.
Tone: practical, instructional.
Stop after the checklist."
Now it is scoped and testable.

Transformation 2: From broad request to a usable tool

Weak prompt:
"Give me best practices for prompts."
Stronger prompt:
"Give me 7 prompt-writing rules for business emails.
For each rule: one sentence rule, one example prompt line.
Include one 'do not' section with 5 items.
Max 350 words."
This converts a broad topic into a usable artifact.

A reusable "scope control" header (paste into prompts)

Use this when you want to prevent broad drift:
"Scope control:
Audience: <who>
Use case: <single scenario>
In scope: <3–6 items>
Out of scope: <3–6 items>
Depth: <overview, intermediate, deep dive>
Output: <format + length + required sections>
If scope is still unclear, ask up to 4 questions before writing."
This makes scope explicit and forces the model to prioritize correctly.

Mini lab: rescue a broad prompt

Take this broad prompt:
"Write about AI prompt engineering."
Rewrite it into three scoped versions:
One-page cheat sheet (max 400 words)
Deep dive on one core pattern (900–1,100 words)

Practical debugging guide for one failure mode (600–800 words)
Compare outputs. You will notice that scoping decisions create better results than "more instructions" ever will.
Overly broad scope is one of the easiest failures to prevent. Decide the lens, define boundaries, pick a deliverable, set depth and length, and the model will stop wandering and start producing work you can actually use.

Hallucination Risk

A hallucination-risk failure happens when the model produces information that is not grounded in your inputs or verifiable sources, then presents it fluently. This can look like:
invented facts, numbers, names, citations, or quotes,
confident explanations for unknown causes,
fabricated references, URLs, or "studies say" claims,
details borrowed from examples or common patterns rather than your data.
Hallucination risk is not random. It increases under predictable conditions, and prompt engineering can reduce it dramatically by changing how the task is framed and what outputs are allowed.
What hallucination risk looks like
Typical symptoms:
specific numbers appear even though you never provided them,
dates, names, or policies are asserted without sources,
citations are listed but cannot be verified,
the model "fills in" missing steps in a process as if it knows them,
it answers ambiguous questions without asking clarifying questions,
it states uncertain content as fact instead of labeling uncertainty.
A common clue is when the output is more specific than the input supports.
Why hallucinations happen
At a practical level, the model is trying to be helpful by completing a coherent response. Risk rises when the prompt pressures it to be complete and confident even when inputs are missing.
Hallucination risk is driven by:
missing context or missing source material,
overly broad scope,
high specificity demands (names, stats, "exact steps") without data,

long multi-part prompts where constraints are missed,
few-shot examples that leak content,
requests for citations or quotes without providing sources,
tasks involving rapidly changing facts where the model cannot verify.

The debugging method: locate the "unsupported claim points"

To fix hallucination risk, first identify where it might invent.
Ask:
Which parts of the output require external facts?
Which details were not in the input?
Which fields are required by the format but missing in the data?
Then choose a mitigation strategy:
allow Unknown,
ask questions,
constrain to provided sources only,
or separate generation from verification.

High-risk prompts and how to rewrite them

Certain prompt wordings encourage hallucination:

High-risk wording

"Give me the exact statistics on…" (without sources)
"Provide citations" (without providing references)
"Be detailed and comprehensive" (with missing data)
"Explain why this happened" (when cause is unknown)
"Fill in the missing parts" (without specifying placeholders)

Lower-risk rewrites

"Use only the provided text. If missing, write Unknown."
"List assumptions and label them."
"Provide hypotheses, not facts, and list what data would confirm them."
"Ask up to 5 questions before concluding."

The professional anti-hallucination toolkit (what to do in the prompt)

1) Declare a source policy

Pick one and state it:
"Use only the provided inputs."
"Use general knowledge allowed, but do not invent specific numbers or citations."
"If you cite sources, only cite the sources I provide."

This single choice matters. Many hallucinations are "source policy ambiguity."

2) Define an Unknown policy

Tell the model what to do when data is missing.

Options:

use "Unknown,"

use null (for JSON),

ask a clarifying question.

Example:

"If a fact is not in the input, write Unknown. Do not guess."

This prevents the model from feeling forced to invent.

3) Separate facts from interpretation

A powerful safety pattern:

Facts (from input)

Assumptions (explicit)

Hypotheses (plausible explanations, labeled)

Next data to verify

This is especially important for diagnosis and analysis tasks.

4) Require evidence mapping

If you provide text, force the model to point to where it got claims.

Example:

"For each key claim, cite the exact sentence from the provided input that supports it."

You can request this during a draft stage, then remove citations in the final.

5) Use intermediate representations

Extract first, write second.

Step 1: extract facts into a table (with Unknown for missing)

Step 2: generate narrative using only the table

This is one of the most reliable anti-hallucination methods.

6) Add a verification step

After generation, force a self-check:

"Scan your output for any claims not supported by inputs. If unsupported, remove or label as assumption."

This turns hallucination control into a test.

Ready-to-use prompt blocks (copy and paste)

Block A: Strict grounding (best for summarization and extraction)

"Grounding rules:

Use only the text I provide as your source of truth.

Do not add facts not present in the text.

If something is missing, write Unknown.

If you must infer, label it clearly as an inference."

Block B: Hypothesis mode (best for 'why' questions)

"If the cause is not directly supported by the data, do not present it as fact. Instead:

list 3 hypotheses labeled Hypothesis,

list what evidence would confirm each,

recommend next steps."

Block C: Fact/assumption split (fast and practical)

"Output in two sections:

Facts from input (bullets)

Assumptions or unknowns (bullets)

Then produce the deliverable using facts only, and clearly label any assumption."

Block D: Content-leak protection for few-shot prompts

"Examples are for style only. Do not reuse any names, numbers, or facts from examples.

Use only the new input for content. Missing info → Unknown."

How to handle citations safely

A major hallucination trap is "provide citations" when you did not provide sources.

Safe options:

If you did not provide sources: ask the model to avoid citations and instead suggest what sources to consult.

If you did provide sources: require citations only from that list.

If you allow web research: separate it as a distinct step and capture sources explicitly.

Prompt line:

"Do not invent citations. If sources are not provided, do not cite."

Before and after transformations

Transformation 1: Risky request becomes grounded output

Weak prompt:
"Write a report on the latest trends in AI prompt engineering with citations."
Problem:
Without sources, citations will be risky.
Stronger prompt:
"Write a trends overview based only on the sources I paste below.
If a trend is not supported by the sources, omit it.
No invented citations.
Output: 6 bullets + 2 risks + 3 questions for further research."

Transformation 2: "Why did this happen?" becomes hypothesis mode

Weak prompt:
"Why did our conversion rate drop last month?"
Problem:
Cause is unknown without data, model will guess.
Stronger prompt:
"Using only the data I provide, identify what changed.
Then provide 3 hypotheses (labeled), the data needed to confirm each, and 5 next actions ranked by impact/effort.
Do not state causes as facts."

Red flags checklist (teach readers to spot hallucination risk)

If any of these are true, risk is high:
you did not provide the underlying text or data,
you asked for specific numbers, names, dates without inputs,
you asked for citations without sources,
the task is broad and "comprehensive,"
you demanded certainty, confidence, or definitive conclusions,
you used few-shot examples containing real facts you do not want repeated.

Mini lab: build a "hallucination-resistant" prompt

Take a risky prompt you have used and add:
source policy,
Unknown policy,
fact vs hypothesis separation,
verification step.
Then test it with incomplete input and confirm it:
asks questions or uses Unknown,
does not invent numbers,

labels hypotheses clearly,
stays within the allowed scope.
Hallucination risk is manageable. The professional approach is to remove the pressure to guess by defining a source of truth, providing an Unknown policy, separating facts from hypotheses, using intermediate representations, and forcing verification. This turns "sounds right" into "is supported."

Bad Format Control

A "bad format control" failure happens when the model gives the right ideas in the wrong shape. You asked for JSON but got prose. You asked for a table but got bullets. You asked for "headings in this order" but it changed the order, added sections, or merged sections. This is one of the most frustrating failures because the content may be useful, yet unusable in your workflow.
The good news is that format control is highly fixable. Most format failures come from unclear format contracts, conflicting instructions, or missing validation.
What bad format control looks like
Common symptoms:
extra commentary before or after structured output,
wrong headings or wrong order,
wrong bullet counts or section counts,
invalid JSON (trailing commas, quotes wrong, extra keys),
tables missing columns or inconsistent rows,
schema drift across runs,
output mixes formats (table plus prose plus summary).
Typical phrases in the output:
"Sure, here is the JSON:" followed by JSON,
"Here's a table:" but it is not a table,
"In conclusion," even though you said "no conclusion."
Why format control fails
Bad format control usually comes from one of these causes:
1) No explicit format contract
Saying "make a table" is not a contract. The model needs:
columns, order, and constraints.

2) Mixed or conflicting format requirements

Example:

"Output JSON" + "Explain your reasoning."

3) Under-specified counts and ordering

If you say "include bullets," the model chooses how many.

4) Too many instructions at once

Long prompts can bury format rules. The model may follow the main request but miss a smaller formatting clause.

5) No validation step

Without validation, small format defects remain.

The professional fix: a format contract

A format contract is a short, explicit specification of what the output must look like. It should include:

output type (JSON/table/headings/bullets),

required sections and their order,

counts (exact bullets, exact rows, exact keys),

allowed and forbidden content,

stop condition,

a validation instruction.

Think of it as an interface definition.

Format contracts that work (copy and paste)

Contract A: Headings and bullets

"Output format contract:

Use exactly these headings in this order:

Summary

Key points

Risks

Next steps

Under each heading, use exactly 4 bullets.

No extra headings, no intro, no conclusion.

Stop after 'Next steps'."

This is far more controllable than "write a structured report."

Contract B: JSON only

"Output format contract:

Return valid JSON only. No markdown, no commentary.

Keys must match this schema exactly: <schema>

No extra keys.
Use null for unknown values.
Validate JSON before outputting."
This prevents the most common JSON failures.

Contract C: Table only

"Output format contract:
Return a markdown table only.
Columns (in order): Week | Milestone | Tasks | Owner role | Risks | Metric
Exactly 4 rows (Week 1–4).
No text outside the table.
Stop after the last row."

The four main format failure categories and fixes

Category 1: Wrong structure (headings missing, order wrong)

Fix:
provide the exact heading list in order,
add "no extra headings,"
include a skeleton the model must fill.
Example skeleton:
Summary:
...
Key points:
...
Risks:
...
Next steps:
...

Category 2: Wrong counts (too many bullets, wrong number of items)

Fix:
specify counts,
specify what to do if information is insufficient.
Example:
"If fewer than 4 items exist, fill remaining bullets with 'Unknown'."
This avoids the model inventing.

Category 3: Extra commentary around structured output
Fix:
add "output only,"
add "no preamble,"
add a stop condition.
For JSON and code-like outputs:
"Return JSON only, nothing else."
For narrative:
"Do not include explanations, only the deliverable."

Category 4: Schema drift and invalid JSON
Fix:
define schema explicitly,
use type constraints,
require a validation step.
Example:
"Validate that:
all keys exist,
no extra keys exist,
types match (string/null/array),
output parses as JSON."

Best practice: separate reasoning from formatting

If you need both thinking and strict formatting, do not combine them in one output. Use a chain:
reasoning or extraction step (bullets or table),
final formatted output (JSON/table only).
Example:
"Step 1: Extract fields into a table.
Step 2: Convert to JSON only."
This removes the most common cause of format failure: mixed output expectations.

Validation prompts: turn format compliance into a test

A professional workflow includes a validator pass:
"Check your output against this format contract.
If any rule fails, fix it and re-check.
Return only the corrected final output."

For strict outputs, add:
"If you cannot comply, say 'FORMAT ERROR' and list the failing rules."
That forces visibility when formatting is impossible due to conflicts.

The "format guardrail" pack (drop-in block)

Use this block whenever format is important:
"Format guardrails:
Output must match the format contract exactly.
No extra text before or after the output.
If information is missing, use Unknown or null, do not invent.
Validate against the contract before returning the final."
This reduces drift, hallucination pressure, and accidental commentary.

Before and after transformations

Transformation 1: From vague to strict structure

Weak prompt:
"Write a report with a summary and recommendations."
Problems:
No order, counts, length, or stop condition.
Stronger prompt:
"Output format:
Summary (max 60 words)
Findings (exactly 5 bullets)
Recommendations (exactly 3 bullets)
Risks (exactly 2 bullets)
No other sections. Stop after Risks."
Now the model knows exactly what "done" looks like.

Transformation 2: Fixing JSON drift

Weak prompt:
"Extract into JSON the owner and due date."
Problems:
It may add explanation, add extra keys, or invent a due date.
Stronger prompt:
"Return valid JSON only. Keys: owner (string or null), due_date (YYYY-MM-DD or null).
No extra keys. Use null if unknown. No commentary."

Mini lab: repair a bad-format prompt

Take a prompt that often returns the wrong shape. Do this:

Write a format contract with:
type, headings/keys/columns, order, counts, stop condition.
Add an Unknown policy.
Add a validation step.
If you need reasoning, split into two steps.
Run it twice. If the output shape becomes consistent, you fixed the root cause.
Bad format control is rarely a model limitation. It is usually a missing contract. When you define the output like an interface, enforce counts and ordering, separate reasoning from strict formatting, and add a validation step, format stops being a fight and becomes reliable.

Debugging workflow

Isolate Variables

Prompt debugging works best when you treat it like engineering: change one thing at a time, observe the effect, and keep what improves reliability.
"Isolate variables" means you do not rewrite the entire prompt at once. You identify the suspected cause of failure, make a minimal change, and test again.
This workflow turns prompt tuning from guesswork into a repeatable method.

Why isolating variables matters

If you change five things at once and the output improves, you will not know why it improved. If it gets worse, you will not know what broke it. Isolating variables gives you:
clear cause and effect,
reusable lessons you can apply elsewhere,
stable templates you can trust.

Step 0: Define the test case (freeze the input)

Before you change the prompt, freeze the conditions:
use the same input text,
use the same task,
keep the same output requirements,
keep the same evaluation checklist.
If your input changes every run, you are not debugging. You are redoing a task.

Step 1: Name the failure in one sentence

Write a single-line diagnosis:

"Wrong goal: it produced a tutorial instead of a checklist."

"Missing context: it assumed the audience."

"Bad format: extra text around JSON."

"Conflicting constraints: short but comprehensive."

"Hallucination risk: invented numbers."

This sentence becomes your debugging target.

Step 2: Extract the "contract" (what must be true)

Convert your prompt into a checklist. This is your evaluation rubric.

Example contract:

Output type: JSON only

Keys: owner, due_date, risk

due_date: YYYY-MM-DD or null

No extra keys

No commentary

Use null for missing facts

Stop after JSON

A contract makes failures objective.

Step 3: Identify the smallest likely cause

Choose one root cause to test first, such as:

unclear objective,

missing constraints,

missing Unknown policy,

missing stop condition,

too much scope,

lack of examples,

need for intermediate extraction.

Pick the smallest change that targets that cause.

Step 4: Apply one change only (a minimal patch)

Make a minimal patch, not a full rewrite.

Examples of single-variable patches:

add a stop condition: "Return JSON only, nothing else."

add Unknown policy: "If missing, use null, do not guess."

specify counts: "Exactly 6 bullets."

add a heading order list: "Use these headings in this order."

add audience line: “Audience: beginners.”

Keep everything else the same.

Step 5: Run controlled tests (two to three trials)

Run the updated prompt more than once. Minor variability can happen, so you want to see if the fix consistently helps.

Evaluate with your contract checklist:

Pass/Fail for each item.

If it passes consistently, keep the patch.

If it fails, revert and try a different variable.

Step 6: Log what changed and what improved

Keep a tiny prompt change log:

Change: added stop condition

Outcome: removed extra commentary 2 out of 2 runs

Keep: yes

This builds a library of reliable fixes you can reuse.

The variable isolation toolkit (what to change, one at a time)

Variable 1: Objective clarity

Patch:

“Deliverable: <exact artifact>.”

Test effect:

Does it stop solving the wrong problem?

Variable 2: Audience specification

Patch:

“Audience: <role and level>.”

Test effect:

Does tone and depth align?

Variable 3: Scope boundaries

Patch:

“In scope: <3 items>. Out of scope: <3 items>.”

Test effect:

Does it stop drifting?

Variable 4: Format contract

Patch:

“Output must be: <schema/headings/table>.”

Test effect:

Does structure become consistent?

Variable 5: Unknown handling
Patch:
"If missing, write Unknown/null. Do not invent."
Test effect:
Does hallucination reduce?
Variable 6: Step separation
Patch:
"Step 1: extract. Step 2: generate final."
Test effect:
Does correctness improve without format drift?
Variable 7: Examples
Patch:
Add one short positive example and one edge case.
Test effect:
Does behavior generalize across input variation?
Variable 8: Verification loop
Patch:
"Check output against checklist, fix until all pass."
Test effect:
Do constraint violations disappear?

A practical "isolate variables" debugging sequence (recommended order)

When you are unsure what is wrong, debug in this order because these fixes have the highest ROI:
Add a clear deliverable line (objective)
Add a format contract (structure, counts, stop)
Add Unknown policy (no guessing)
Add scope boundaries (in scope, out of scope)
Add a verification checklist
Add a two-step chain (extract then generate)
Add examples (few-shot) if still unstable
Each step changes one major variable and tests impact.

Example: isolating variables on a bad-format JSON prompt

Initial prompt:
"Extract owner and due date into JSON."

Failure:

Extra text and inconsistent keys.

Patch 1 (format contract only)

"Return valid JSON only. Keys: owner, due_date. No extra text."

Result:

Still invents due_date sometimes.

Patch 2 (Unknown policy only)

"Use null if unknown. Do not invent dates."

Result:

Stops invention, but sometimes adds extra key.

Patch 3 (no extra keys)

"No extra keys. Validate schema."

Result:

Now stable.

Notice each patch addressed one failure mode and you kept the ones that worked.

Example: isolating variables on an overly broad prompt

Initial prompt:

"Write a comprehensive guide to prompt engineering."

Failure:

Too generic.

Patch 1 (use case lens)

"Focus only on prompt debugging for beginners."

Result:

More relevant but still long and unfocused.

Patch 2 (structure contract)

"Sections: Symptoms, Causes, Fix patterns, 2 examples, Checklist. 900–1,100 words."

Result:

Now scoped and usable.

Again: one change at a time.

The "control prompt" technique (baseline comparison)

Keep a baseline prompt as your control. For each test, compare:

baseline output vs patched output,

using the same input and checklist.

This helps you measure improvements objectively.

A ready-to-use prompt debugging harness

When debugging, you can ask the model to help you isolate variables:

"Here is my prompt and the output it produced.

Identify the top 3 failure causes.

Propose three minimal patches, each changing one variable only.

Predict what each patch will improve.

Then apply Patch #1 and produce the revised output."

This keeps the process disciplined.

Mini lab: isolate variables in three rounds

Pick one prompt that fails often. Do three rounds:

Round 1: add a format contract only.

Round 2: add an Unknown policy only.

Round 3: add a verification checklist only.

Run each round twice and score pass/fail. You will learn which lever matters most for that prompt type.

Isolating variables is how you become an expert prompt debugger. You stop rewriting prompts randomly and start making controlled changes that you can measure, keep, and reuse.

Reduce Prompt

"Reduce the prompt" means shrinking your prompt to the smallest version that still reproduces the failure. This is one of the fastest ways to debug because it removes noise, reveals the true cause, and makes fixes obvious. Professionals use prompt reduction the same way engineers reduce a bug to a minimal reproducible example.

Why reducing the prompt works

Long prompts often contain:

redundant rules,

buried constraints,

conflicting instructions,

unnecessary examples,

multiple goals.

When output fails, it can be unclear which part caused the failure. Reduction helps you:

isolate the exact trigger,

discover contradictions you did not notice,
avoid "fixing" the wrong thing,
build a clean prompt you can reuse.

The reduction mindset: strip until the failure disappears

Your job is to remove prompt parts one by one until either:
the failure stops happening, or
the prompt becomes too small to perform the task.
The part you removed right before the failure stops is likely the source of the problem.

The step-by-step reduction workflow

Step 1: Freeze the test case

Use the same:
input text,
target output type,
evaluation checklist.
Do not change inputs while reducing. Otherwise you cannot compare results.

Step 2: Define the failure precisely

Write it in one sentence:
"It adds commentary around JSON."
"It ignores the word limit."
"It follows the wrong goal."
"It changes the heading order."
A clear failure statement tells you what to test for.

Step 3: Copy your prompt and remove obvious clutter

Remove anything that is not essential to the task:
repeated instructions,
motivational text,
long explanations,
extra examples,
optional nice-to-haves.
Keep only:
objective,
required output format,
key constraints,
the input.
This gives you the first reduced version.

Step 4: Apply the 50 percent cut rule

Make a bold reduction pass:
cut the prompt roughly in half,
keep the hardest requirements.
Then test:
if the failure still occurs, continue reducing,
if the failure disappears, the removed half contained the trigger.
This is faster than removing one line at a time from the start.

Step 5: Reduce by sections in a controlled order

To find the trigger quickly, remove in this order:
stylistic instructions (tone, voice)
background context (history, narrative)
optional constraints (nice-to-have)
examples (few-shot)
intermediate steps (if any)
finally, core constraints and format contract (do not remove these too early)
Why this order works:
style and background rarely cause core failures,
examples often cause leakage or drift,
conflicting constraints usually hide in the "nice-to-have" layer.

Step 6: Convert remaining text into a format contract

Once your prompt is short, rewrite it as a contract:
Deliverable: <what to output>
Format: <headings/schema/table>
Constraints: <must include, must avoid>
Unknown policy: <Unknown/null/questions>
Stop condition: <where to stop>
This makes failures measurable.

Step 7: Add back only what earns its keep

After you have a minimal prompt that works, reintroduce one feature at a time:
add tone requirements, test
add one example, test
add an edge case example, test
add a verification loop, test
If the failure reappears after adding something, you found a trigger.

What reduction reveals most often (the real root causes)

Hidden conflict

You discover that the prompt says:

"ask questions first" and "deliver final answer now,"

"be concise" and "cover everything in detail,"

"JSON only" and "explain reasoning."

Reduction makes these conflicts easier to see because there is less noise.

Buried format rules

In a long prompt, format rules can get lost. Reduction forces you to put format first.

Fix:

Move format contract to the top and shorten it.

Example leakage or topic anchoring

Few-shot examples can cause the model to copy names, numbers, or topics.

Reduction test:

Remove examples. If the issue disappears, rebuild examples with placeholders and add an anti-leak rule.

Too many instructions competing

Long prompts create instruction overload.

Reduction fix:

Keep only 5 to 7 high-impact rules and convert the rest into a checklist or post-validation.

Reduction patterns for common failures

Bad format control (JSON/table issues)

Minimal prompt to test:

"Return valid JSON only. Keys: <...>. No extra text. Use null if missing. Input: <...>."

If this works, the failure was caused by extra instructions or examples.

Hallucination risk

Minimal prompt to test:

"Use only the provided text. If missing, write Unknown. List facts only."

If hallucination stops, the earlier prompt was pressuring completeness or allowing assumptions.

Wrong goal

Minimal prompt to test:

"Deliverable: <exact artifact>. Output format: <...>. Stop after <...>."

If the goal aligns, the earlier prompt had ambiguous objective wording.

Before and after example: reducing a bloated prompt

Bloated prompt (typical)

"Write a comprehensive, detailed, professional guide with examples, make it short, include citations, use a table, also output JSON for key points, keep it friendly, ask me questions if needed, and make sure it is perfect."

This contains multiple conflicts and too many goals.

Reduced prompt (debug version)

"Deliverable: 6-bullet cheat sheet for beginners.
Format: bullets only, max 180 words.
Must include: one prompt formula, one example, one checklist.
Must avoid: citations, JSON, tables.
Stop after the checklist."

This version is testable and stable. Once it works, you can add back one feature at a time.

The "minimum prompt" templates (quick starting points)

Minimum template for structured writing

"Deliverable: <what>
Audience: <who>
Format: <headings/order/counts>
Constraints: <must include/must avoid>
Stop: <end point>
Input: <text>"

Minimum template for extraction

"Return <JSON/table> only.
Schema/columns: <...>
Unknown policy: <null/Unknown>
No extra text.
Input: <text>"

Mini lab: reduce a failing prompt in 10 minutes

Choose a prompt that fails often.
Freeze one input example.
Make a 50 percent cut and test.
Remove examples and test.
Convert to a format contract and test.
Add back one feature at a time until failure returns.

Keep only the features that survive.
Result: you end up with a clean prompt that is shorter, clearer, and more reliable than the original.
Reducing the prompt is a professional debugging habit. It exposes what is essential, removes hidden conflicts, and gives you a minimal working core that you can confidently extend.

Add Tests

A prompt is not "good" because one output looked good. A prompt is good because it behaves predictably across many realistic inputs. That is why professional prompt debugging includes tests.
Adding tests means you create a small, reusable test suite that checks:
correctness,
format compliance,
grounding,
edge-case handling,
and stability across runs.
With tests, you stop relying on intuition and start measuring prompt quality.
Why prompt tests matter
Without tests, you debug by feelings:
"It seems better."
"It worked this time."
With tests, you debug by evidence:
"It passed 9 out of 10 cases."
"It failed only on missing-data inputs."
"It breaks when the input is short."
Tests give you:
faster iteration,
fewer regressions,
reusable prompt templates,
consistent performance across a team.
What makes a good prompt test
A good test is:
short and realistic,
designed to expose a specific failure mode,

measurable (pass/fail or scored),
repeatable.
Bad tests are:
unrealistic,
too easy,
or impossible to evaluate objectively.

Step-by-step workflow: add tests to your prompt debugging

Step 1: Write a prompt contract (your acceptance criteria)

A test suite needs a clear target.
Create a compact contract:
deliverable type,
required structure and order,
counts (bullets, sections, keys),
length range,
forbidden content,
source policy,
unknown policy,
stop condition.
Example contract:
Output: JSON only
Keys: owner, due_date, risk
Types: string or null
No extra keys, no extra text
due_date format: YYYY-MM-DD or null
Without a contract, you cannot test reliably.

Step 2: Identify the top failure modes to test

Pick 5 to 8 failure modes you care about most, such as:
wrong goal,
missing context,
conflicting constraints,
overly broad scope,
hallucination risk,
bad format control,
wrong tone,
incomplete coverage.
Each test case should map to one failure mode.

Step 3: Build a small test suite (start with 8–12 cases)

A practical starter suite has 8 to 12 tests. Include:

Core cases

2 normal cases (typical input)

2 messy cases (real-world noise, mixed formatting)

Edge cases

2 missing-data cases (critical fields absent)

1 conflicting-data case (contradictory statements)

1 boundary case (shortest acceptable input or borderline classification)

Stress cases (optional but useful)

1 long input case (length pressure)

1 adversarial phrasing case (tempts the model to break rules)

This mix reveals where the prompt is brittle.

Step 4: Label each test with what it is designed to break

Every test should have:

a name,

a purpose,

and clear pass/fail criteria.

Example label:

"Test 6: Missing due date. Purpose: verify null/Unknown handling. Pass if due_date is null and no invented date appears."

This makes debugging fast when something fails.

Step 5: Create an evaluation checklist (pass/fail)

A test is only useful if you can score it.

Pass/fail checklist examples

Format:

correct headings order,

correct bullet counts,

no extra text.

Grounding:

no facts beyond input,

unknowns labeled.

Constraints:

word count in range,

forbidden content absent.

If you need nuance, use a simple 0–2 rubric per criterion.

Step 6: Run tests after every prompt change (regression testing)

Once tests exist:

run them after each change,

compare results to the previous version.

If a change improves one case but breaks two others, you decide whether to:

revert,

or add a targeted guardrail.

This prevents "fix one thing, break another."

Test patterns you can reuse (templates)

Pattern A: Format compliance tests

Use for JSON, tables, strict headings.

Test inputs:

normal data,

missing field,

extra irrelevant line,

conflicting values.

Pass criteria:

schema holds,

no extra text,

unknown policy applied.

Pattern B: Hallucination resistance tests

Use incomplete inputs deliberately.

Test input:

gives only partial facts.

Pass criteria:

model does not invent specifics,

uses Unknown or questions-first.

Pattern C: Scope control tests

Use prompts that tempt drift:

"cover everything,"

multiple topics in one input.

Pass criteria:

output stays within in-scope list,

out-of-scope content omitted.

Pattern D: Stability tests

Run the same test case two or three times.

Pass criteria:
structure remains identical,
key decisions consistent,
only minor wording differences.

Example: a ready-to-use 10-case test suite (generic)

You can adapt this to many prompts by swapping the input content.
Normal case, clean input
Normal case, different topic
Messy input (bullets + fragments)
Messy input (long paragraph)
Missing critical field A
Missing critical field B
Conflicting statements
Very short input (minimum)
Very long input (stress)
Adversarial phrasing ("also add citations," "be comprehensive," etc.)
For each case, define:
expected structure,
unknown handling,
forbidden content.

How to use red-team tests

Once your base suite passes, add 3 to 5 red-team tests designed to break it:
"Ask for JSON but tempt it to explain reasoning."
"Ask for short output but include many required sections."
"Provide ambiguous terms like 'best' and 'optimize'."
"Include a misleading number to see if it propagates."
Red-team tests harden the prompt.

Building a test harness prompt (meta prompt)

If you want the model to help you create tests, use:
"Create a test suite for this prompt.
Include 10 test inputs covering: normal, messy, missing data, conflicting data, long input, and adversarial phrasing.
For each test, provide pass/fail criteria tied to the prompt's contract.
Prompt to test:
<paste prompt>"
This is a fast way to bootstrap testing.

Common mistakes when adding tests (and fixes)

Mistake 1: Tests are too easy

Fix:

Add missing-data and conflicting-data cases. Those reveal real brittleness.

Mistake 2: No objective pass/fail rules

Fix:

Write a contract with measurable criteria: counts, order, schema rules.

Mistake 3: Tests are unrealistic

Fix:

Base tests on actual inputs you see in your workflow.

Mistake 4: You never rerun tests

Fix:

Run the suite after every meaningful prompt change.

Mini lab: add tests to one of your prompts

Choose a prompt you use often.

Write a 6-item contract (format, counts, unknown, forbidden, stop).

Create 8 test inputs: 2 normal, 2 messy, 2 missing, 1 conflict, 1 long.

Run them and log pass/fail.

Fix the prompt and rerun the same suite.

That is professional prompt debugging: not one perfect answer, but predictable performance across cases.

Adding tests turns prompt engineering into an engineering discipline. You stop optimizing for one example and start building prompts that hold up under real-world messiness, missing information, and edge conditions.

Add Constraints

Adding constraints is one of the fastest ways to turn a "sometimes good" prompt into a reliable one. When a prompt fails, the model is often not being "bad." It is operating in an under-specified space. Constraints shrink that space so the model has fewer ways to go wrong.

This section teaches you how to add constraints systematically, without turning your prompt into a giant wall of text.

What "constraints" mean in prompt debugging

Constraints are explicit rules that limit:

what the output must contain,

what it must not contain,
how it must be structured,
what sources it can use,
and when it must stop.
A constraint is effective when it is testable:
pass/fail, not "kind of."

When you should add constraints

Add constraints when you see:
inconsistent structure across runs,
missing required sections,
extra sections you did not request,
hallucinations or invented details,
output that is too long or too short,
mixed formats (JSON plus commentary),
wrong tone or audience mismatch.
If the output is "good but unpredictable," constraints are the fix.

The constraint ladder (add in this order)

Do not add everything at once. Add constraints in a sequence from highest impact to lower impact.

Level 1: Goal and deliverable constraints

These prevent wrong-goal failures.
Add:
Deliverable type: checklist, outline, report, JSON, email
Audience: who it is for
Success criteria: what "done" means
Example:
"Deliverable: a 1-page beginner cheat sheet. Audience: novices. Success: includes 5 rules, 3 examples, 1 checklist."

Level 2: Format contract constraints

These prevent bad format control.
Add:
required headings and order,
counts (exact bullets, exact items),
length limits,
stop condition.

Example:
"Use headings A, B, C in that order. Under each, exactly 4 bullets. Total 400–500 words. Stop after C."

Level 3: Source and grounding constraints

These reduce hallucination risk.
Add:
source-of-truth rule,
Unknown policy,
inference labeling.
Example:
"Use only the provided inputs. If missing, write Unknown. Do not invent names, numbers, or citations."

Level 4: Content boundaries (non-goals and forbidden content)

These prevent scope creep and unwanted tone.
Add:
in scope, out of scope,
forbidden content list.
Example:
"Out of scope: history of AI, vendor comparisons. Forbidden: hype, emojis, invented stats."

Level 5: Quality constraints (validation and revision)

These keep outputs compliant.
Add:
self-check list,
revise-until-pass loop.
Example:
"Check output against this checklist. Fix any violations. Return final only."

The four types of constraints (and how to write them)

1) Structural constraints

Define the shape.
Good structural constraints:
"Exactly 6 bullets."
"Headings must be in this order."
"Return JSON only."
Weak structural constraints:
"Make it well structured."

2) Quantitative constraints

Define measurable limits.

Examples:

"120–160 words."

"2 examples, 1 checklist."

"Max 12 lines."

"No more than 3 sentences per paragraph."

Quantitative constraints are powerful because they are easy to verify.

3) Content constraints

Define what must and must not appear.

Examples:

"Must include: risks, mitigation, owner, next step."

"Must not include: personal opinions, moralizing, marketing tone."

"Do not mention tools or brands."

4) Process constraints

Define how the model should behave.

Examples:

"Ask up to 4 clarifying questions if inputs are missing."

"Use a two-step process: extract facts, then write."

"Verify against schema before final output."

Process constraints are especially useful for complex tasks.

How to add constraints without bloating the prompt

The secret is to write constraints as a compact contract block. Keep it short and reusable.

Constraint contract template (copy and fill)

Deliverable: <what to produce>

Audience: <who>

Format: <headings/schema/table>

Counts: <bullets/examples/sections>

Length: <range>

Source policy: <allowed sources>

Unknown policy: <Unknown/null/questions>

Must include: <3–7 items>

Must avoid: <3–7 items>

Stop: <where to stop>

This is enough for most tasks.

Common constraint mistakes (and fixes)

Mistake 1: Contradictory constraints

Example:

"Be short and comprehensive and deeply detailed."

Fix:

Declare priorities:

"Priority: format and grounding, then completeness, then style."

Or split into stages:

summary first, deep dive second.

Mistake 2: Constraints are not testable

Example:

"Make it professional."

Fix:

Translate into measurable rules:

"no emojis, no hype, short paragraphs, neutral tone."

Mistake 3: Constraints force hallucinations

Example:

"Fill all fields even if missing."

Fix:

Add Unknown policy:

"Use null/Unknown when missing, do not guess."

Mistake 4: Too many constraints at once

Fix:

Start with 5–7 core constraints, then add one at a time only when a failure appears.

Before and after transformations

Transformation 1: Fixing format drift

Weak prompt:

"Summarize these notes in a structured way."

Add constraints:

"Output format:

Summary (max 60 words)

Decisions (exactly 4 bullets)

Action items (table: Task | Owner role | Due date | Risk)

Unknown for missing due dates. Stop after the table."

Result:
Reliable structure and no guessing.

Transformation 2: Reducing hallucination risk

Weak prompt:
"Write a report and include key metrics."
Add constraints:
"Use only the provided text. Do not invent metrics.
If metrics are missing, write 'Unknown' and list what data is needed.
Must include: findings, risks, recommendations.
Length: 800–1,000 words."
Result:
Grounded output and transparent unknowns.

Debugging workflow: add constraints step-by-step (practical routine)

When a prompt fails, do this routine:
Add a deliverable line (goal)
Add a format contract (structure + stop)
Add an Unknown policy (no guessing)
Add must include / must avoid boundaries
Add a verification checklist and revise loop
Test after each addition. Keep what fixes the failure.

Mini lab: constraint hardening in three rounds

Pick a prompt that outputs inconsistently.
Round 1: Add format contract only.
Round 2: Add Unknown policy only.
Round 3: Add verification checklist only.
Run the same test input twice each round and evaluate pass/fail. You will see which constraint class has the biggest impact for that task.

Adding constraints is not about making prompts longer. It is about making them clearer and more testable. A short, well-written constraint contract plus an Unknown policy and a stop condition often produces more reliable results than paragraphs of guidance.

Add Examples

Adding examples is one of the most effective debugging moves when a prompt is conceptually clear but the model still behaves inconsistently.

Examples reduce interpretation. They show the model exactly what you mean by "like this," including structure, tone, boundaries, and edge-case handling.

This section teaches how to add examples systematically, without causing content leakage or making the prompt too long.

When examples are the right fix

Add examples when you see these symptoms:

the model understands the task but outputs vary in structure,

it keeps missing a specific section or formatting rule,

it struggles to match your house style,

it mislabels borderline cases in classification tasks,

it does not follow "do not" instructions reliably,

it needs to learn a transformation pattern (rewrite, extract, reformat).

Examples are less useful when:

the prompt has a wrong goal (objective unclear),

the input data is missing (context issue),

constraints conflict (examples cannot fix impossible requirements).

Fix the objective and constraints first. Then add examples.

The purpose of examples in debugging

Examples can teach four things:

Output shape: headings, bullet counts, schema keys

Content boundaries: what to include and what to exclude

Decision rules: how to classify or choose

Edge-case behavior: what to do when information is missing or conflicting

A good example set is not about being long. It is about being representative.

The example ladder (add in this order)

Do not jump to five examples immediately. Add the smallest example that fixes the failure.

Level 1: Output skeleton

First, try a skeleton with placeholders.

Example:

"Use this exact structure:

Title:

Summary:

…

Actions:
…
Stop."
This often fixes format drift without full few-shot examples.

Level 2: One positive example (one-shot)
Add one short input and one correct output.
Best for:
tone imitation,
formatting stability,
simple transformations.
Level 3: Two positives with variety (recommended default)
Add two examples that differ in topic or input style but produce the same structure.
This improves generalization and reduces overfitting.
Level 4: Add one edge-case example
If you still see failures, add one example that demonstrates:
missing info → Unknown/null,
ambiguous info → ask questions,
conflicting info → flag and choose a rule.
This is one of the highest ROI moves in professional prompting.
Level 5: Add one negative example (wrong vs correct)
If the model keeps making the same mistake, show it:
a short "bad output" and why it is wrong,
the corrected output.
Keep the negative example compact. You are teaching a boundary.
How to design examples that actually debug the problem
Rule 1: Keep examples aligned with the contract
Examples must reflect:
the same format contract,
the same constraints,
the same Unknown policy.
If the example violates your own rules, the model will copy that behavior.
Rule 2: Make examples minimal
Examples should contain only what is necessary to teach the pattern.
short inputs,

short outputs,
consistent labels.
Long examples increase noise and risk content transfer.

Rule 3: Use placeholders to prevent content leakage

If you use real names, numbers, or unique stories, the model may reuse them.
Use:
<NAME>, <DATE>, <AMOUNT>, <PRODUCT>.
Then explicitly instruct:
"Examples are for style and structure only. Do not reuse example content."

Rule 4: Vary the input, keep the output structure identical

This teaches the model what is invariant:
the output format.
Example variation:
one input is bullet notes,
one input is a paragraph,
output still follows the same schema.

Rule 5: Include one boundary case for the failure you are seeing

If the failure is hallucination, your edge-case example should show Unknown usage.
If the failure is wrong format, your example should show strict structure and no extra text.
If the failure is wrong classification, your edge-case should show a borderline label.

Debugging workflow: add examples step-by-step

Step 1: Identify the repeated failure

Write it as:
"The model keeps doing X instead of Y."
Examples:
"keeps adding commentary around JSON"
"keeps missing the Risks section"
"keeps using a chatty tone"
"keeps confusing labels A and B"

Step 2: Add an example that demonstrates the correct behavior

Start with one positive example.
Then test. If the failure persists, do not immediately add more examples. Add variety or an edge case next.

Step 3: Add one edge-case example targeted to the failure
Edge-case examples are more valuable than adding many normal examples.
Step 4: Add one negative example if the same mistake repeats
Show the wrong pattern and correct it.
Step 5: Retest with your test suite
Do not judge based on one input. Run at least:
one normal case,
one messy input case,
one missing-data case.
If examples improve one case but break another, your examples may be too narrow or too specific.
Copy-paste example blocks (useful patterns)
Pattern A: Few-shot for strict formatting
"Follow the format shown in the examples exactly.
Examples are for format only, do not reuse their content.
Example 1
Input: <...>
Output: <exact structure>
Example 2
Input: <...>
Output: <exact structure>
Now do this input: <...>
Output:"
This pattern makes the example boundary explicit.
Pattern B: Few-shot for missing data behavior
Example shows:
missing field becomes Unknown/null.
Example:
Input: "Owner: <NAME>. Due date not provided."
Output: {"owner":"<NAME>","due_date":null}
Now the model learns not to invent dates.
Pattern C: Few-shot for classification boundaries
Examples should include:
clear cases,
borderline case,
"none of the above" case if relevant.

This reduces label confusion.

Pattern D: Negative example for recurring failure

"Bad output (wrong): <short snippet>
Why wrong: violates <rule>
Correct output: <short snippet>"

This is a direct behavioral correction.

Common mistakes when adding examples (and fixes)

Mistake 1: Examples teach the wrong thing

Fix:

Make sure examples match your desired output contract exactly.

Mistake 2: Examples are too long and dilute the pattern

Fix:

Compress to micro-examples and skeletons.

Mistake 3: Content leakage from examples

Fix:

Use placeholders and add an anti-leak rule:

"Do not reuse any names, numbers, or facts from examples."

Mistake 4: Too many examples, still unstable

Fix:

Add a validator step instead of more examples:

"Check output against the contract and fix violations."

Mistake 5: Examples conflict with constraints

Fix:

Update examples after you change the contract. Stale examples are a common cause of regressions.

Mini lab: debug a prompt by adding examples

Choose a prompt that fails in a repeated way.

Add a skeleton output. Test.

If still failing, add one positive example. Test.

Add one edge-case example for missing data or borderline cases. Test.

If needed, add one negative example for the recurring failure.

Run three tests: normal, messy, missing-data.

You will learn a key professional lesson: one well-chosen edge-case example often fixes more than five generic examples.

Adding examples is not about making prompts longer. It is about making intent visible. A small, carefully designed example set can lock structure, prevent common errors, teach boundary behavior, and dramatically reduce variability.

Lab, a "prompt clinic" with 15 broken prompts

This lab is a hands-on "prompt clinic." You will diagnose and repair 15 intentionally broken prompts. Each case trains a specific debugging skill: spotting the failure mode, identifying the root cause, and applying a minimal fix that makes the prompt reliable.

How to use this lab:

Read the broken prompt.

Predict the failure mode.

Apply the "clinic fix" prompt.

Test with the suggested input.

Compare results and iterate if needed.

The clinic framework (use for all 15 cases)

Step A: Diagnose

Answer three questions:

What did the prompt ask for?

What will likely go wrong?

Which information or constraint is missing or conflicting?

Step B: Patch

Apply a minimal patch using one or more:

Goal + deliverable clarification

Format contract

Scope boundaries

Unknown policy

Examples (few-shot)

Validation checklist

Step C: Test

Use a test input and score pass/fail against the contract.

The 15 broken prompts

Case 1: Wrong goal

Broken prompt

"Help me with prompt engineering."

Likely failure

Generic overview, not a usable deliverable.

Clinic fix

"Deliverable: a one-page beginner cheat sheet on prompt engineering.
Must include: 5 rules, 3 examples, 1 checklist.
Audience: beginners.
Length: 350–450 words.
Stop after checklist."

Test input

None needed, this is content generation.

Case 2: Missing context

Broken prompt

"Write a chapter section about temperature."

Likely failure

Wrong depth and audience assumptions.

Clinic fix

"Audience: beginners, plain language.
Objective: explain determinism vs randomness and what temperature changes.
Length: 800–1,000 words.
Must include: 2 analogies, 1 mini lab, 1 checklist.
Out of scope: math-heavy derivations."

Test input

None.

Case 3: Conflicting constraints

Broken prompt

"Write a comprehensive, detailed explanation in 120 words."

Likely failure

Too long or too shallow.

Clinic fix

"Output in two parts:
Part 1: 120-word summary.
Part 2: 6 bullets for detail.
No extra sections."

Test input
Any topic.

Case 4: Overly broad scope
Broken prompt
"Explain everything about prompt debugging."
Likely failure
Shallow, wandering content.
Clinic fix
"Focus only on debugging 'missing context' prompts.
Output: Symptoms, Causes, Fix patterns, 2 before/after examples, Checklist.
Length: 700–900 words."
Test input
None.

Case 5: Bad format control
Broken prompt
"Extract tasks and owners into JSON."
Likely failure
Extra text, invalid JSON, invented due dates.
Clinic fix
"Return valid JSON only.
Schema: [{task: string, owner_role: string|null, due_date: string|null}]
No extra keys. Use null if unknown.
Input: <paste notes>"
Test input
Provide 6 lines of meeting notes with missing due dates.

Case 6: Hallucination risk
Broken prompt
"Give me the exact statistics and citations about prompt engineering trends."
Likely failure
Invented stats and fake citations.
Clinic fix
"If you do not have sources provided, do not cite.
Instead: list 6 plausible trends labeled 'Hypothesis,' and list what sources to

check.
No numbers unless provided."

Test input

None.

Case 7: Undefined audience

Broken prompt

"Write this more professionally."

Likely failure

Tone changes meaning or becomes too formal.

Clinic fix

"Revise without changing meaning.
Audience: external customer.
Tone: calm, helpful, direct.
Constraints: keep commitments and dates unchanged.
Return revised version only."

Test input

Paste a messy customer email draft.

Case 8: Ambiguous words

Broken prompt

"Optimize this prompt and make it better."

Likely failure

Random changes, unclear improvement goal.

Clinic fix

"Define 'better' as:
fewer than 140 words
includes exact output format
includes Unknown policy
includes stop condition
Rewrite the prompt to meet these criteria."

Test input

Paste any vague prompt.

Case 9: Mixed deliverables

Broken prompt

"Give me a table, a summary, and JSON, and also explain everything."

Likely failure

Messy mixed output.

Clinic fix

"Two-stage workflow.
Stage 1: produce the table + short summary.
Stage 2: produce JSON only.
No explanation in stage 2."

Test input

Paste a short dataset or notes.

Case 10: Too many rules, buried priorities

Broken prompt

A long prompt with 20 instructions and no priority order.

Likely failure

Important constraints ignored.

Clinic fix

"Rewrite this prompt into a compact contract with priorities:
Priority order: (1) source policy, (2) output format, (3) required sections, (4) forbidden content, (5) length, (6) style.
Return the revised prompt only."

Test input

Paste the long prompt.

Case 11: Few-shot content leakage

Broken prompt

Includes examples with real names, dates, and numbers.

Likely failure

The model reuses example facts.

Clinic fix

"Examples are for style only. Do not reuse names, numbers, dates, or facts from examples.
Replace specifics with placeholders in all examples: <NAME>, <DATE>,

<AMOUNT>.
Then generate output for the new input."

Test input

Provide a new input and see if old names appear.

Case 12: Missing stop condition

Broken prompt

"Output JSON with these keys: …" (no mention of extra text)

Likely failure

Adds preamble and postscript.

Clinic fix

"Return JSON only, no markdown, no commentary. Stop immediately after the closing brace."

Test input

Any extraction.

Case 13: Missing evaluation criteria

Broken prompt

"Write a good prompt for extracting requirements."

Likely failure

Generic prompt, not verifiable.

Clinic fix

"Create a prompt template that includes: objective, inputs, schema, Unknown policy, validation step.
Also provide a 6-item checklist to evaluate whether the extraction prompt is correct."

Test input

Paste a requirements paragraph.

Case 14: Wrong level of detail

Broken prompt

"Explain chain-of-thought prompting."

Likely failure

Either too advanced or too shallow, and may invite unwanted internal reasoning.

Clinic fix

"Explain multi-step prompting in plain language.
Do not include private reasoning.
Include: 1 analogy, 1 4-stage workflow, 1 short example.
Length: 500–650 words."

Test input

None.

Case 15: No handling for missing or conflicting inputs

Broken prompt

"Summarize these notes and list next steps." (notes are messy and contradictory)

Likely failure

Invented "next steps" or false certainty.

Clinic fix

"First, extract facts into a table: Decision | Owner role | Due date | Confidence.
Use 'Low confidence' for unclear items.
Then propose next steps as options, not facts.
Do not invent dates or owners."

Test input

Paste messy meeting notes with contradictions.

Clinic scoring sheet (quick, use across all cases)

Score each fixed prompt 0–2 on:
Goal clarity
Format control
Scope boundaries
Unknown handling and grounding
Testability (clear pass/fail)
Total out of 10. Aim for 8+.

Bonus: build your own "prompt clinic" library

After you complete the 15 cases:
save each fixed prompt as a template,
label it by failure mode,

add one test input you can reuse.

Over time, you will have a personal prompt playbook:

"JSON extraction template"

"Question-first workflow template"

"Strict format contract template"

"Hallucination-resistant analysis template"

That is how novices become experts: not by memorizing tricks, but by building a tested set of prompt patterns that solve predictable failures.

Chapter 11. Managing hallucinations and reliability

When Hallucinations Happen Most

Hallucinations are most likely when the model is pressured to be specific, complete, and confident while the inputs do not fully support that specificity. The model's job is to produce plausible continuations, so when information is missing or the task is under-specified, it may "fill in" details to keep the output coherent.

This section teaches you to recognize the highest-risk situations so you can design prompts and workflows that reduce hallucinations before they appear.

The core pattern: high demand, low grounding

Hallucination risk spikes when these conditions combine:

High demand: you ask for detail, citations, exactness, or a complete plan.

Low grounding: you provide limited or ambiguous source material.

If you reduce demand or increase grounding, risk drops.

The highest-risk situations (when hallucinations happen most)

1) You ask for facts that are not in the input

Examples:

"What was the exact revenue last quarter?" without a source

"List the steps in our internal process" without documentation

"Summarize the report" without pasting the report

Why it triggers hallucinations:

The model tries to be helpful and complete. Without facts, it guesses.

Risk-reducing move:

Use a strict source policy:

"Use only provided text. If missing, say Unknown."

2) You request citations, quotes, or references without providing sources

Examples:

"Add citations," "include references," "quote the policy" with no source list.

Why it triggers hallucinations:
The format strongly implies sources exist, so the model may fabricate plausible citations or quotes.
Risk-reducing move:
provide sources explicitly, or
forbid citations and ask for "what sources to consult."

3) You ask "why did this happen?" with insufficient data
Examples:
"Why did sales drop?"
"Why is our model failing?"
"Why did the customer churn increase?"
Why it triggers hallucinations:
Causal explanations are tempting to complete as a narrative, even when multiple causes are plausible.
Risk-reducing move:
Switch to hypothesis mode:
"List hypotheses, label them, and state what evidence would confirm each."

4) You demand completeness under tight length limits
Examples:
"Be comprehensive in 150 words."
"Include everything but keep it brief."
Why it triggers hallucinations:
To feel "complete," the model may compress too hard, drop caveats, or insert confident claims without support.
Risk-reducing move:
Split deliverables:
short summary, then bullets or appendix.

5) You ask for "best," "optimal," or "most accurate" without a rubric or constraints
Examples:
"What's the best strategy?"
"Optimize this plan."
"Give the most accurate answer."

Why it triggers hallucinations:
The model must choose criteria and may invent justification to support a recommendation.
Risk-reducing move:
Provide evaluation criteria:
"Rank options using this rubric."

6) You provide vague, ambiguous, or incomplete instructions
Examples:
"Make it professional."
"Improve this."
"Explain AI."
Why it triggers hallucinations:
Ambiguity forces the model to assume audience, scope, and success criteria. Assumptions can become "facts" inside the output.
Risk-reducing move:
Add a context packet:
objective, audience, format, constraints, stop condition.

7) The output format requires fields that the input does not contain
This is common in extraction tasks.
Example:
You ask for JSON with fields like:
owner, due date, budget, risk
But your notes only mention owner.
Why it triggers hallucinations:
The model tries to fill required fields rather than leaving them empty.
Risk-reducing move:
Define an Unknown policy:
"Use null for unknown. Do not invent."

8) Few-shot examples contain real facts that the model can copy
Examples:
training examples include real names, dates, numbers, and the model repeats them.

Why it triggers hallucinations:
The model treats examples as part of the context and may reuse details, especially when the new input is thin.
Risk-reducing move:
Use placeholders and anti-leak rules:
"Examples are for style only. Do not reuse example facts."

9) The task is broad, open-ended, and "comprehensive"
Examples:
"Write a complete guide,"
"cover all aspects of,"
"everything you know about."
Why it triggers hallucinations:
The model must select content across a huge space and may stitch together plausible-sounding material that is not grounded.
Risk-reducing move:
Narrow scope:
one audience, one use case, defined boundaries, defined length.

10) The topic involves rapidly changing facts
Examples:
current events, laws, product specs, policies, schedules.
Why it triggers hallucinations:
The model may not have the latest info and may produce outdated or incorrect specifics.
Risk-reducing move:
Require verification:
"Use provided sources," or
"List what must be verified and do not guess."

11) Long conversations with conflicting instructions
If the context includes:
earlier rejected drafts,
contradictory constraints,
multiple versions of requirements,
the model may blend them and generate inconsistent or incorrect details.

Risk-reducing move:
Keep context clean:
carry forward only one "source of truth" context packet.

12) The prompt pressures confidence and authority

Examples:
"Answer decisively," "be very confident," "no uncertainty."
Why it triggers hallucinations:
It discourages the model from admitting unknowns.
Risk-reducing move:
Allow uncertainty explicitly:
"If unsure, say so and list missing information."

A practical risk meter (quick self-check)

Before you run a prompt, check these questions:
Did I provide the source text or data?
Am I asking for citations without sources?
Am I asking for causes without evidence?
Am I demanding "complete" under tight length?
Does the format require fields I did not provide?
Did I include examples with real facts?
Did I define what to do when info is missing?
If you answer "yes" to any, hallucination risk is high unless you add guardrails.

What to do when you know risk is high

Use one of these three strategies:

Strategy A: Grounded-only mode

"Use only the provided inputs. If missing, say Unknown. No extra facts."

Strategy B: Hypothesis mode

"Provide labeled hypotheses, not factual claims, and list evidence needed."

Strategy C: Two-step workflow

Step 1: extract facts into a table with Unknown.
Step 2: generate output using only the table.
These are reliable professional patterns.

Hallucinations happen most when the model is forced to complete a story without enough grounded material. Your job is to either supply the missing grounding or change the task so it is allowed to be incomplete in a controlled way, using Unknown, questions, hypotheses, and verification steps.

“Unknown” behavior, forcing the model to say “I don’t know”

A professional prompt does not only tell the model what to produce. It tells the model what to do when it cannot know. “Unknown behavior” is the discipline of preventing confident guessing by giving the model a safe, explicit way to respond when information is missing, ambiguous, or unverifiable.

This section teaches how to design prompts that reliably produce:
“Unknown,” “Not provided,” or null,
clarifying questions,
or labeled assumptions and hypotheses,
instead of fabricated details.

Why “Unknown behavior” matters

Without an Unknown policy, the model is incentivized to be fluent and complete. If you ask for:
a filled table,
a complete report,
a strict schema,
or a definitive explanation,
and the input lacks necessary facts, the model may fill gaps to make the output look finished.

Unknown behavior flips the incentive:
missing data is allowed,
and guessing is penalized.

This is the single most effective reliability guardrail for many real-world tasks.

When to enforce “I don’t know”

Use Unknown behavior when:
you have partial or messy inputs,
you are extracting structured data,
you are summarizing documents with strict grounding,

you are dealing with compliance, policy, legal, medical, financial topics,
you are requesting citations, dates, numbers, or named entities,
you are doing root cause analysis without full data.

The three "Unknown modes" (choose one)

Different tasks need different Unknown responses. Pick one and state it.

Mode 1: Explicit Unknown tokens (best for text deliverables)

Use:
"Unknown," "Not specified," "Insufficient information."
Best for:
reports, explanations, memos, chapter writing.
Example rule:
"If the input does not specify it, write 'Unknown' and move on."

Mode 2: Null values (best for JSON and extraction)

Use:
null in JSON, empty field, or "N/A" per schema rules.
Best for:
automation, APIs, datasets.
Example rule:
"If a field is missing, set it to null. Do not infer."

Mode 3: Questions-first (best when missing info blocks progress)

Use:
ask up to N clarifying questions before drafting.
Best for:
custom plans, recommendations, decisions.
Example rule:
"If critical info is missing, ask up to 5 questions and do not draft until answered."

A hybrid option (often best in practice)

You can also use:
"best-effort draft + Unknown + questions."
Example:
"Draft what you can, label unknowns, then ask 3 questions to complete it."

This preserves momentum without guessing.

How to force "Unknown" reliably (prompt patterns)
Pattern A: The Unknown policy block (drop-in)
"Unknown policy:
If a required detail is not in the provided input, do not guess.
Write 'Unknown' (or null) instead.
Do not fill gaps using common sense.
If you need it to proceed, ask a clarifying question."
This is the core guardrail.

Pattern B: "No citation, no claim"
Use when grounding matters.
"If a claim cannot be supported by the provided sources, omit it or mark it Unknown. Do not fabricate citations."
This prevents invented facts and invented references.

Pattern C: Field-level rules (strongest for structured outputs)
For tables and schemas, specify Unknown behavior per field.
Example:
"Fields:
Owner: must be a name or null
Due date: YYYY-MM-DD or null
Budget: number or null
Rule: do not infer any field. Unknown → null."
Field-level rules reduce ambiguity.

Pattern D: Confidence labeling (useful when info is messy)
"Label each key statement as:
Confirmed (explicit in input)
Inferred (logical from input, explain briefly)
Unknown (not supported)"
Then instruct:
"Final deliverable must not include Unknown items as facts."
This teaches the model to separate certainty levels.

Pattern E: "Stop and ask" trigger
Add a condition that forces the model to pause when a critical item is missing.
Example:
"If objective, audience, or constraints are missing, ask questions first and do not draft."
This prevents wrong-goal plus hallucination.

Where Unknown behavior is most critical
1) Extraction tasks (JSON, tables, databases)
Most hallucinations here happen because the schema demands completeness.
Fix:
null policy,
no inference rule,
optional: include a "missing_fields" array.
Example schema pattern:

```
{
"owner": null,
"due_date": null,
"missing_fields": ["owner", "due_date"]
}
```

2) "Why" questions and root cause analysis
Unknown behavior prevents false causality.
Fix:
Switch to hypothesis mode:
"If the cause is not in the data, provide hypotheses labeled Hypothesis, not facts. List evidence needed."

3) Recommendations
Recommendations can be risky if constraints are missing.
Fix:
Ask questions-first or provide options with assumptions:
"Provide 3 options, list assumptions for each, and ask questions to confirm."

4) Citations and quotes
Unknown behavior prevents fake references.
Fix:
"Do not invent citations. If sources are not provided, say 'No source provided' and list what to verify."

"Unknown" without being unhelpful
Forcing "I don't know" should not mean stopping work. The professional move is: be maximally helpful within the known boundary.
Use one of these output patterns:
Pattern 1: Known facts + Unknown list + next questions
Output:
What we know
What we do not know
Questions to resolve unknowns
Pattern 2: Best-effort draft with explicit placeholders
Output includes:
[UNKNOWN: due date]
[UNKNOWN: budget]
Then ask:
"Provide these missing values."
Pattern 3: Options with assumptions
Output:
Option A (assumes X)
Option B (assumes Y)
What data to confirm
This produces progress without pretending certainty.

Hardening rules: phrases that reduce guessing
Add these phrases to increase compliance:
"Do not guess."
"If not explicitly stated, mark Unknown."
"Common knowledge is not allowed unless stated."
"Use only provided inputs as source of truth."
"If you must infer, label it as inference and keep it minimal."
"No invented numbers, dates, names, or citations."

These are simple but effective.

Validation prompts: catch and remove hidden guessing

Even with an Unknown policy, add a final audit step:

"Audit your answer for any specific claim that is not supported by the input. For each unsupported claim, either remove it or mark it Unknown. Then return the final."

This turns Unknown behavior into a test.

Before and after transformations

Transformation 1: Prevent invented dates in action items

Weak prompt:

"Extract action items with owner and due date."

Risk:

Invented owners or due dates.

Stronger prompt:

"Extract action items into JSON only.

Keys: task (string), owner (string | null), due_date (YYYY-MM-DD | null).

Rule: If owner or due date is not explicitly stated, set to null. Do not infer.

Return JSON only, no extra text."

Transformation 2: Prevent fake causes

Weak prompt:

"Why did engagement drop?"

Risk:

Confident narrative guessing.

Stronger prompt:

"Using only the data provided, list confirmed changes.

If cause is not directly evidenced, list 3 hypotheses labeled Hypothesis and the data needed to confirm each.

Do not state causes as facts."

Mini lab: build an Unknown-safe prompt in 5 minutes

Take a prompt you use often.

Add an Unknown policy block.

Add field-level null rules if structured.

Add a final audit step: "remove or mark unsupported claims."
Test with an incomplete input and verify:
it uses Unknown/null,
it asks questions,
it does not invent specifics.

A reusable "Unknown behavior" block (ready to paste)

"Unknown behavior:
If a detail is not explicitly in the input, do not guess.
Mark it as Unknown (or null) and continue.
If the missing detail is required to complete the task, ask up to 4 clarifying questions.
Before finalizing, audit for unsupported specifics and remove or label them."
This block is a professional reliability upgrade for almost any prompt.
Forcing the model to say "I don't know" is not about limiting output. It is about keeping outputs trustworthy. Once Unknown is allowed and guessing is discouraged, the model becomes far more reliable, and your prompts become safer to use in real workflows.

Verification prompts, cross-check, compare, sanity checks

Verification prompts turn a model from a fast generator into a quality-controlled assistant. Instead of trusting the first answer, you ask the model to prove its output is consistent with inputs, constraints, and basic logic. This dramatically reduces hallucinations, format drift, and subtle errors that "sound right."

This section gives you a practical verification toolkit: cross-checking, comparing, and sanity checks, plus ready-to-use prompt templates.

Why verification works

Most failures are not dramatic. They are small:
a missed constraint,
a number copied wrong,
an invented detail to fill a gap,
a heading out of order,
a claim stated with too much certainty.
Verification works because it forces the model to shift into evaluator mode with explicit tests. The model can catch many of its own mistakes when you give it a checklist and a source of truth.

The three verification families

1) Cross-check prompts

Cross-check means: verify the output against a reference.
References can be:
your provided source text,
a table of extracted facts,
a schema or format contract,
a policy excerpt,
a rubric.
Goal: "No claim without support."

2) Compare prompts

Compare means: generate two or more independent outputs or perspectives and reconcile differences.
Examples:
two different drafts,
two solution strategies,
model output vs your expected answer,
summary vs extraction table consistency.
Goal: "If two routes disagree, investigate."

3) Sanity-check prompts

Sanity checks are fast plausibility tests:
math consistency,
unit consistency,
timeline coherence,
internal contradictions,
"too good to be true" detection.
Goal: "Catch obvious nonsense before it ships."

Cross-check prompts: the reliability backbone

A) Grounding cross-check: cite or mark Unknown

Use when you have source text.

Template

"Cross-check the answer against the sources below.
For each key claim in the answer:
mark Supported or Unsupported,
cite the exact source ID that supports it,
if unsupported, revise the answer to remove the claim or mark it Unknown.
Return only the corrected answer."
This forces grounding and removes invented details.

B) Constraint cross-check: pass/fail against the contract

Use when format and constraints matter.

Template

"Verify the output against this contract.
Contract:
<rule 1>
<rule 2>
<rule 3>
If any rule fails, fix the output and re-check.
Return:
Pass/Fail list
Final corrected output"
For production, you can request final output only and keep the pass/fail internal.

C) Schema cross-check for JSON and structured outputs

Use when outputs feed tools or pipelines.

Template

"Validate the JSON against this schema:
required keys: <...>
types: <...>
no extra keys
unknown values must be null
If invalid, fix it.
Return valid JSON only, no extra text."
This reduces "almost JSON" failures.

D) Extraction-to-summary cross-check (high ROI)
A professional pattern is:
extract facts into a table,
write narrative from that table,
cross-check narrative back to the table.
Template
"Cross-check the narrative against the facts table.
Identify any statement that is not in the table. Remove it or label it as assumption.
Return the corrected narrative only."
This is one of the best anti-hallucination workflows.

Compare prompts: independent routes to detect mistakes
A) Dual-draft compare
Generate two drafts with different strategies, then compare.
Template
"Create two versions of the output:
Version A: concise, structured
Version B: detailed, explanatory
Then compare them:
list any factual differences or conflicting claims
choose the most accurate phrasing
Return the final reconciled version only."
Differences reveal weak points that need checking.

B) Advocate vs skeptic (controlled red-team compare)
Useful for high-stakes recommendations.
Template
"Write the recommendation. Then switch roles:
Skeptic: list the top 5 risks, missing info, and counterarguments
Revise the recommendation to address valid critiques without adding new facts.
Return final only."
This catches overconfident claims and missing caveats.

C) Summary vs bullets compare

Great for clarity and completeness.

Template

"Produce:
a 100-word summary
8 bullets of key points
Then check: does every bullet appear in the summary?
If not, revise the summary to include the missing points or remove the bullet if it is not supported.
Return the final summary and bullets."

This prevents summary drift.

Sanity checks: fast tests that catch "sounds right" errors

A) Consistency sanity check (internal contradictions)

Template

"Sanity check for contradictions:
conflicting numbers, dates, or claims
duplicated points
inconsistent terminology
List issues and fix them. Return final only."

B) Math sanity check (arithmetic and units)

Use for budgets, percentages, time estimates.

Template

"Sanity check the calculations:
recompute totals, percentages, and averages
verify units
If any mismatch, correct the numbers and update the narrative accordingly.
Return corrected output only."

C) Timeline sanity check

Use for plans, project schedules, case histories.

Template

"Sanity check the timeline:
ensure dates are in correct order
ensure dependencies make sense

flag missing milestones
Revise to fix any issues, without inventing dates. Use 'TBD' if missing."

D) Plausibility sanity check (too specific without evidence)
Template
"Scan for suspicious specificity:
precise numbers without sources
named entities not provided
confident causal claims without evidence
For each, either cite support, soften with uncertainty, or mark Unknown."
This catches hallucinations disguised as detail.

A complete verification workflow (plan, generate, verify, finalize)
For professional reliability, combine verification steps in a chain:
Generate draft
Cross-check against sources and constraints
Sanity check for contradictions and suspicious specificity
Finalize output
All-in-one template
"Produce the deliverable. Then run verification:
Contract check (pass/fail)
Grounding check (unsupported claims removed or marked Unknown)
Sanity check (contradictions, suspicious specificity, math/timeline)
Revise until all checks pass.
Return only the final output."
If you want transparency while training, ask for the check results too.

How to write verification criteria that work
Verification fails when criteria are vague. Make them testable.
Instead of:
"Make sure it's correct."
Use:
"Every numerical claim must have a source or be removed."
"Exactly 4 headings in this order."
"No extra keys in JSON."
"If data is missing, use Unknown or null."

"Stop after section X."
The model cannot reliably verify fuzzy instructions.

Common mistakes with verification prompts (and fixes)
Mistake 1: Verifying against the same messy input
Fix:
Create a "source of truth" first:
extracted facts table,
approved outline,
schema contract.
Verify against that, not against a long conversation.
Mistake 2: Verification adds new claims
Fix:
Add:
"Do not add new facts during verification. Only remove, correct, or label Unknown."
Mistake 3: Over-verifying everything
Fix:
Verify the load-bearing claims:
numbers, definitions, steps, compliance rules, decisions.
Mistake 4: No stop condition
Fix:
"Return final only. No notes."

Mini lab: build a verification harness for any prompt
Take a prompt you use often and add a verification harness:
Write a 6-item contract (format, length, must include, must avoid, unknown policy, stop).
Add a grounding rule (use only sources or label Unknown).
Add one sanity check relevant to the task:
math, timeline, contradictions, suspicious specificity.
Add: "revise until all checks pass."
Run it on a messy input and compare to the non-verified version. The verified version will usually be:
more compliant,
less hallucinated,

more consistent in structure,
safer to reuse.

Verification prompts are the professional upgrade from "generate" to "deliver." Cross-checking keeps claims grounded, comparison exposes disagreements that require attention, and sanity checks catch the subtle errors that fluency can hide.

Guardrails, "If unsure, ask a question"

The simplest way to reduce hallucinations is to remove the pressure to guess. A powerful guardrail is making the model ask clarifying questions when it lacks required information. This turns uncertainty into a controlled interaction instead of a confident fabrication.
This section teaches how to implement the "If unsure, ask a question" guardrail in a way that is reliable, efficient, and not annoying.

Why this guardrail works

Most hallucinations are caused by missing inputs, ambiguous requirements, or unclear success criteria. If the model is allowed to ask first, it can:
confirm the goal and audience,
request missing constraints,
clarify ambiguous terms,
avoid inventing details,
and produce an output that fits the real need.
Think of it as requirements gathering built into the prompt.

When to use "ask a question" guardrails

Use it when:
the task depends on user-specific facts,
the prompt contains vague terms (best, optimize, detailed),
missing information would change the result,
you are requesting plans, recommendations, or decisions,
the output must be grounded in documents you have not provided,
the format requires fields the input may not contain.
Do not use it when:
you want a fast generic draft,

your input is complete and well-structured,
you are running automated batch prompts where questions are not practical.
In those cases, prefer an Unknown policy or a best-effort draft with labeled assumptions.

The three styles of question guardrails
Style 1: Questions-first (strict)
The model must ask questions before drafting.
Best for:
high-stakes work,
customized outputs,
unclear requirements.
Rule:
"Do not draft until questions are answered."

Style 2: Best-effort + questions (practical default)
The model drafts what it can, but marks unknowns and asks questions to finalize.
Best for:
keeping momentum,
partial inputs,
real-world workflows.
Rule:
"Draft with placeholders, then ask questions."

Style 3: Conditional questions (smart gate)
The model only asks questions if certain critical fields are missing.
Best for:
structured extraction,
routine templates,
faster interactions.
Rule:
"If any critical field is missing, ask questions, otherwise proceed."

How to write question guardrails that do not annoy users

If you tell the model "ask questions," it may ask too many. Professional guardrails make questions:

limited in number,

prioritized,

specific and answerable,

and tied to output decisions.

The 4 rules of good clarifying questions

Cap the number: 3–6 max

Ask only high-impact questions

Use multiple-choice options when possible

Request missing facts in a structured way

Example:

"Ask up to 5 questions, ordered by impact. Use multiple-choice when possible."

The question ladder (what to ask first)

When unclear, the most valuable questions usually follow this order:

Objective: what outcome do you want

Audience: who will use it

Constraints: length, format, must include, must avoid

Inputs: what sources to use

Success criteria: what "good" looks like

Edge cases: what to do when data is missing

If the model asks about these first, you avoid waste.

Copy-paste guardrail templates

Template A: Strict questions-first

"Before you answer, check if you have enough information to do the task correctly.

If anything important is missing, ask up to 5 clarifying questions and wait.

Do not produce the deliverable until I answer."

Use when correctness depends on user info.

Template B: Best-effort plus questions (recommended)
"Draft what you can using the provided information.
For any missing critical details, insert [UNKNOWN] placeholders instead of guessing.
Then ask up to 4 clarifying questions needed to produce the final version."
Use when you want progress immediately.

Template C: Conditional gate (critical fields)
"If any of these are missing: objective, audience, output format, or source text, ask questions first.
Otherwise proceed with the deliverable."
This prevents unnecessary questions on complete prompts.

Template D: Intake form style (fast answers)
"Ask up to 6 questions using this intake form format:
Objective (choose one): inform, persuade, decide, teach
Audience: beginner, intermediate, expert
Output type: checklist, template, report, table, JSON
Length: short (150–250), medium (400–700), long (900–1,200)
Must include: <free text>
Must avoid: <free text>"
This produces quick, structured replies.

How to combine "ask questions" with anti-hallucination rules
Questions help, but you also need a non-guessing rule.
Add:
"Do not guess facts."
"Use Unknown or placeholders."
"No invented names, numbers, citations."
A strong combined block:
"If unsure, ask. If you proceed without an answer, label assumptions and use Unknown for missing facts."

Examples: turning risky prompts into question-first prompts
Example 1: Vague request

Risky:
"Write a marketing plan for my product."
Question-first rewrite:
"Before writing, ask up to 5 questions about product, audience, channel, budget, and timeline.
Do not draft until answered."
Why it reduces hallucinations:
The model stops guessing the product and market.

Example 2: Extraction with missing data

Risky:
"Extract owner and due date for each task."
Guardrail rewrite:
"Extract tasks into JSON. Use null for missing owner or due_date.
If more than 30 percent of tasks have missing owner or due_date, ask up to 4 questions to clarify."
Why it works:
It proceeds safely but escalates when missingness is too high.

Example 3: Root cause analysis

Risky:
"Why did conversion drop?"
Guardrail rewrite:
"If the data does not identify a cause, do not claim one.
Ask up to 4 questions about timeframe, segments, tracking changes, and campaigns.
Meanwhile, list 3 hypotheses labeled Hypothesis and the data needed to confirm each."
This prevents confident causal hallucinations.

The "question budget" technique (keeps it efficient)

A professional prompt sets a budget and prioritization:
"Ask at most 4 questions.
Order by impact on correctness.
If a question is optional, do not ask it."
This keeps the interaction fast and avoids the model turning into a questionnaire.

A verification twist: ask questions only when constraints fail

You can combine guardrails with validation:
"Generate a draft. Validate against the contract.
If any requirement cannot be satisfied due to missing info, ask targeted questions.
Otherwise return the final."
This makes questions conditional on real need.

Mini lab: convert 5 tasks into question-first guardrails

Give readers these tasks and require question-first prompts:
"Write a policy summary"
"Create a project plan"
"Recommend the best option"
"Extract tasks into JSON"
"Rewrite this email professionally"
For each, the learner should:
define 3–5 critical unknowns,
write a 4-question guardrail,
add Unknown policy,
add stop condition.

A reusable guardrail block (ready to paste)

"If you are missing information needed for correctness, do not guess.
Ask up to 4 clarifying questions, ordered by impact.
If you can proceed partially, draft with [UNKNOWN] placeholders and label assumptions.
Before finalizing, remove any unsupported specifics or mark them Unknown."
This single block dramatically improves reliability across many tasks.

The "If unsure, ask a question" guardrail is a professional reliability tool. It shifts the model from guessing to gathering requirements, which reduces hallucinations, increases alignment, and produces outputs that are correct for the real situation, not the imagined one.

Practice, build a fact-check routine for a research summary

A research summary is only as trustworthy as its claims. A professional routine does not rely on "seems right." It enforces a repeatable pipeline that:
extracts claims from sources,
checks each claim against evidence,
separates facts from interpretation,
labels unknowns,
and produces a final summary with traceability.
This practice section gives you a complete fact-check routine you can teach and reuse.

The fact-check routine (the 6-stage pipeline)
Stage 1: Set the source policy and scope
Before summarizing, decide what counts as truth.
Define:
Allowed sources: provided papers only, or web allowed, or no external research.
Output scope: what the summary should cover and what it should ignore.
Citation style: source IDs like [S1], [S2] or author-year.
Prompt block
"Source policy: Use only the sources I provide. Do not add external facts.
If a claim is not supported, mark it Unknown or omit it.
Scope: summarize methods, key findings, limitations, and implications.
Out of scope: unrelated background and unsupported speculation."
This prevents the summary from drifting into general knowledge or invented context.

Stage 2: Extract "claim candidates" before writing prose
Do not start with a narrative. Start with claims.
Goal: produce a list of checkable statements.
Prompt template
"From the sources, extract 12–20 claim candidates as short bullets.
For each claim:
label type: Finding, Method, Data, Limitation, Definition, Implication
include source ID [S#]

include a short supporting quote snippet (max 12 words)
If no quote supports it, label the claim Unsupported."
This stage is your evidence inventory.

Stage 3: Normalize claims into a fact table (make checking easy)

Convert extracted claims into a structured table so you can see gaps.
Recommended columns:
Claim ID
Claim text (one sentence)
Claim type
Source ID
Quote snippet
Confidence: High/Medium/Low
Notes (what could be misread)

Prompt template

"Convert the claim bullets into a table with columns:
ID | Claim | Type | Source | Evidence snippet | Confidence | Notes.
Mark Confidence as Low if wording is ambiguous or evidence is indirect."
Tables make hallucinations obvious because unsupported claims stand out.

Stage 4: Cross-check and remove "unsupported specificity"

This is the most important verification step.

What to check:

Any numbers, dates, effect sizes, sample sizes
Strong causal language (causes, proves)
Generalizations beyond the study scope
Claims that combine two different sources incorrectly
Details that are not present in quotes

Prompt template

"Verification pass:
Scan the claim table for suspicious specificity: numbers, dates, named entities, strong causal claims.
For each, confirm the evidence snippet supports it exactly.
If not supported, rewrite the claim to be accurate or mark Unsupported.
Return the corrected claim table only."
This eliminates "sounds right" detail.

Stage 5: Write the research summary using only verified claims

Now you write prose, but with strict boundaries.

Recommended structure for a research summary

One-paragraph overview (what the study is about)

Methods (what they did)

Key findings (what they found)

Limitations (what to be cautious about)

Implications (what it might mean, labeled carefully)

Prompt template

"Write a research summary using only claims marked Supported or Verified in the table.

Rules:

Every key claim must include a citation [S#].

Do not introduce new facts.

Use cautious language for implications (may, suggests) unless the source states otherwise.

If something is not in the table, omit it.

Output format:

Overview (80–120 words)

Methods (4 bullets)

Findings (6 bullets)

Limitations (4 bullets)

Implications (3 bullets)"

This forces grounding and keeps the summary auditable.

Stage 6: Final audit, "no citation, no claim"

Do a last check after writing.

Prompt template

"Final audit:

List any sentence that lacks a citation or is not supported by the claim table.

Remove or rewrite those sentences.

Ensure numbers match the sources exactly.

Return only the final corrected summary."

This catches last-minute drift.

Practice exercise: build your routine with a mini dataset

To practice, use 2–3 short papers or reports. Assign each a source ID:
[S1] Paper 1
[S2] Paper 2
[S3] Paper 3
Then run the stages:
claim extraction,
claim table,
verification pass,
summary writing,
final audit.
Repeat twice with different topics to build the habit.

A compact "fact-check harness" prompt (one block)

If you want a single reusable prompt to run as a workflow:
"Fact-check routine for research summary.
Sources:
[S1] <paste>
[S2] <paste>
[S3] <paste>
Step 1: Extract 15 claim candidates with type and evidence snippet (max 12 words) and source ID.
Step 2: Build a claim table: ID | Claim | Type | Source | Evidence snippet | Confidence | Notes.
Step 3: Verify: flag suspicious specificity, causal claims, and generalizations. Fix or mark Unsupported.
Step 4: Write the summary using only Verified claims, with citations [S#] on each key claim.
Format:
Overview 80–120 words
Methods 4 bullets
Findings 6 bullets
Limitations 4 bullets
Implications 3 bullets
Step 5: Final audit: no citation, no claim. Return final summary only."
This is ideal for teaching because it makes each stage explicit.

Sanity checks to add (choose based on your domain)

Numerical sanity checks

totals add up,
percentages plausible,
effect sizes not mixed across studies.
Prompt add-on:
"Recompute any derived numbers. If not computable from sources, remove them."

Scope sanity checks

population, setting, timeframe match the claims,
no generalization to broader contexts unless stated.
Prompt add-on:
"Confirm each finding matches the study population and setting."

Terminology sanity checks

terms used consistently,
definitions match the source.
Prompt add-on:
"List key terms and ensure usage matches sources."

Common failure points (and how your routine prevents them)

Failure: summary includes "common knowledge" not in papers

Fix in routine:
Stage 1 source policy plus Stage 5 "table-only claims."

Failure: invented numbers or wrong sample size

Fix in routine:
Stage 4 suspicious specificity scan plus Stage 6 audit.

Failure: implications overstated as conclusions

Fix in routine:
Stage 5 cautious language rules and limitation section.

Failure: mixing results across papers incorrectly

Fix in routine:
Claim table ties each claim to a specific source.

Scoring rubric for the final summary (quick)

Score 0–2 each:

Grounding: every key claim has a citation

Accuracy: no unsupported specificity

Separation: facts vs implications clearly separated

Coverage: includes methods, findings, limitations

Clarity: readable, structured, concise

Target: 8/10 or higher.

This practice routine teaches expert reliability habits: extract claims first, verify them, then write. When you build summaries from verified claim tables and enforce "no citation, no claim," hallucinations drop sharply and your research summaries become genuinely trustworthy.

Chapter 12. Tone, voice, and audience control

Audience specs that work (role, knowledge level, sensitivity)

Audience control is one of the most practical prompt skills. The same content can succeed or fail depending on who reads it. A professional prompt does not say "write professionally." It specifies an audience profile the model can reliably target.

A strong audience spec has three parts:

Role: what the reader does and what they care about

Knowledge level: what they already understand and what they do not

Sensitivity: what tone risks to avoid (legal, emotional, cultural, privacy)

When you provide these, the model stops guessing and your tone becomes consistent.

1) Role: who the reader is and what they need

Role is not a job title alone. It is a goal plus constraints.

What to specify

reader role and decision power

what they are trying to accomplish

what they value (speed, accuracy, risk avoidance, practicality)

what they dislike (jargon, long explanations, sales tone)

Examples of role specs (good)

"Audience: Product manager deciding whether to ship this feature next sprint."

"Audience: Customer support agent responding to a frustrated user."

"Audience: Executive sponsor who wants risks and next steps, not implementation details."

"Audience: Compliance reviewer looking for policy alignment and caveats."

Role-driven formatting (high impact)

Different roles want different output shapes:

executives: short summary, risks, decision, next steps

engineers: requirements, edge cases, acceptance criteria

customers: empathy, clarity, reassurance, concrete steps

researchers: methods, evidence, limitations

Add role plus "what they want first":
"Lead with the decision and risk, then details."

2) Knowledge level: how much context and jargon to use

Knowledge level is the dial for:
definitions,
step-by-step explanations,
assumed terminology,
and depth.

The three-level model (simple and reliable)

Beginner

define terms
avoid acronyms or explain them
provide examples and checklists
keep sentences shorter
Prompt phrases:
"Assume no prior knowledge."
"Define terms the first time."
"Use an analogy and a simple example."

Intermediate

skip basics, but clarify key terms
focus on practical steps and tradeoffs
include common pitfalls and edge cases
Prompt phrases:
"Assume they know the basics."
"Focus on how to apply it."
"Include pitfalls and troubleshooting."

Expert

concise, technical language acceptable
focus on constraints, failure modes, and decision criteria
omit hand-holding
Prompt phrases:
"Assume expert familiarity."
"Be compact and technical."
"Prioritize edge cases and rigorous definitions."

The most common knowledge-level mistake

People specify "beginner-friendly" but then ask for:
"advanced strategies,"
"full coverage,"
"in-depth details,"
in a short space. That creates conflict.
Fix:
Choose one:
beginner + narrow scope, or
advanced + deeper scope, or
layered output (beginner summary + expert appendix).

3) Sensitivity: tone risk management

Sensitivity is the safety rail for tone. It covers:
emotional tone,
legal or compliance risk,
cultural or reputational risk,
privacy and confidentiality,
workplace dynamics.

Sensitivity controls that actually work

Specify:
emotional state of the reader (calm, confused, angry, anxious)
what must be avoided (blame, judgment, certainty, medical/legal advice)
escalation behavior (ask questions, recommend professional review)
Examples:
"Sensitivity: reader may be frustrated; use empathy, avoid blame, avoid sarcasm."
"Sensitivity: compliance context; use cautious language, include caveats, avoid absolute claims."
"Sensitivity: internal conflict; keep neutral tone, avoid naming individuals, focus on behaviors and next steps."
"Sensitivity: privacy; remove personal identifiers and do not infer identity."

Useful tone constraints for sensitive contexts

"Use neutral language."
"Avoid moral judgments."
"Do not speculate about motives."
"Use 'may' or 'could' when uncertain."

"Offer options, not ultimatums."

The audience spec card (the format to teach and reuse)

Use a compact "audience spec card" in prompts. This is short but powerful.

Audience spec card template

Role: <who they are and what decision/action they need>
Knowledge level: <beginner/intermediate/expert + assumptions>
Sensitivity: <what to avoid + emotional tone + risk posture>
What they want first: <summary, steps, risks, recommendation>
Tone: <neutral, friendly, firm, empathetic, executive concise>

You can paste this into any prompt and it will immediately improve tone control.

Examples: audience specs that work

Example A: Executive stakeholder

Role: VP sponsor deciding funding
Knowledge level: intermediate, not technical
Sensitivity: risk-focused, time-limited
What they want first: bottom line and risks
Tone: concise, confident, no hype
Output style:
6-bullet brief, risks, recommendation, next step
Prompt line:
"Audience spec: executive sponsor; lead with decision, then top 3 risks, then rationale."

Example B: Beginner learner (your book reader)

Role: novice learning prompt engineering
Knowledge level: beginner
Sensitivity: avoid intimidation, avoid jargon
What they want first: simple formula and examples
Tone: encouraging, clear, direct
Output style:
short sections, examples, checklists, practice drill
Prompt line:
"Assume the reader is new; define terms and include two simple examples."

Example C: Customer support response

Role: support agent writing to a frustrated user
Knowledge level: user is non-technical
Sensitivity: user upset; avoid blame; empathize
What they want first: fix steps
Tone: calm, helpful, step-by-step
Output style:
empathy sentence, numbered steps, escalation path
Prompt line:
"Start with empathy, then 5 numbered steps, then how to escalate if not resolved."

Example D: Technical peer review

Role: engineer reviewing a design
Knowledge level: expert
Sensitivity: avoid condescension; be precise
What they want first: issues and tradeoffs
Tone: direct, technical
Output style:
assumptions, constraints, edge cases, tests
Prompt line:
"Be technical and compact; focus on failure modes and test cases."

How audience specs interact with voice

Audience spec controls what the reader needs. Voice controls how it sounds. Professional voice instructions should be measurable:
sentence length
vocabulary level
amount of hedging
use of headings and bullets
do/don't lists
Examples:
"Use short paragraphs, average sentence under 20 words."
"Use plain words, define acronyms."
"Avoid metaphors" (for compliance contexts)
"Use one metaphor" (for beginners)

Debugging tone problems with audience specs

If tone keeps missing the mark, check which audience element is missing:

Problem: too technical

Missing:

knowledge level definition

Fix:

"Beginner level, define all terms, avoid acronyms."

Problem: too long

Missing:

what they want first and length constraint

Fix:

"Executive: 150–200 words, lead with decision."

Problem: too casual

Missing:

sensitivity and tone boundaries

Fix:

"Neutral professional tone, no jokes, no emojis."

Problem: sounds judgmental

Missing:

sensitivity constraints

Fix:

"Avoid blame, focus on behaviors and solutions."

A reusable audience block you can paste anywhere

"Audience spec:
Role: <...>
Knowledge level: <...>
Sensitivity: <...>
Tone rules:
prioritize what they need first
avoid jargon beyond their level
avoid speculation and strong claims if uncertain
keep within <length>
Output format: <...>"

This block upgrades tone control immediately.

Audience specs work when they are concrete: role with goals, knowledge level with assumptions, and sensitivity with explicit tone risks to avoid. Once you teach readers to write an audience spec card, they stop fighting tone and start controlling it on purpose.

Style constraints, formal, casual, technical, persuasive

Style constraints are the rules that control how the output sounds. They sit on top of your audience spec and act like a "house style." Professionals do not say "make it good." They specify a style profile with concrete, testable behaviors.

A strong style constraint defines:
vocabulary level,
sentence and paragraph shape,
tone posture (neutral, warm, firm),
persuasion stance (inform, recommend, sell),
formatting patterns (headings, bullets),
and things to avoid (hype, slang, legal risk phrases).
Below are four common style modes with reliable constraint sets and copy-paste templates.

1) Formal style constraints

Formal means: polished, neutral, respectful, careful wording, minimal emotion.

When to use

business communication,
executive memos,
policy documents,
stakeholder updates,
sensitive topics.

Observable constraints that work

Use complete sentences, no slang, no emojis.
Prefer precise nouns and verbs over intensifiers.
Keep tone neutral and professional.
Use cautious language for uncertainty (may, appears, likely) when appropriate.

Avoid dramatic claims or hype.
Use headings and bullets for clarity.

Formal style prompt block

"Style: formal and professional.
Rules:
no slang, no emojis, no jokes
neutral, respectful tone
use clear headings and short paragraphs
avoid hype words (amazing, revolutionary, game-changing)
if uncertain, use cautious language and state limits
Length: <range>"

Common failure and fix

Failure: formal becomes stiff or vague.
Fix: add clarity constraints:
"Prefer concrete verbs, avoid vague phrases like 'various' or 'many.'"

2) Casual style constraints

Casual means: friendly, approachable, conversational, but still clear and purposeful.

When to use

onboarding, tutorials, community posts, internal chats, friendly emails.

Observable constraints that work

Use simple words and short sentences.
Use contractions (you'll, we're) if appropriate.
Keep paragraphs short.
Use a friendly tone, but avoid being overly playful for serious topics.
Give examples and practical steps.

Casual style prompt block

"Style: casual, friendly, and clear.
Rules:
use simple words and short sentences
optional contractions are OK
keep paragraphs to 2–3 sentences
be warm but not overly playful

include practical steps or examples
Avoid: slang that could confuse non-native speakers, sarcasm, and exaggeration."

Common failure and fix

Failure: casual becomes unprofessional.
Fix: add a boundary:
"Friendly but still workplace-appropriate."

3) Technical style constraints

Technical means: precise, structured, unambiguous, assumes domain familiarity or defines it.

When to use

engineering docs, specifications, SOPs, debugging guides, research notes.

Observable constraints that work

Use definitions for key terms.
Use exact steps and acceptance criteria.
Prefer active voice and explicit subject (who does what).
Include edge cases and failure modes.
Use consistent terminology.
Use structured formats: lists, tables, schemas, numbered steps.

Technical style prompt block

"Style: technical and precise.
Rules:
define key terms on first use
use consistent terminology throughout
include assumptions and constraints explicitly
include edge cases and failure modes
use structured format: numbered steps, bullets, or a table
avoid metaphors and vague adjectives
Output must be actionable (a reader can implement it)."

Common failure and fix

Failure: technical becomes too dense.
Fix: layer it:
"Start with a 3-bullet overview, then details."

4) Persuasive style constraints

Persuasive means: designed to influence a decision, with clear rationale and anticipated objections. It can be ethical and evidence-based, not manipulative.

When to use

proposals, stakeholder buy-in, product justifications, fundraising, internal advocacy.

Observable constraints that work

State the recommendation early.

Provide 2–4 strong reasons linked to audience priorities.

Address risks and objections.

Include evidence, examples, or quantified impact when available.

End with a clear call to action.

Keep claims grounded. Avoid overpromising.

Persuasive style prompt block

"Style: persuasive but evidence-based.

Structure:

Recommendation (1–2 sentences)

Benefits (3 bullets tied to audience priorities)

Risks and mitigations (2 bullets)

Objection handling (2 bullets)

Call to action (one clear next step)

Rules:

avoid hype and absolute claims

do not invent data

use cautious language when evidence is limited."

Common failure and fix

Failure: persuasion becomes salesy.

Fix:

"Tone: calm, credible, and grounded. No marketing language."

Choosing the right style mode (fast guide)

Use this mapping:

Formal: credibility, sensitivity, external communication

Casual: approachability, internal learning, community tone

Technical: implementation, accuracy, repeatability
Persuasive: decision-making, alignment, buy-in
If unsure, pick formal for safety, then adjust warmth.

Style mixing without chaos (layered style)

Sometimes you need two styles at once. Avoid mixing randomly. Use a layered structure:
Example: executive + technical
Section 1: formal, concise summary
Section 2: technical appendix
Prompt:
"Output two sections:
A) Executive summary, formal, max 120 words
B) Technical appendix, precise steps and edge cases"
This preserves clarity and prevents tone drift.

Style constraints as measurable "dials"

To make style reliable, define dials:

Length and density

"Max 180 words"
"Average sentence under 18 words"
"No paragraph longer than 3 sentences"

Vocabulary level

"Plain language, avoid jargon"
"Technical vocabulary allowed, define terms once"

Tone posture

"Neutral and cautious"
"Warm and supportive"
"Firm and direct"

Formatting

"Use headings and bullets"
"Use JSON only"
"Use exactly 6 bullets"
Measurable dials produce consistent style.

Verification prompt: check style compliance

Style is easier to control if you validate it.

Style check template

"Verify the draft against these style rules:
<rule list>
List violations and revise to fix them.
Return final only."

This catches drift like slang in formal writing or hype in persuasive writing.

Mini lab: rewrite the same content in four styles

Exercise for readers:

Take one paragraph and request four versions:

Formal (policy memo tone)
Casual (friendly tutorial tone)
Technical (specification tone)
Persuasive (proposal tone)

Each version must preserve meaning, only change style and structure. This teaches controlled style shifts.

Copy-paste universal style card

Use this as a general template:

"Style constraints:
Mode: <formal/casual/technical/persuasive>
Tone: <neutral/warm/firm>
Vocabulary: <plain/technical>
Structure: <headings/bullets/table/schema>
Length: <range>
Avoid: <slang/hype/jargon/absolute claims/extra commentary>
If unsure, ask 2–4 clarifying questions before drafting."

With a style card like this, you can reliably steer voice without rewriting your entire prompt every time.

Consistency across long documents

Long documents fail when the voice drifts. Early chapters sound friendly and later chapters sound academic. One section uses "you," another uses "the reader." Some chapters use bullets and checklists; others are dense paragraphs. Consistency is not just style. It is structure, terminology, depth, and tone stability across hundreds of pages.

This section gives you a practical system to keep voice consistent across long documents using prompt design, reusable style anchors, and verification routines.

What "consistency" really means in a long book

You are keeping multiple layers consistent:

Audience alignment: same reader assumptions throughout

Voice: same personality of the narrator

Terminology: same words for the same concepts

Depth level: predictable level of detail per section type

Structure patterns: recurring templates (labs, checklists, examples)

Formatting rules: headings, bullets, callouts, and code blocks

Policy boundaries: how you handle uncertainty, sources, and claims

You do not need the document to sound identical everywhere. You need it to feel like one book written by one person.

The professional approach: create a "voice contract"

A voice contract is a short spec you reuse for every chapter. It contains:

audience spec (role, knowledge level, sensitivities)

tone (formal/casual/technical balance)

vocabulary rules (jargon allowed, define terms, no hype)

recurring structure templates

do/don't list

stance on uncertainty and sources

Voice contract template (copy and use)

"Voice contract for this book:

Audience: beginner to intermediate learners, practical focus

Voice: clear, confident, supportive, not salesy

Tone: professional and friendly, no hype, no sarcasm

Vocabulary: plain language first, define terms once, then reuse consistently

Structure defaults:

each section starts with a short purpose paragraph

then 3–7 bullet key points

then examples

ends with a checklist or mini lab when appropriate
Do not: use emojis, exaggeration, or vague adjectives like 'amazing'
Uncertainty: if not supported, label as Unknown or 'Needs verification'
Formatting: use consistent headings, short paragraphs (2–3 sentences)"
Put this at the top of your prompt every time you generate new content.

Build a "style bible" in 1 page

A style bible is not a long document. One page is enough if it is specific.
Include:
preferred terms and forbidden terms
standard section templates
example of your ideal paragraph and ideal bullet list
punctuation and casing conventions
citation policy if used

What to define (high impact)

Second person vs third person: "you" vs "the reader"
Sentence length: short and direct vs long and academic
Headings style: Title Case vs sentence case
List style: how many bullets per list, how long they should be
Example formatting: "Prompt:" blocks, "Output:" blocks
How you introduce formulas and steps
Once defined, reuse it to prevent drift.

Use recurring "section patterns" to keep the book coherent

Long documents stay consistent when sections follow predictable templates. Pick a small set and reuse.
Examples of reusable patterns:
Concept section: definition, why it matters, do/don't, example, checklist
Lab section: setup, steps, expected output, scoring rubric
Debugging section: symptoms, causes, fixes, before/after prompts
Pattern section: when to use, template, variations, pitfalls, exercises
If every chapter uses the same 3–5 templates, the book feels unified even when topics change.

Maintain a terminology map

Terminology drift is a silent consistency killer.

Create a small glossary table you keep stable:

term

definition

preferred phrasing

avoid phrasing

related terms

Examples:

prefer "format contract" instead of alternating with "output schema," unless you define both

prefer "Unknown policy" instead of switching between "uncertainty handling" and "IDK rule"

Prompt line you can reuse:

"Terminology: use the book's standard terms. Do not introduce new synonyms for existing concepts."

Control the narrator voice with "voice anchors"

A voice anchor is a short sample that represents your ideal tone. You provide it once, then ask the model to match it.

How to use:

write a 120–200 word anchor paragraph in your preferred voice,

include it in prompts as "Voice reference,"

instruct: "match tone and sentence rhythm, not content."

Prompt block:

"Voice anchor:

<paste your anchor paragraph>

Instruction:

Match the voice and rhythm of the anchor. Do not reuse anchor content."

This is extremely effective for long projects.

Use "chapter briefs" to prevent local drift

Each chapter should start from a brief that includes:

chapter objective,

target audience level for this chapter,

what is in scope and out of scope,

required section pattern,

approximate length.
Prompt block:
"Chapter brief:
Goal: <...>
Reader level: <...>
In scope: <...>
Out of scope: <...>
Required pattern: <template name>
Length: <range>"
This prevents the model from over-expanding or changing tone to fill space.

Keep context clean across generations
Consistency breaks when the model is given too much messy history: multiple drafts, contradictory notes, or old guidelines.
Professional method:
keep one "source of truth" voice contract,
keep one glossary,
keep one chapter brief,
provide only the necessary previous excerpt for continuity.
Prompt line:
"Use the voice contract and glossary as the only style authority. Ignore earlier drafts unless pasted here."

Use verification prompts to enforce consistency (the missing piece)
After generating a section, run a consistency check.
Consistency audit prompt
"Consistency audit:
Check the draft against:
voice contract (tone, formality, no hype)
structure template (required sections present)
terminology map (preferred terms used consistently)
formatting rules (headings, bullets, prompt blocks)
List violations and revise. Return final only."
This is how you prevent gradual drift.

Handle intentional variation without losing consistency

Some parts of a book should sound different:
case studies,
interviews,
checklists,
labs.
The trick is to constrain variation explicitly:
"Keep the narrator voice consistent, but switch format to a lab worksheet."
Use "format variation, voice constant."

Common consistency failures and how to fix them

Failure 1: Tone shifts between chapters

Cause:
Different prompts, missing voice contract.
Fix:
Always include the voice contract plus a short anchor excerpt.

Failure 2: Depth level drifts

Cause:
Some prompts say "comprehensive," others say "quick."
Fix:
Define depth bands:
overview, practical, deep dive, and assign each chapter one band.

Failure 3: Terminology synonyms multiply

Cause:
Model tries to vary language stylistically.
Fix:
Add a terminology rule:
"Prefer standard terms, avoid synonyms for key concepts."

Failure 4: Formatting is inconsistent

Cause:
No templates, no format contract.
Fix:
Use section templates and require them by name.

Failure 5: Examples vary in structure
Cause:
No example format standard.
Fix:
Define one example format:
"Example format must be: Scenario, Prompt, Output, Why it works."

Practice: a simple long-document workflow you can teach
Here is a reliable routine for each chapter:
Provide voice contract + glossary (short)
Provide chapter brief
Generate outline using standard templates
Draft section by section with the same structure pattern
Run consistency audit after each section
After chapter completion, run a chapter-level audit:
tone, terminology, formatting, and cross-references
Prompt line for step 6:
"Scan for repeated phrases, inconsistent terms, and shifts in tone.
Normalize."

Mini lab: consistency checkpoint exercise
Ask your readers to do this:
Write a voice contract in 8–12 lines.
Create a glossary of 10 key terms.
Draft two sections on different topics using the same template.
Run a consistency audit prompt.
Revise until both sections:
use the same tone,
reuse the same terminology,
follow the same structure.
This builds the habit of treating voice as a spec, not a feeling.

Consistency across long documents is achieved by standardization: a voice contract, a small style bible, reusable templates, a terminology map, and verification audits. When you treat voice like an interface and enforce it with checklists, your book reads as one coherent work instead of many separate drafts.

Reusable voice profiles

A reusable voice profile is a compact, copy-paste spec that reliably produces the same tone, rhythm, and level of detail across many prompts. Think of it as a "voice preset." Instead of re-explaining your style every time, you select a profile and attach it to the task.

Voice profiles help you:

keep a consistent narrator voice across a book,
switch tone deliberately without drifting,
scale writing across chapters and contributors,
reduce editing time.

What a voice profile includes

A professional voice profile is short but specific. It covers:

Audience: role, knowledge level, sensitivity
Tone posture: neutral, warm, firm, cautious, confident
Vocabulary: plain language vs technical, jargon rules
Structure defaults: headings, bullets, examples, checklists
Rhythm rules: sentence length, paragraph size
Boundaries: do not do list (no hype, no sarcasm, no speculation)
Uncertainty policy: Unknown behavior, citations policy if needed
Keep it under 12–16 lines so it stays usable.

The "voice profile card" format (copy and paste)

Use this standard card for all profiles:

Voice Profile: <NAME>
Audience: <role + knowledge level>
Sensitivity: <tone risks to avoid>
Tone: <adjectives that describe voice>
Vocabulary: <plain/technical + rules>
Structure defaults: <sections + patterns>
Rhythm: <sentence/paragraph rules>
Do not: <forbidden style elements>
Uncertainty: <Unknown / questions / grounding rules>

This structure makes profiles consistent and easy to compare.

Eight reusable voice profiles (ready to use)
1) Beginner-friendly teacher
Voice Profile: Beginner Teacher
Audience: new learners, no prior knowledge
Sensitivity: avoid intimidation, avoid jargon overload
Tone: clear, patient, encouraging, practical
Vocabulary: plain language; define terms on first use; minimal acronyms
Structure defaults: short intro, 5–7 bullets, 1 simple example, mini checklist
Rhythm: short sentences; paragraphs 2–3 sentences
Do not: hype, sarcasm, long theory dumps
Uncertainty: if not known, say Unknown and ask 1–3 questions

2) Professional instructor (book narrator)
Voice Profile: Practical Book Narrator
Audience: beginner to intermediate readers learning a skill
Sensitivity: avoid hype and absolute claims
Tone: confident, supportive, direct, methodical
Vocabulary: plain first, then technical with definitions; consistent terms
Structure defaults: purpose paragraph, key points, templates, pitfalls, practice drill
Rhythm: medium sentences; use headings; bullets for steps
Do not: filler, motivational fluff, slang
Uncertainty: label assumptions; no invented facts; suggest verification when needed

3) Executive brief
Voice Profile: Executive Brief
Audience: leaders making decisions quickly
Sensitivity: risk-aware, time-limited
Tone: concise, calm, credible
Vocabulary: non-technical; business outcomes and tradeoffs
Structure defaults: decision, 3 key points, risks, recommendation, next step
Rhythm: very short paragraphs; bullets preferred

Do not: deep implementation detail, long background
Uncertainty: state limits clearly; avoid speculation; list what to verify

4) Technical specification
Voice Profile: Technical Spec
Audience: engineers implementing or reviewing
Sensitivity: precision matters, avoid ambiguity
Tone: neutral, exact, structured
Vocabulary: technical allowed; define terms; consistent naming
Structure defaults: assumptions, requirements, non-goals, steps, edge cases, acceptance criteria
Rhythm: numbered lists; tables for constraints
Do not: metaphors, vague adjectives, hand-wavy claims
Uncertainty: Unknown becomes TBD; never invent numbers, versions, or APIs

5) Diagnostic debugger
Voice Profile: Debugging Coach
Audience: practitioner troubleshooting output or systems
Sensitivity: avoid blame, focus on fixes
Tone: analytical, practical, reassuring
Vocabulary: pragmatic; explain terms briefly
Structure defaults: symptoms, likely causes, minimal fix, tests, prevention checklist
Rhythm: short sections; action-oriented bullets
Do not: theory-heavy detours, vague advice
Uncertainty: present hypotheses labeled clearly; ask targeted questions

6) Persuasive proposal
Voice Profile: Persuasive Proposal
Audience: stakeholders evaluating a recommendation
Sensitivity: credibility first, avoid sales tone
Tone: confident, evidence-based, respectful
Vocabulary: benefits framed to audience priorities
Structure defaults: recommendation, rationale, risks/mitigations, alternatives,

call to action
Rhythm: tight paragraphs; bullets for reasons
Do not: exaggerated claims, certainty without evidence
Uncertainty: qualify claims; separate facts from assumptions; suggest proof points

7) Customer support response
Voice Profile: Support Reply
Audience: non-technical customer
Sensitivity: customer may be frustrated, avoid blame
Tone: empathetic, calm, helpful, step-by-step
Vocabulary: simple, no jargon; define necessary terms
Structure defaults: empathy line, numbered steps, expected outcome, escalation path
Rhythm: short sentences; one instruction per line
Do not: sarcasm, technical deep dive
Uncertainty: ask clarifying questions before diagnosing; avoid guessing root causes

8) Research summary and analysis
Voice Profile: Research Synthesizer
Audience: analysts and informed readers
Sensitivity: accuracy and uncertainty handling
Tone: neutral, careful, evidence-led
Vocabulary: technical terms allowed with definitions when needed
Structure defaults: question, method, findings, limitations, implications
Rhythm: headings + bullets; clear claim separation
Do not: overgeneralize, causal claims without support
Uncertainty: "no citation, no claim" when sources provided; otherwise label needs verification

How to use voice profiles in prompts (the practical method)
Step 1: Pick a profile name
Example:
"Use Voice Profile: Practical Book Narrator."
Step 2: Add task-specific constraints below it

Keep voice separate from task rules.
Example structure:
Voice profile card
Task objective
Input material
Output format contract
Constraints and stop condition
This prevents voice rules from getting lost inside the task description.

Switching voices safely (without losing meaning)
When you rewrite content in a new voice, you want the meaning to remain stable.
Add a meaning-preservation constraint:
"Keep meaning unchanged. Only adjust tone, vocabulary, and structure."
For technical or policy text:
"Do not change commitments, numbers, or requirements."

Voice drift prevention in long documents
Reusable profiles work best with two extra tools:
1) A voice anchor snippet
Provide a short sample paragraph that represents your ideal voice and instruct the model to match it.
Rule:
"Match tone and rhythm, do not reuse content."
2) A consistency audit prompt
After drafting:
"Check against the voice profile. Fix any violations. Return final."
This keeps the profile stable across chapters.
Practice: build your own custom voice profile
Exercise for readers:
Choose a target persona (book narrator, executive brief, technical spec).
Fill the voice profile card with:
3 tone adjectives,
3 do not rules,
1 uncertainty rule,
1 structure default.

Test it on the same topic three times:
explanation,
checklist,
example prompts.
Refine until outputs feel consistently "yours."

Quick checklist: what makes a voice profile reusable
short enough to paste often
contains measurable rules (structure, rhythm, do not list)
has an uncertainty policy
separates voice rules from task requirements
includes consistent terminology rules if writing a series
Reusable voice profiles turn tone control into a system. Once you define a handful of strong profiles, you can produce consistent writing across chapters, formats, and audiences with minimal prompt changes.

Exercises, rewrite a piece for 6 audiences with strict constraints

This exercise trains one of the most valuable professional skills in prompt engineering: rewriting the same content for different audiences while keeping meaning stable and following strict rules. You will practice controlling role, knowledge level, sensitivity, tone, and format, without drifting into new claims or losing key details.

Exercise overview
You will take one base piece of text and produce six rewrites for six audiences. Each rewrite must follow strict constraints so you can score it objectively.
Learning goals
keep meaning stable while changing tone and structure
adjust vocabulary for different knowledge levels
control sensitivity and risk posture
follow format contracts precisely
reduce hallucination and drift during style transfer

Step 1: Choose the base piece (use one of these options)

Option A: Use this provided base piece (recommended for the lab)

Base piece (about prompt engineering reliability):

"AI outputs can sound confident even when they are wrong. This happens when the prompt is missing key context or when the model is pressured to be complete. To reduce errors, define your objective, provide the needed inputs, and specify the output format. If a fact is not available, the model should say 'Unknown' instead of guessing. For high-stakes work, add a verification step that checks claims against sources and constraints."

Keep this base piece unchanged as your source of truth.

Option B: Use your own base piece

Pick 120–160 words from your draft and paste it as the base.

Rule:

Do not change the meaning across rewrites.

Step 2: Global strict constraints (apply to all 6 rewrites)

These constraints prevent drift and make scoring possible.

Global constraints

Preserve meaning. Do not add new claims, stats, examples, or names.

Keep all key points:

confidence vs correctness

missing context and pressure to be complete

objective + inputs + output format

Unknown policy

verification step

No vendor names. No citations.

No rhetorical questions.

No emojis. No hype words (amazing, revolutionary, game-changing).

Use consistent terminology: objective, inputs, output format, Unknown, verification.

If you cannot satisfy a constraint, mark the conflicting part as "Unknown" rather than inventing.

Step 3: The six audiences and their strict output contracts

Produce one version for each audience. Follow the exact format and length limits.

Audience 1: Executive sponsor (non-technical)
Audience spec
Role: decides funding and priorities
Knowledge: low technical
Sensitivity: time-limited, risk-aware
Strict constraints
90–110 words
4 bullets only, no headings
Each bullet max 18 words
Must end with a clear next step in the last bullet
What this trains
Compression without losing key points.

Audience 2: New learner (beginner)
Audience spec
Role: first-time learner
Knowledge: beginner
Sensitivity: avoid intimidation
Strict constraints
140–170 words
Exactly 2 short paragraphs
Include exactly 1 simple analogy (one sentence)
Define "Unknown" in plain words once
What this trains
Clarity and teaching voice.

Audience 3: Engineer (technical peer)
Audience spec
Role: builds systems and checks correctness
Knowledge: expert
Sensitivity: precision over friendliness
Strict constraints
8–10 bullets
No bullet longer than 16 words
Must include one bullet labeled "Assumption policy:"
Must include one bullet labeled "Verification:"

No analogies

What this trains

Technical framing and explicit policies.

Audience 4: Customer support response (empathetic)

Audience spec

Role: support agent responding to a confused or frustrated user

Knowledge: user is non-technical

Sensitivity: empathy, avoid blame

Strict constraints

120–150 words

Start with one empathy sentence

Then a numbered list of exactly 4 steps

End with one reassurance sentence

No technical jargon beyond "objective" and "output format"

What this trains

Tone control under emotional constraints.

Audience 5: Compliance or risk reviewer

Audience spec

Role: checks for accuracy and risk

Knowledge: intermediate

Sensitivity: avoid overclaiming

Strict constraints

130–160 words

Headings required in this order:

Purpose

Controls

Limits

Under Controls: exactly 3 bullets

Under Limits: exactly 2 bullets

Use cautious language (may, can) where appropriate

What this trains

Cautious language and structured risk posture.

Audience 6: Persuasive internal proposal (credible, not salesy)
Audience spec
Role: convince a team to adopt reliability practices
Knowledge: mixed
Sensitivity: credibility, avoid hype
Strict constraints
160–190 words
Must follow this structure:
Recommendation (2 sentences)
Rationale (3 bullets)
Risks and mitigations (2 bullets)
Call to action (1 sentence)
No absolute claims
What this trains
Persuasion with guardrails.

Step 4: How to run the exercise as a prompt
Here is a single prompt you can reuse to generate all six outputs:
"Task: Rewrite the base piece for 6 audiences.
Base piece:
<paste the base piece>
Global constraints:
Preserve meaning, do not add new claims
Keep these points: confidence vs correctness; missing context/pressure; objective+inputs+output format; Unknown; verification
No citations, no vendor names, no hype, no emojis, no rhetorical questions
Use consistent terms: objective, inputs, output format, Unknown, verification
Now produce 6 versions, labeled A–F, following these strict contracts:
A) Executive: 90–110 words, 4 bullets only, each bullet <=18 words, last bullet is next step
B) Beginner: 140–170 words, exactly 2 paragraphs, include 1 analogy sentence, define Unknown once
C) Engineer: 8–10 bullets, each <=16 words, include 'Assumption policy:' and 'Verification:' bullets, no analogies
D) Support: 120–150 words, empathy sentence + 4 numbered steps +

reassurance sentence, minimal jargon
E) Compliance: 130–160 words, headings Purpose/Controls/Limits, Controls=3 bullets, Limits=2 bullets, cautious language
F) Persuasive: 160–190 words, structure Recommendation(2 sentences), Rationale(3 bullets), Risks(2 bullets), Call to action(1 sentence), no absolutes"

Step 5: Scoring rubric (fast and objective)

Score each version 0–2 on each item:
Contract compliance (length, structure, counts)
Audience fit (role and sensitivity)
Meaning preserved (no new claims, no missing key points)
Vocabulary alignment (beginner vs expert)
Tone control (formal, empathetic, cautious, persuasive as required)
Target score: 8/10 or higher per version.

Step 6: Common failure patterns (and fixes)

Failure: meaning drift, new claims appear

Fix:
Add:
"Do not introduce new facts. If tempted, omit or mark Unknown."

Failure: contract violations (word count, bullets)

Fix:
Add:
"Validate counts and length before finalizing. If off, revise."

Failure: engineer version becomes too explanatory

Fix:
Add:
"Bullets only, no narrative sentences."

Failure: persuasive version becomes hype

Fix:
Add:
"Use calm, credible language. No superlatives."

Bonus challenge: stabilize across multiple runs

Run the same six-audience prompt twice and compare. If outputs vary too much:
add a tighter voice profile,

add a stricter format skeleton,
add a verification step:
"Check each version against its contract and fix before returning."

This exercise builds real-world skill: you learn to specify audience and style as measurable constraints, preserve meaning under rewriting pressure, and produce consistent outputs across contexts that demand different tones and structures.

Chapter 13. Summarization, extraction, and transformation

Summarize vs extract vs rewrite, and how to choose

These three tasks sound similar, but they produce very different outcomes. Many "bad prompts" fail because the user asked for the wrong operation. Professionals decide first: do I want a **summary**, an **extraction**, or a **rewrite**. Then they design the prompt accordingly.

A simple rule:

Summarize when you want *less text with the same meaning.*

Extract when you want *structured facts pulled out.*

Rewrite when you want *the same content expressed differently.*

Definitions you can teach

1) Summarize

Summarization compresses. It answers:

"What are the most important points?"

What it keeps:

main ideas, key decisions, major findings, high-level context.

What it may drop:

minor details, examples, edge cases, exact wording.

Best outputs:

executive summary, key takeaways, meeting recap, abstract.

Best prompt ingredients:

target audience, length limit, required sections, priorities, and what to omit.

2) Extract

Extraction pulls specific pieces of information into a structured format. It answers:

"What are the fields I need, and what values fill them?"

What it keeps:

explicit facts in the source.

What it should not do:

infer missing values, invent details, or "smooth" the story.

Best outputs:

JSON, tables, spreadsheets, labeled fields, databases.

Best prompt ingredients:
schema, types, Unknown policy (null/Unknown), and "no extra text."

3) Rewrite
Rewrite transforms expression, not meaning. It answers:
"How should this sound or be formatted for a new purpose?"
What it keeps:
the same facts and commitments.
What changes:
tone, clarity, structure, level of jargon, or format.
Best outputs:
email rewrite, simplify language, convert bullets to paragraph, change voice, translate style.
Best prompt ingredients:
"preserve meaning" constraint, audience spec, style constraints, and what must not change.

The most common confusion (and how to avoid it)
People ask for a summary when they really need extraction, or ask for a rewrite when they need a summary.
You want extraction, not summary, when:
you need owners, due dates, action items, requirements, risks, metrics, or entities.
the output will go into a tool, spreadsheet, or workflow.
You want summary, not extraction, when:
you need a human-readable overview, decisions, and narrative context.
You want rewrite, not summary, when:
the content is correct but the style is wrong, too long, too harsh, too technical, or poorly organized.
A professional prompt starts with: "Operation: summarize/extract/rewrite."

How to choose: the decision guide
Step 1: What will you do with the output?
If you will **read it** to understand quickly → **Summarize**
If you will **store it, track it, or automate** → **Extract**
If you will **send it or publish it** → **Rewrite**

Step 2: Do you need coverage or precision?

Need broad coverage of key ideas → **Summarize**

Need exact values, names, dates, counts → **Extract**

Need the same content with different tone or structure → **Rewrite**

Step 3: Is missing info acceptable?

Summaries can omit minor details.

Extraction must handle missing values explicitly (Unknown/null).

Rewrites must not invent missing content; they should preserve what exists.

If missing info is common, extraction needs an Unknown policy, and summarization should include "what's missing" as a section if relevant.

What to specify for each task (prompt components)

Summarization prompt checklist

Include:

audience (executive, beginner, technical)

length (word count or bullets)

required sections (decisions, risks, next steps)

prioritization rule (top 5 key points)

scope boundaries (in scope, out of scope)

grounding rule if needed (use only provided text)

Example prompt pattern:

"Summarize for <audience> in <length>. Include <sections>. Prioritize <criteria>. Use only the provided text."

Extraction prompt checklist

Include:

schema (JSON keys or table columns)

types and formats (date format, number format)

Unknown policy (null/Unknown, no guessing)

strict output rule (no extra text)

validation step (check schema compliance)

Example prompt pattern:

"Extract into JSON with this schema. Use null if missing. No extra keys. Return JSON only."

Rewrite prompt checklist
Include:
what must not change (facts, numbers, names, commitments)
audience and tone (formal, casual, empathetic)
format target (email, memo, outline)
constraints (length, forbidden phrases, reading level)
optional: preserve original meaning and intent
Example prompt pattern:
"Rewrite for <audience> with <tone>. Preserve meaning. Do not change <items>. Output in <format>."

Examples: same source text, three different operations
Source text:
"Meeting notes: Launch slipped due to vendor delay. Alex will update the timeline. New target is mid-April. Main risk is integration testing. Next meeting Friday."
A) Summarize
Output goal:
Short human overview.
Request:
"Summarize in 3 bullets for executives. Include decisions and risks."
Expected output:
launch delay reason and impact
new target
risk and next step

B) Extract
Output goal:
Structured tracking.
Request:
"Extract into JSON: {owner, task, due_date, risk}. Use null if missing. JSON only."
Expected output:
owner: Alex
task: update timeline
due_date: null

risk: integration testing

C) Rewrite
Output goal:
Send message to stakeholders.
Request:
"Rewrite as a formal stakeholder email. Preserve facts. 120–160 words. Include next meeting date. No hype."
Expected output:
Polished email, same facts, clearer tone.

When to combine tasks (and how to do it safely)
Sometimes you need more than one operation. The safe way is staged prompting.
Safe combination patterns
Pattern 1: Extract then summarize
Best when you want a trustworthy summary based on facts.
Workflow:
Extract key facts into a table
Summarize using only that table
This reduces hallucinations.

Pattern 2: Summarize then rewrite
Best when the original is long, and you need a short message.
Workflow:
Summarize to the key points
Rewrite the summary into an email or memo
This prevents rewriting from preserving unnecessary detail.

Pattern 3: Extract then rewrite
Best for converting notes into a clean artifact.
Workflow:
Extract action items and decisions
Rewrite into SOP, plan, or email

Common failure modes by task type

Summarization failures

too generic, misses key decisions

Fix: require sections and priorities.

adds facts not in source

Fix: grounding rule, "no new facts."

Extraction failures

invents missing values

Fix: Unknown policy, null allowed.

adds commentary around JSON

Fix: "JSON only, stop after closing brace," validation step.

Rewrite failures

changes meaning

Fix: "preserve meaning, do not change names, dates, numbers."

becomes overly formal or too casual

Fix: specify voice profile and examples.

Quick selection cheat sheet

Choose **Summarize** if you want:

understanding quickly, less text, key ideas.

Choose **Extract** if you want:

fields, tables, JSON, tracking, automation.

Choose **Rewrite** if you want:

same content, different voice, clearer structure, ready to send.

If you are unsure, ask for a two-step output:

extraction of facts,

summary or rewrite built from those facts.

That is the professional default for reliability.

Practice, build a "document intake pipeline" prompt set

A document intake pipeline is a repeatable set of prompts you run on any document to turn it into usable outputs: a quick understanding, structured metadata, key facts, actions, and reusable artifacts. Professionals do not rely

on one giant prompt. They use a pipeline that separates extraction from interpretation, then verifies, then publishes.
This practice section gives you a ready-to-use prompt set you can teach and reuse for reports, meeting notes, policies, research papers, contracts, tickets, and emails.

What the intake pipeline produces
A good intake pipeline outputs six things:
Document ID card (metadata and classification)
Executive summary (short, human-readable)
Structured extraction (JSON or table for automation)
Action and decision log (owners, due dates, risks)
Open questions and unknowns (what's missing)
Verification report (what is supported vs uncertain)
You can run all steps, or pick only the outputs you need.

Pipeline design principles (the rules)
Separate **extract** from **summarize**.
Use a clear **Unknown policy** (Unknown/null, no guessing).
Use a **format contract** for each step.
Keep outputs small, consistent, and labeled.
Add at least one **verification pass** for reliability.
Maintain a stable taxonomy for classification.

The document intake prompt set (copy and paste)
Step 0: Document normalization (optional but useful)
Use when documents come messy: OCR, email threads, notes.
Prompt
"Normalize this document text without changing meaning.
Rules:
remove obvious formatting noise (duplicate headers/footers)
keep original wording, do not paraphrase
preserve lists and section headings
Return cleaned text only.
Document:
<PASTE>"

Output becomes cleaner input for all other steps.

Step 1: Document ID card (classification + metadata)
Goal: tag the document so downstream steps know how to treat it.
Prompt
"Create a Document ID Card.
Output format (YAML):
doc_title: <string or Unknown>
doc_type: <one of: policy, meeting_notes, report, research_paper, email_thread, contract, ticket, other>
domain: <one of: product, engineering, operations, legal, compliance, marketing, finance, HR, research, other>
date_in_document: <YYYY-MM-DD or Unknown>
author_or_sender: <string or Unknown>
intended_audience: <string or Unknown>
confidentiality: <public, internal, restricted, Unknown>
one_sentence_purpose: <string>
keywords: [<5 to 10 keywords>]
risk_level: <low, medium, high> # based on impact if wrong
Rules:
Use only what is explicit in the document. If missing, use Unknown.
No extra fields.
Document:
<PASTE>"
Why this works: it creates a consistent top-level index.

Step 2: Executive summary (fast understanding)
Goal: provide a short, reliable overview for humans.
Prompt
"Write an executive summary using only the document content.
Output format:
Summary (80–120 words)
Key points (5 bullets)
Decisions (up to 5 bullets, or 'None found')
Action items (up to 5 bullets, include owner if stated, otherwise Unknown)
Risks (3 bullets)

Rules:
Do not add new facts.
If a detail is missing, write Unknown or omit that item.
Keep bullets short.
Document:
<PASTE>"

Step 3: Structured extraction (for tracking and automation)

Goal: capture facts into JSON for downstream systems.

Prompt

"Extract structured data into JSON only.
Schema:
{
"entities": {
"people": [string],
"teams": [string],
"orgs": [string],
"products": [string]
},
"dates": [{"date": "YYYY-MM-DD", "context": string}],
"metrics": [{"name": string, "value": string, "context": string}],
"requirements": [string],
"decisions": [string],
"action_items": [{"task": string, "owner": string|null, "due_date": "YYYY-MM-DD"|null, "status": string|null}],
"risks": [{"risk": string, "severity": "low"|"medium"|"high"|null}],
"open_questions": [string]
}
Rules:
Return valid JSON only, no markdown or commentary.
Use null when unknown. Do not guess.
Include only information explicit in the document.
No extra keys.
Document:
<PASTE>"

Step 4: Action and decision log (operational view)

Goal: convert content into a practical log you can execute.

Prompt

"Create an Action and Decision Log.
Output format:
Decisions:
D1: <decision> | Owner: <name or Unknown> | Date: <YYYY-MM-DD or Unknown>
Actions:
A1: <task> | Owner: <name or Unknown> | Due: <YYYY-MM-DD or Unknown> | Dependency: <if stated, else Unknown> | Risk: <if stated, else Unknown>
Rules:
Use only what is explicit in the document.
If missing, use Unknown. Do not infer owners or dates.
Max 8 decisions, max 12 actions.
Document:
<PASTE>"

This step is easier for humans than raw JSON.

Step 5: Unknowns and clarifying questions (requirements gap)

Goal: prevent guessing and prepare follow-up.

Prompt

"Identify what is missing or ambiguous.
Output format:
Unknowns (bullets): list missing critical info required to act.
Clarifying questions (max 6): ask the highest-impact questions first.
Assumptions to avoid (bullets): list tempting guesses you will not make.
Rules:
Questions must be specific and answerable.
Do not propose solutions yet.
Document:
<PASTE>"

This step is your anti-hallucination safety net.

Step 6: Verification pass (cross-check for reliability)

Goal: detect unsupported claims or drift.

Prompt

"Verification pass.

Inputs:

Document: <PASTE DOCUMENT>

Draft outputs: <PASTE THE OUTPUTS FROM STEPS 2–4>

Task:

Flag any statement in the draft outputs that is not supported by the document.

For each flagged item, mark as:

Unsupported (remove it)

Needs clarification (move to open_questions)

Supported but overstated (rewrite with cautious language)

Return corrected versions of:

Executive summary

Action and Decision Log

Structured extraction JSON (if needed)

Rules:

Do not add new facts.

If unsure, mark Unknown or add a clarifying question.

Return corrected outputs only."

This is what makes the pipeline professional.

Optional add-ons (useful variants)

Add-on A: Role-specific summary

For different readers, generate different views.

Prompt:

"Produce two summaries:

Exec view: 90–120 words + risks

Operator view: actions + owners + deadlines

No new facts."

Add-on B: Create a filing name and tags

Prompt:

"Generate a file name and tags:

file_name: YYYY-MM-DD_<doc_type>_<short_title>
tags: 6–10 tags
Use Unknown if date missing."

Add-on C: Convert to a reusable artifact

Turn intake into something usable, like a SOP or brief.
Prompt:
"Transform the verified action log into a SOP.
Preserve meaning. Do not invent steps not mentioned. Use TBD where missing."

How to teach the pipeline as a routine

Tell readers to run it in this order:
ID card
Executive summary
Structured extraction
Action and decision log
Unknowns and questions
Verification pass
If time is short, run:
summary + action log + unknowns.
If automation is needed, include JSON extraction.

Practice assignment (hands-on)

Give learners two documents:
one clean report,
one messy meeting notes dump.
For each document:
Run steps 1–5.
Compare extracted action items vs summary action items.
Run step 6 verification and note what got removed or downgraded.
Record improvements you want in schemas and tags.
Success criteria:
no invented owners or dates,
clear Unknowns,
consistent output format,
action log is executable.

Common failure points and quick fixes

Failure: action items invent owners or due dates

Fix:

Strengthen Unknown policy:

"Owner and due_date must be explicit, else Unknown/null."

Failure: summaries add "helpful" background not in document

Fix:

Add:

"Use only the document. No general knowledge."

Failure: JSON includes extra keys or commentary

Fix:

"Return JSON only. No extra text. Validate schema."

Failure: pipeline outputs inconsistent terminology

Fix:

Add a terminology rule:

"Use these terms exactly: decision, action, risk, unknown."

A compact "pipeline runner" prompt (single message)

If you want one prompt to run all steps at once:

"Run the document intake pipeline on the text below.

Outputs required, in this order:

Document ID Card (YAML, fixed fields)

Executive summary (5 sections)

Structured extraction (JSON only, fixed schema)

Action and Decision Log (max limits)

Unknowns + clarifying questions (max 6)

Rules:

Use only the document.

Unknown/null for missing info, no guessing.

Follow formats exactly, no extra commentary.

Document:

<PASTE>"

Then run a separate verification pass if reliability is critical.

This prompt set teaches a professional habit: treat documents like inputs to a controlled process, not a one-off chat. When you separate extraction from summarization, enforce Unknown behavior, and add a verification pass, you get consistent, auditable outputs that scale from novice workflows to expert-grade reliability.

Chapter 14. Reasoning tasks, planning, and decision support

Getting options, tradeoffs, and risk assessments

When you ask an AI model to help with decisions, the biggest risk is not "bad writing." It is false certainty. Decision support requires structure: options, tradeoffs, risks, assumptions, and a clear recommendation logic. A professional prompt does not ask, "What should I do?" It asks for a decision package.

This section teaches how to prompt for:
multiple options,
explicit tradeoffs,
risk assessments,
and decision-ready outputs that are grounded in your constraints.

What a "decision package" should contain

A reliable decision output usually includes:
Decision statement (what you are deciding)
Constraints (budget, time, people, policy, must-haves)
Options (2–5 distinct paths)
Tradeoffs (pros, cons, what you give up)
Risks (likelihood, impact, mitigations)
Assumptions and unknowns (what would change the answer)
Recommendation (with rationale and conditions)
Next steps (what to do this week)
If the model outputs only a single recommendation, it is not decision support. It is advice.

Step 1: Provide a decision context packet

Options are only useful when they respect your reality. Give a short context packet:
objective and success metrics
timeline
resources (people, tools)
budget range
constraints and non-goals

risk tolerance (conservative vs aggressive)
stakeholders and what they care about
what has already been tried

Context packet template (copy and paste)

"Decision context:
Decision: <one sentence>
Objective: <what success looks like>
Time horizon: <date or weeks>
Constraints: <budget, time, policy, tools>
Must-haves: <3–5>
Non-goals: <3–5>
Stakeholders: <who + priorities>
Risk tolerance: <low/medium/high>
Known facts: <bullets>
Unknowns: <bullets>"

A good context packet prevents the model from inventing assumptions.

Step 2: Ask for options that are genuinely different

Many outputs provide "options" that are just small variations. Make the model separate options by strategy.

Prompt pattern

"Generate 3–5 options that are meaningfully different approaches, not minor variations.
Each option must include:
summary (2 sentences)
prerequisites
estimated effort (S/M/L)
timeline (short estimate)
when it works best
when it fails"

This forces real variety.

Step 3: Force tradeoffs, not just pros and cons

Pros and cons are often shallow. Tradeoffs are comparative: what you gain and what you lose.

Tradeoff prompts that work

"For each option, list the primary tradeoff in one sentence: 'We gain X but give up Y.'"
"Compare options pairwise on the top 3 criteria."
"State second-order effects: what happens later if we choose this now."
Decision criteria prompt
"Use this rubric for comparison:
Speed
Cost
Quality
Risk
Maintainability
Stakeholder impact
Score each 1–5 with one-line justification."
Rubrics make tradeoffs visible and testable.

Step 4: Ask for risk assessments the professional way
A risk list without likelihood, impact, and mitigation is not useful.
Risk assessment structure
For each option:
Risk description
Likelihood (Low/Med/High)
Impact (Low/Med/High)
Early warning signals
Mitigation plan
Residual risk after mitigation
Risk prompt template
"For each option, provide a risk table with:
Risk | Likelihood | Impact | Early signal | Mitigation | Residual risk.
No invented numbers. Use Low/Med/High if you cannot quantify."
Add a risk tolerance alignment:
"Align mitigations with our risk tolerance: <low/medium/high>."

Step 5: Require assumptions and "what would change the recommendation"
This is one of the best hallucination controls for planning tasks.
Prompt block

"List the key assumptions behind your recommendation.
Then list 'decision changers': 5 facts that, if different, would change the recommendation."
This makes uncertainty explicit and guides follow-up questions.

Step 6: Ask for a recommendation with conditions
A professional recommendation is conditional, not absolute.
Recommendation prompt
"Recommend one option, but include:
why it wins under our constraints
the conditions under which you would choose a different option
the minimum additional information needed to confirm"
This produces a decision that can be defended.

Output formats that work best
Format A: Options comparison table (fast and decision-ready)
Columns:
Option | Summary | Cost | Time | Complexity | Key tradeoff | Biggest risk | Best for
Use when:
you need to decide quickly.

Format B: One-page decision memo (stakeholder-friendly)
Sections:
Decision
Context
Options
Recommendation
Risks and mitigations
Next steps
Use when:
you need alignment and approvals.

Format C: Risk register (operations-focused)
A risk table for each option.
Use when:

reliability and compliance matter.

Copy-paste prompts (ready to use)
Prompt 1: Options and tradeoffs pack

"Using the context below, produce 4 options that are meaningfully different strategies.
For each option include:
2-sentence summary
prerequisites
key tradeoff ('gain X but give up Y')
effort (S/M/L) and rough timeline
Then provide a comparison table scored 1–5 on:
Speed, Cost, Quality, Risk, Maintainability, Stakeholder impact.
Finally recommend one option and list conditions when another option is better.
Context:
<PASTE CONTEXT PACKET>"

Prompt 2: Risk assessment pack

"For each option listed below, produce a risk table:
Risk | Likelihood | Impact | Early signal | Mitigation | Residual risk.
Use Low/Med/High ratings. Do not invent statistics.
Close with the top 3 cross-option risks and how to reduce them.
Options:
<PASTE OPTIONS>"

Prompt 3: Conservative vs aggressive planning

"Provide two plan variants:
Conservative plan: minimizes risk, slower, higher certainty
Aggressive plan: faster, accepts higher risk
For each, list tradeoffs, failure modes, and guardrails."
This is great when leadership wants speed but you need safety.

Common failure modes in decision prompting (and fixes)
Failure 1: The model picks one option too early

Fix:
"Do not recommend until you list at least 3 options."
Failure 2: Options are not distinct
Fix:
"Options must differ by strategy: outsource vs build, phased rollout vs big bang, manual vs automated."
Failure 3: Risks are generic
Fix:
Ask for "early signals" and "mitigations." Generic risks cannot produce early signals.
Failure 4: Hidden assumptions
Fix:
Require assumptions and decision changers.
Failure 5: Overconfident recommendation
Fix:
"State uncertainty and what to verify. Use conditional language."

Practice lab: build a decision package (repeatable exercise)
Pick any scenario, for example:
selecting a summarization pipeline for your team,
deciding whether to adopt a new model tool,
planning a training program,
choosing between two product approaches.
Steps:
Write a context packet (10 lines).
Ask for 4 distinct options.
Add a rubric scoring table.
Ask for risk tables per option.
Ask for recommendation plus decision changers.
Convert the output into a one-page decision memo.
Success criteria:
at least 3 distinct strategies,
explicit tradeoffs,
risks with likelihood, impact, and mitigations,
recommendation is conditional and auditable.

Decision support prompting is not about getting the "right answer." It is about getting a structured set of options, tradeoffs, and risks that makes the decision clearer, exposes uncertainty, and helps you choose deliberately. When you force distinct options, use a rubric, and require risk tables plus assumptions, you get outputs that are genuinely useful and far more reliable.

Avoiding false precision

False precision happens when an output looks exact and confident but is not truly supported by evidence. In planning and decision support, this is one of the most dangerous failure modes because it can make weak guesses feel like facts, especially when the model provides specific numbers, timelines, probabilities, or "definitive" rankings.

A professional prompt actively prevents false precision by:
constraining what can be quantified,
requiring uncertainty labels,
separating facts from assumptions,
and using ranges or qualitative ratings when data is missing.

What false precision looks like

Watch for these signals:
exact dates without inputs: "Finish by March 12."
exact hours and costs without data: "This will take 37 hours and cost $4,820."
precise probabilities: "There's a 73 percent chance this will succeed."
overly specific metrics: "Engagement will increase by 14.2 percent."
confident causal claims: "The reason is X," with no evidence
detailed citations without sources
These outputs can be well-written and still wrong. Professional prompting should reduce their occurrence.

Why models produce false precision

Common causes:
You asked for a plan that implies specifics, but you did not provide enough data.
You requested "best" or "optimal," forcing the model to pick a winner.
You demanded completeness, encouraging it to fill gaps.

You did not specify an Unknown policy, ranges, or acceptable uncertainty.
You asked for estimates but gave no baseline, constraints, or reference points.
The fix is not "tell it to be accurate." The fix is to change the task into a grounded output with controlled uncertainty.

The professional rules to prevent false precision
Rule 1: Use ranges, not point estimates, unless you provide data
Instead of:
"Give the time estimate."
Ask:
"Provide a range (best case, typical, worst case) and list assumptions."
Prompt line:
"Use ranges. Do not give single-number estimates unless the input contains sufficient data."

Rule 2: Require assumptions next to every estimate
Estimates must be traceable.
Prompt line:
"For each estimate, list 2–4 assumptions that drive it."
Example format:
Time: 2–4 weeks (assumes 1 engineer, stable requirements, existing tooling)
This is one of the highest-impact anti-false-precision constraints.

Rule 3: Separate facts, inferences, and guesses
Force the output to label what it is doing.
Prompt line:
"Separate:
Confirmed facts (from inputs)
Inferences (supported reasoning)
Assumptions (not confirmed)
Do not present assumptions as facts."
This prevents "quiet guessing."

Rule 4: Use qualitative risk ratings when probabilities are not defensible

Probability numbers are rarely justified without historical data.

Prompt line:

"Use Low/Medium/High likelihood and impact. Avoid numeric probabilities unless provided."

Add:

"If you do provide numeric probabilities, explain the basis and data source."

Rule 5: Force "Unknown" behavior for missing information

Prompt line:

"If required information is missing, say Unknown and ask a clarifying question. Do not guess."

For structured outputs:

"Use null for unknown fields."

Rule 6: Add a "suspicious specificity" audit

Make the model scan for fake exactness.

Prompt line:

"Before finalizing, scan for precise numbers, dates, or claims not supported by inputs. Replace with ranges or Unknown."

Practical prompting patterns that avoid false precision

Pattern A: Estimate with bands

Ask for banded estimates instead of a single number.

Template

"Provide estimates in bands:

Best case

Typical case

Worst case

For each band, list key assumptions and primary risk drivers.

Do not provide a single-point estimate."

This produces realistic planning outputs.

Pattern B: Decision criteria scoring with explanations, not exact math

Rubric scoring helps, but it can create false precision if treated as "scientific."

Use:

1–5 scores with one-line justification

or qualitative labels like Strong/Medium/Weak

Prompt line:

"Scores are directional, not statistical. Provide justifications and sensitivity notes."

Pattern C: Confidence tags per claim

Template

"Tag each major claim with confidence:

High (explicit in input), Medium (reasonable inference), Low (speculation).

Do not include Low-confidence claims in the final recommendation unless labeled clearly."

This helps readers interpret certainty.

Pattern D: "What would change this plan"

Template

"List decision changers:

5 pieces of missing information that would change the plan or recommendation."

This turns unknowns into actionable questions.

Examples: turning false precision into professional uncertainty

Example 1: Timeline estimate

Risky request:

"Create a project plan and give exact dates."

Safer request:

"Create a project plan with relative timelines (Week 1, Week 2–3).

Provide best/typical/worst ranges.

Only convert to calendar dates if I provide the start date and team capacity."

This prevents invented dates.

Example 2: Risk probability

Risky request:
"What's the chance this will fail?"
Safer request:
"Assess risk using likelihood and impact (Low/Med/High).
List early warning signals and mitigations.
Do not provide numeric probabilities without historical data."

Example 3: ROI and metrics

Risky request:
"Estimate how much revenue this will generate."
Safer request:
"Provide a simple scenario model:
conservative, baseline, optimistic
State assumptions for each.
If any assumption is unknown, label it Unknown and ask a question."
This replaces fake exactness with transparent scenarios.

The "precision permission" concept (a simple teaching model)

Teach readers this rule:
Precision must be earned.
Precision is permitted only when:
you provide numbers, constraints, or historical baselines,
you specify the formula or method,
you accept uncertainty and assumptions.
Otherwise, the model should default to:
ranges, bands, qualitative ratings, or Unknown.
You can encode this as a prompt policy:
"Precision permission:
If data is provided, compute precisely.
If data is missing, use ranges and label assumptions.
If critical data is missing, ask questions."

Add a built-in false precision filter (copy-paste)

Use this guardrail block in planning and decision prompts:
"False precision guardrail:

Do not invent exact numbers, dates, probabilities, or citations.
Use ranges (best/typical/worst) when estimating.
Label assumptions next to each estimate.
Use Low/Medium/High for likelihood and impact unless data supports numeric probabilities.
If missing info blocks accuracy, mark Unknown and ask up to 4 clarifying questions.
Before finalizing, scan for suspicious specificity and replace with justified ranges or Unknown."
This single block hardens most planning outputs.

Practice: convert an overconfident plan into a reliable one

Exercise for readers:
Ask the model for a plan without guardrails.
Highlight instances of false precision:
exact dates, exact hours, precise probabilities.
Rerun with the false precision guardrail block.
Compare outputs:
are estimates now ranges, with assumptions, and Unknowns?
Success criteria:
no unsupported exact dates or numbers,
assumptions are explicit,
risks are measurable with likelihood/impact,
recommendation is conditional.

Avoiding false precision is not about being vague. It is about being honest and decision-useful. When you force ranges, assumptions, confidence labels, and Unknown behavior, you get outputs that are safer, more reliable, and easier to validate, which is exactly what professional decision support requires.

Lab, create a decision rubric and apply it to 3 scenarios

This lab teaches you how to turn fuzzy decisions into structured, repeatable evaluations. You will build one reusable decision rubric, then apply it to three different scenarios. The focus is not on the "perfect answer." It is on a process that makes your decision logic visible, comparable, and less vulnerable to overconfidence.

Part 1: Build a reusable decision rubric

Step 1: Define the decision type

Choose one decision type for your rubric. Common categories:

selecting a tool or platform

choosing a plan or strategy

prioritizing projects

choosing a workflow or process

hiring or vendor selection

Your rubric should work for a whole class of decisions, not a single one.

Step 2: Pick 6–8 criteria that matter most

A strong rubric has a small number of criteria that are:

relevant across scenarios,

easy to understand,

and scorable with minimal ambiguity.

Recommended criteria set (general-purpose):

Impact on objective

Feasibility with current resources

Time to value

Cost and operational burden

Risk and reversibility

Maintainability and scalability

Stakeholder alignment

Evidence strength (how well-supported the choice is)

You can use 6 criteria for speed or 8 for nuance.

Step 3: Define scoring levels for each criterion

Do not use "good" and "bad." Define what 1, 3, and 5 mean so scoring stays consistent.

Example definitions (1–5 scale):

1) Impact on objective

1: small improvement

3: meaningful improvement

5: major improvement tied directly to success metrics

2) Feasibility

1: requires new capabilities or major dependencies

3: feasible with some ramp-up
5: feasible now with current team and tools
3) Time to value
1: value in months
3: value in weeks
5: value in days
4) Cost and burden
1: high ongoing cost or heavy operations
3: moderate cost and manageable operations
5: low cost and minimal overhead
5) Risk and reversibility
1: high risk, hard to reverse
3: moderate risk, partially reversible
5: low risk, easy rollback
6) Maintainability and scalability
1: fragile or costly to maintain
3: manageable maintenance
5: robust, scalable, low maintenance
7) Stakeholder alignment
1: likely pushback, misaligned incentives
3: mixed support
5: strong buy-in and clear ownership
8) Evidence strength
1: mostly assumptions
3: some evidence or precedent
5: strong evidence, data, or proven track record

Step 4: Add weights (optional but powerful)
Weights reflect priorities. Keep it simple: weights sum to 100.
Example default weights:
Impact: 20
Feasibility: 15
Time to value: 15
Cost and burden: 10
Risk and reversibility: 15
Maintainability: 10

Stakeholder alignment: 10
Evidence strength: 5
If your environment is risk-sensitive, increase risk and evidence weights.

Step 5: Add guardrails against false precision

Rubrics can create a fake sense of math certainty. Add rules:
Scores are directional, not scientific.
Every score must include a one-line justification.
If information is missing, mark Unknown and lower evidence strength.
Include a sensitivity note: "If X changes, the ranking may change."

The final rubric template (copy and paste)

Decision Rubric (1–5 score, with weights)

Criteria	Weight	1 means	3 means	5 means
Impact on objective	20	Small impact	Meaningful	Major
Feasibility	15	Hard now	Some ramp	Feasible now
Time to value	15	Months	Weeks	Days
Cost and burden	10	High/ongoing	Moderate	Low
Risk and reversibility	15	High/hard	Moderate	Low/easy
Maintainability	10	Fragile	Manageable	Robust
Stakeholder alignment	10	Pushback	Mixed	Strong
Evidence strength	5	Assumptions	Some evidence	Strong evidence

Scoring rules:
Provide 1-line justification per criterion.
Use Unknown where needed and reduce Evidence strength.
Provide a sensitivity note for the top choice.

Part 2: Apply the rubric to 3 scenarios

Below are three realistic scenarios for prompt engineering and knowledge work. For each, you will evaluate three options using the rubric, then pick a recommendation.

You can do this lab by hand or by prompting an AI to produce the scored table and then reviewing it.

Scenario 1: Choosing a summarization workflow for a team

Decision

Your team processes long documents weekly. You need a reliable workflow.

Constraints

mixed skill levels

limited time per doc

high risk if facts are wrong

Options

A) One-step summary prompt

B) Two-step: extract facts table, then summary from table

C) Multi-step: extract, verify, summarize, then produce action log

Task

Score A, B, C using the rubric. Then:

rank options,

recommend one,

list the top two risks and mitigations,

add a sensitivity note: what would change your decision.

Scenario 2: Deciding how to control output format for automation

Decision

You need structured outputs (JSON) that will feed an internal tool.

Constraints

JSON must validate

missing fields are common

failure should be detectable

Options

A) Ask for JSON only with a schema

B) Ask for JSON plus a validation self-check pass

C) Extract into a table first, then convert table to JSON, then validate

Task

Score A, B, C using the rubric. Then:

pick the best option for reliability,

explain tradeoffs,

specify "Unknown policy" and "stop condition" as part of the recommendation.

Scenario 3: Planning a training path for beginners vs advanced users
Decision
You are splitting content into two tracks and need a teaching plan.
Constraints
beginners need quick wins
advanced track needs depth and rigor
consistent terminology across both
Options
A) Single mixed book with beginner and advanced chapters interleaved
B) Two separate books with shared glossary and templates
C) One core book plus a separate workbook of labs and drills
Task
Score A, B, C using the rubric. Then:
recommend one option,
list who benefits and who struggles,
include a rollout plan in 3 steps.

Part 3: How to run this lab as a prompt (ready to use)
Prompt to generate the rubric and score scenarios
"Create a decision rubric for evaluating options. Use 6–8 criteria with clear 1/3/5 definitions and weights summing to 100. Include anti-false-precision guardrails.
Then apply the rubric to these 3 scenarios. For each scenario:
score each option 1–5 per criterion with one-line justification
compute weighted totals
rank options
recommend one option
list top two risks and mitigations
include a sensitivity note: what missing info could change the ranking
Scenarios:
Summarization workflow: A one-step, B extract-then-summarize, C extract-verify-summarize-action log

JSON automation: A schema-only, B schema + validation, C table → JSON → validate
Training path: A mixed book, B two books shared glossary, C core book + workbook"

Part 4: Scoring and reflection
After you complete the lab, review:
Did any option win because of a single heavily weighted criterion?
Were any scores based on assumptions? If yes, were they labeled?
Would different stakeholders choose different weights?
What is your decision changer list, the 3 facts you wish you had?
This reflection step is the difference between using a rubric and being controlled by it.

What success looks like
You know you did this lab correctly when:
your criteria definitions prevented vague scoring,
each score had a justification,
missing info reduced evidence strength,
the final recommendation included conditions and risks,
and you could explain the decision in one minute using the rubric.
This lab builds decision discipline: options become comparable, uncertainty becomes visible, and recommendations become auditable.

Chapter 15. Creative prompting without losing control

Divergent vs convergent phases

Creative work with AI is most effective when you separate it into two distinct phases:
Divergent phase: generate many possibilities without judging too early.
Convergent phase: evaluate, refine, and select the best ideas using constraints and tests.
Most "creative prompting problems" happen when people mix these phases. They ask for originality and strict precision in one step, then get outputs that are either bland or chaotic. Professionals run creativity like a pipeline: explore first, then narrow.

The mental model: creativity as a controlled funnel

Think of your process as a funnel:
Open up: produce variety, angles, metaphors, options, and drafts.
Narrow down: apply constraints, rubrics, and edits to produce a final deliverable.
Lock in: validate format, tone, and requirements.
Your prompt should match the phase.

Phase 1: Divergent prompting (generate options)

What divergent prompting is for

Use divergence when you need:
many ideas quickly,
different concepts or styles,
alternative headlines, hooks, structures, names, metaphors, story arcs,
multiple ways to explain the same concept.
Success in divergence is measured by:
variety, not perfection.

Divergent constraints that help (yes, you still use constraints)

Divergent prompts still need guardrails, just different ones. You constrain:
breadth and coverage,
categories,

novelty requirements,
and output format for easy comparison.

Useful divergent constraints

"Give 20 ideas across 5 categories."
"Each idea must be meaningfully different."
"Include 5 counterintuitive options."
"Include 3 'wild' options and label them."
"No repeats, no synonyms as separate ideas."
"Each idea must fit in one sentence."
"Include a short 'why it might work'."
These rules increase creativity while keeping the output organized.

High-performing divergent prompt templates

Template A: Idea expansion by categories

"Generate 25 ideas for <goal>.
Split them into 5 categories: <cat1>…<cat5>.
Rules:
each idea is one sentence
no repeats
include at least 5 unusual options
Output format:
Category name, then numbered list."

Template B: Constraint-driven creativity

"Generate 15 concepts for <goal> under these constraints:
must work with <constraint>
must avoid <non-goal>
must target <audience>
For each concept: name + 1-sentence pitch + 1 risk."
This produces creativity that stays relevant.

Template C: "Angles and hooks"

"Give 12 different angles to explain <topic>.
Each angle must use a different framing: analogy, story, data-driven, skeptical, contrarian, how-to, myth-busting, etc."
This prevents repetitive outputs.

Common divergent failures and fixes

Failure: ideas are repetitive

Fix:

Add a novelty rule:

"Each idea must differ by mechanism, not wording."

Failure: ideas ignore the audience

Fix:

Repeat audience in the prompt and add:

"Reject any idea that would confuse this audience."

Failure: output is too long to review

Fix:

Force compactness:

"Each idea max 18 words."

Phase 2: Convergent prompting (select and refine)

What convergent prompting is for

Use convergence when you need:

one best answer,

an implementation-ready plan,

a polished section,

consistent tone and format,

risk-controlled decisions.

Success in convergence is measured by:

compliance, clarity, and usefulness.

Convergent constraints that matter most

In convergence, you narrow using:

a rubric,

must-haves and non-goals,

format contracts,

length limits,

grounding and Unknown policy,

verification checks.

Useful convergent constraints

"Score each option using this rubric."

"Pick top 3, explain why."

"Combine two ideas if synergy is clear."
"Produce final output in this exact structure."
"Do not introduce new claims."
"Validate against checklist and revise."
Convergent prompts should be testable.

High-performing convergent prompt templates

Template D: Rubric selection

"Evaluate the ideas below using this rubric:
Fit to audience (1–5)
Novelty (1–5)
Feasibility (1–5)
Risk (1–5, lower is better)
Pick the top 3 and justify briefly.
Then choose 1 final direction and explain the tradeoff."

Template E: Rewrite to a strict deliverable

"Using idea #7, write the final <deliverable>.
Constraints:
length <range>
tone <style>
include sections: <...>
must avoid: <...>
Stop after final section."

Template F: Iterative refinement loop

"Draft version 1.
Then run a checklist audit and fix issues.
Then produce version 2 as final."
This reduces drift and improves compliance.

Common convergent failures and fixes

Failure: the model keeps adding new ideas while refining

Fix:
Add:
"Do not introduce new concepts. Use only selected ideas."

Failure: selection rationale is vague

Fix:
Require scores and evidence:
"Provide scores and one-line justification per criterion."
Failure: final output drifts from the chosen option
Fix:
Pin the chosen option:
"Use only option #3 as the source. Quote its key points before writing the final."

The professional workflow: divergence → convergence → lock
Here is a reliable 3-step pipeline you can reuse:
Step 1: Diverge (generate)
"Generate 20 options under these constraints, organized by categories."
Step 2: Converge (select)
"Score options with a rubric. Pick top 3. Choose 1 direction."
Step 3: Lock (deliver)
"Produce the final deliverable with strict format, length, do-not rules, and verification."
This keeps creativity high and control strong.

A complete "creative funnel" prompt set (ready to paste)
Prompt 1: Divergent generation
"Divergent phase.
Goal: <...>
Audience: <...>
Constraints: <...>
Generate 20 distinct ideas.
Rules:
group into 4 categories
each idea: 1 sentence + 1 risk
avoid repeats and near-duplicates"
Prompt 2: Convergent selection
"Convergent phase.
Score each idea 1–5 on: audience fit, novelty, feasibility, risk.
Select top 3. Explain tradeoffs.
Pick 1 final direction and state why it wins."

Prompt 3: Final deliverable lock
"Production phase.
Using only the final direction, write the deliverable.
Format: <exact>
Length: <exact>
Must include: <...>
Must avoid: <...>
Unknown policy: do not invent facts
Before finalizing: check against contract and fix."

Practice lab: apply divergence and convergence to one task
Choose a task, for example:
"Write a chapter opening,"
"Create a metaphor to explain context windows,"
"Design a workshop exercise,"
"Generate book titles or section names."
Run the funnel:
Diverge: 20 options, one line each.
Converge: score and pick top 3.
Lock: produce final output with strict format and tone.
Success criteria:
you see real variety in divergence,
you can explain why the final was chosen,
and the final output meets constraints without inventing facts.

Creative prompting stays controllable when you separate exploration from selection. Divergence gives you breadth without judgment. Convergence turns breadth into a decision using rubrics and constraints. Then you lock the output with a strict format contract and verification. This structure keeps creativity high while keeping outcomes reliable.

Constraints that improve creativity

Constraints do not reduce creativity. They focus it. In professional work, the most original and usable ideas usually come from well-chosen constraints, not from unlimited freedom.
When prompts are too open, the model often produces:

generic ideas,
repetitive variations,
content that drifts off-target,
or "creative" outputs that cannot be used.
The goal is to use constraints as creative fuel while preserving variety.

Why constraints increase creativity

Constraints help in three ways:

They define the problem shape

Creativity needs a target. Constraints say what "fits."

They force tradeoffs

Tradeoffs create originality. If you must satisfy X while avoiding Y, you get novel solutions.

They reduce noise

The model stops filling space and starts making choices.
Professionally, the best constraints are:
concrete,
testable,
and tied to the audience and deliverable.

The "right amount" of constraint

Think of constraint like a dial:
Too little: generic, wandering, repetitive
Too much: stiff, formulaic, no novelty
Just right: focused originality
A good rule:
Constrain the **outcome and boundaries**, not every sentence.

Constraint categories that reliably improve creativity

1) Audience constraints

Audience constraints force relevance and tone fit, which increases usable creativity.
Examples:
"Audience: beginners, avoid jargon, teach with everyday examples."
"Audience: executives, focus on decisions and risks."
"Audience: skeptical engineers, emphasize tradeoffs and edge cases."

Why it boosts creativity:
It forces the model to invent ideas that make sense for a specific reader, not an imaginary average reader.

2) Format constraints (creative structure)
Format constraints are powerful because they shape outputs into comparable units.
Examples:
"20 ideas, each one sentence."
"For each idea: name + pitch + risk."
"Group into 4 categories."
"Return a table: Idea | Mechanism | Why it works | Risk."
Why it boosts creativity:
The model must produce multiple distinct units, not one rambling piece.

3) Mechanism constraints (the originality engine)
This is one of the most effective creativity constraints.
Prompt line:
"Each idea must be different by mechanism, not wording."
Mechanism examples:
teach by analogy vs teach by checklist
interactive quiz vs workbook exercise
story-first vs data-first
roleplay lab vs debugging clinic
template-based vs case-study-based
Why it boosts creativity:
It prevents shallow rephrases and forces concept diversity.

4) Category constraints (coverage and diversity)
Examples:
"Split ideas into these categories: quick wins, long-term, low-risk, high-risk."
"Give 5 ideas each for: education, tools, community, workflow, metrics."
Why it boosts creativity:
The model must explore multiple regions of the idea space.

5) Non-goal constraints (what not to do)
Creativity improves when you forbid clichés.
Examples:
"Avoid generic advice like 'be clear' or 'use examples.'"
"Do not propose 'just use AI' solutions."
"No 'top 10 tips' format."
Why it boosts creativity:
Blocking default patterns forces alternative solutions.
Professional tip:
List 3–6 non-goals max. Too many makes the output brittle.

6) Resource constraints (realism constraints)
Constraints like time, budget, and people produce practical creativity.
Examples:
"Assume one person, 2 hours total, no paid tools."
"Assume a small team, 2 weeks, minimal engineering."
"No external data collection."
Why it boosts creativity:
It forces clever simplification and prioritization.

7) Tradeoff constraints (choose what to optimize)
Instead of asking for "best," define the tradeoff.
Examples:
"Optimize for speed over polish."
"Optimize for reliability over creativity."
"Optimize for simplicity and teachability."
"Minimize risk even if slower."
Why it boosts creativity:
It forces coherent direction and prevents unfocused outputs.

8) Novelty constraints (anti-repetition rules)
Use these when outputs feel generic.
Examples:
"Include 5 counterintuitive ideas."
"Include 3 'wild' ideas labeled WILD, but still feasible."
"No two ideas may share the same opening verb."

"No repeats of the same format."
Why it boosts creativity:
It pushes the model out of its default patterns.

9) Timebox constraints (short bursts)
Creativity improves when you cap the response.
Examples:
"Give 12 ideas only, no explanations."
"One sentence per idea, max 15 words."
Then do a second pass to expand only the best ideas.
Why it boosts creativity:
Short bursts encourage exploration and prevent over-polished sameness.

10) Evaluation constraints (design with the selection step in mind)
If you plan to score ideas later, include scoring-ready fields now.
Examples:
"For each idea include:
impact (H/M/L)
effort (S/M/L)
risk (H/M/L)"
Why it boosts creativity:
It nudges the model to produce ideas that can survive a real selection process.

Practical constraint recipes (copy-paste)
Recipe A: High-variety idea list
"Generate 20 ideas for <goal>.
Constraints:
audience: <...>
each idea one sentence, max 18 words
each must be distinct by mechanism
include one risk per idea, max 10 words
avoid clichés: <3 banned patterns>
Group into 4 categories."
Use when you want breadth fast.

Recipe B: Realistic constraints, practical creativity

"Generate 12 ideas for <goal> under these limits:

budget: <$X or none>

time: <Y hours/days>

team: <size>

tools: <allowed>

For each idea: pitch + why it fits constraints + risk."

Use when ideas must be implementable.

Recipe C: Novelty push

"Generate 15 ideas, with quotas:

5 conventional

5 unusual

5 counterintuitive

Rules:

no duplicates

distinct mechanisms

one sentence each

Label each idea type."

Use when you keep getting safe outputs.

Recipe D: Ban the defaults

"Generate 10 ideas for <goal>.

Hard bans:

no 'top tips' lists

no generic advice

no repeated formats

Each idea must include a concrete artifact: template, worksheet, checklist, rubric, or lab."

Use when you want concrete outputs.

Common mistakes with constraints (and how to fix them)

Mistake 1: Over-constraining too early

Symptoms:

Ideas feel robotic, all similar.

Fix:
Run two rounds:
Round 1: light constraints for breadth
Round 2: tighter constraints for relevance

Mistake 2: Constraints that conflict
Example:
"Be extremely creative" and "follow strict corporate tone" and "use zero metaphors."
Fix:
Prioritize:
"Primary: corporate tone and clarity. Secondary: creative variety within constraints."

Mistake 3: Vague constraints
Example:
"Make it innovative."
Fix:
Translate to measurable rules:
"include 3 counterintuitive ideas"
"use 4 distinct mechanisms"
"avoid these clichés"

Practice: constraint tuning exercise
Start with an open prompt and generate 15 ideas.
Add one constraint category at a time:
audience,
mechanism diversity,
format,
non-goals,
resource limits.
Compare outputs after each constraint:
Did variety increase?
Did relevance improve?
Did ideas become more usable?
Success criteria:

fewer near-duplicates,
clearer fit to audience,
ideas are concrete and implementable.

Constraints are not the enemy of creativity. They are the steering wheel. When you constrain audience, mechanism diversity, format, non-goals, resources, and tradeoffs, you get ideas that are both original and usable, which is exactly what professional creative prompting aims for.

Idea generation prompts

Idea generation is the divergent phase of creative prompting. The goal is volume and variety, not perfection. The risk is chaos: repetitive ideas, off-topic tangents, or outputs that are hard to compare. Professional idea generation prompts solve this by using light but firm structure, novelty rules, and output formats that make evaluation easy.
This section gives you practical idea-generation prompt patterns, plus guardrails that preserve creativity while keeping outputs usable.

What makes an idea-generation prompt "professional"

A professional prompt for ideation includes five elements:
Target: what you want ideas for, in one sentence
Audience: who the ideas are for
Constraints: the boundaries that matter (time, budget, tone, domain)
Variety requirements: how ideas must differ from each other
Output format: a structured list you can review and score
If any of these are missing, results often drift or repeat.

The idea-generation toolbox (prompt patterns)

Pattern 1: Category grid (best default)
Use when you want coverage across different angles.
Prompt template
"Generate <N> ideas for <goal>.
Audience: <audience>.
Constraints: <3–5 constraints>.

Organize ideas into these categories: <cat1>, <cat2>, <cat3>, <cat4>.
Rules:
no repeats or near-duplicates
each idea is one sentence
each idea must be distinct by mechanism, not wording
Output:
Category heading + numbered list."
Why it works:
Categories force diversity and make review faster.

Pattern 2: Angle rotation (forces novelty)
Use when you keep getting the same type of idea.
Prompt template
"Give 12 ideas for <goal>. Each idea must use a different angle:
analogy
contrarian take
step-by-step how-to
story hook
data framing (no invented numbers)
checklist framing
myth-busting
cautionary framing
minimalist version
premium version
beginner-friendly version
expert-focused version
Each idea: one sentence + one risk."
Why it works:
You prevent the model from staying in one groove.

Pattern 3: Constraint-driven ideation (creative but relevant)
Use when creativity must stay inside strict boundaries.
Prompt template
"Generate 15 ideas for <goal> that satisfy:
Must-haves:
<must-have 1>

<must-have 2>
Non-goals:
<non-goal 1>
<non-goal 2>
For each idea include:
Name, one-sentence pitch, and why it fits the constraints."
Why it works:
Constraints become a creativity engine, not a limiter.

Pattern 4: "Bad ideas" warm-up (unlock originality)
Use when ideas are safe and generic.
Prompt template
"First generate 8 intentionally bad ideas for <goal> (label them BAD and explain why).
Then generate 12 good ideas that avoid those failure reasons.
Rules:
good ideas must be distinct
each idea is one sentence."
Why it works:
Bad ideas reveal clichés and help the model escape them.

Pattern 5: Morphological matrix (systematic exploration)
Use when the space is complex and you want controlled variety.
How it works
Define key dimensions, then combine choices.
Example dimensions:
audience segment (beginner, intermediate, expert)
format (checklist, story, template, quiz)
tone (formal, friendly, technical)
channel (PDF, slide deck, email series)
goal (teach, persuade, onboard)
Prompt template
"Create a morphological matrix for <goal> with these dimensions:
Audience: A/B/C
Format: X/Y/Z

Tone: M/N/O
Generate 12 concept combinations (mix different cells).
For each: name + one-sentence pitch + one risk."
Why it works:
Systematic variety, minimal repetition.

Pattern 6: Divergent variations on one seed idea
Use when you already have one good idea and need alternatives.
Prompt template
"Starting from this seed idea:
<seed>
Generate 10 variations that differ in at least one of:
audience
tone
format
mechanism
length
Return a table: Variation | What changes | Why it could work | Risk."
Why it works:
You keep relevance while increasing creative range.

Pattern 7: "Yes, and" expansion (rapid iteration)
Use when you want to build breadth quickly.
Prompt template
"Generate 10 initial ideas for <goal>.
Then for each idea, add one 'Yes, and' improvement that makes it more original or more useful.
Output format:
Idea 1: …
Yes, and: …"
Why it works:
It creates a second layer of novelty without losing the base.

Pattern 8: Audience-specific idea generation (tone control built-in)

Use when audience fit matters more than novelty.

Prompt template

"Generate 12 ideas for <goal> for this audience:
Role: <role>
Knowledge level: <level>
Sensitivity: <tone risks>
Each idea must include:
one-sentence pitch
one-sentence why it fits this audience
No repeats."

Why it works:

Stops the model from producing ideas that are clever but unusable.

Guardrails that keep ideation useful (without killing creativity)

Guardrail 1: "Distinct by mechanism"

Add this line to reduce repetition:

"Each idea must be different by mechanism, not just phrasing."

Mechanism examples:

teach by analogy vs teach by checklist
interactive quiz vs workbook exercise
storytelling vs rubric evaluation
template-based vs case-study-based

Guardrail 2: Length caps

Caps keep lists scannable:

"Each idea max 18 words."

"Pitch must be one sentence."

This improves review speed.

Guardrail 3: Include a risk or downside

A one-line risk prevents fantasy ideas and makes evaluation easier.

Prompt line:

"For each idea, include one risk or limitation."

Guardrail 4: No invented facts rule

Ideation often triggers fake stats. Prevent it:
"Do not invent numbers, research findings, or citations."

Guardrail 5: Anti-duplication check

Add:
"Before finalizing, remove near-duplicates and replace them with new ideas."
This improves variety in one shot.

Output formats that make evaluation easy

Best formats for ideation review

Category lists (fast scanning)
Tables (quick comparison)
Score-ready lists (idea + risk + audience fit)
Example table columns:
Idea | Category | Pitch | Why it fits | Risk

A reusable "idea generator" master prompt (copy and paste)

"Idea generation mode.
Goal: <what you want ideas for>
Audience: <role + knowledge level>
Constraints: <3–5 must-haves>
Non-goals: <3–5 must-not>
Generate 20 ideas, organized into 4 categories you choose.
Rules:
each idea is one sentence (max 18 words)
each idea must be distinct by mechanism
include 1 risk per idea (max 12 words)
no invented facts, numbers, or citations
remove near-duplicates before returning
Output:
Category heading + numbered ideas."

Mini lab: generate, then prepare for convergence

Practice routine:
Run Pattern 1 (category grid) to generate 20 ideas.

Run Pattern 2 (angle rotation) to generate 12 more.
Combine lists, remove duplicates, and keep the best 15.
Only then move to the convergent phase:
"Score and select top 3 using a rubric."
Success criteria:
you can point to at least 5 ideas that differ by mechanism,
you can quickly see risks,
and the list is structured enough to evaluate.

Idea generation prompts work best when they are structured enough to prevent repetition and drift, but open enough to allow novelty. Categories, angle rotation, mechanism diversity, and compact formats give you creative breadth without losing control.

<u>Practice, generate 30 ideas, then converge to 3 with a rubric</u>

This practice drill teaches a repeatable creative workflow: produce a wide set of ideas (divergent phase), then narrow them to a small set of winners (convergent phase) using a rubric. The goal is not just "more ideas." The goal is controlled creativity you can ship.
You will do this in two passes:
Generate 30 ideas with diversity guardrails.
Score and select the top 3 with a decision rubric, then refine them.

Part 1: Divergent phase, generate 30 ideas
Step 1: Choose a creative target
Pick a target that is realistic and concrete. Examples:
30 exercise ideas for a prompt engineering workbook
30 metaphors to explain hallucinations and verification
30 chapter section hooks for "AI Prompt Engineering"
30 mini labs for controlling output format
30 product feature ideas for a prompt tool
For this lab, you can use this default target:
"Generate 30 practice drills for prompt engineering learners."

Step 2: Apply diversity constraints (to prevent repetition)
Use guardrails that force variety without restricting creativity.

Recommended diversity rules

Organize into 6 categories, 5 ideas per category.
Each idea must be distinct by mechanism, not wording.
Each idea must fit in one sentence.
Include one risk or limitation per idea.
Avoid generic advice or duplicated formats.

Divergent prompt (copy and paste)

"Divergent phase.
Goal: Generate 30 ideas for: <YOUR TARGET>.
Audience: <role + knowledge level>.
Constraints: <3–5 boundaries, e.g., time, tools, tone>.
Output requirements:
Create 6 categories of your choice, with 5 ideas each (total 30).
Each idea must be one sentence, max 18 words.
Each idea must be distinct by mechanism, not just rephrasing.
For each idea, add a short 'Risk' (max 10 words).
No invented facts or citations.
Remove near-duplicates before returning.
Output format:
Category:
Idea … | Risk: …
Idea … | Risk: …"

What good output looks like

you can quickly scan and compare,
categories are meaningfully different,
risks are realistic,
ideas are not repeated in different words.

Part 2: Convergent phase, score down to 3 with a rubric

Step 3: Create a rubric that fits your goal

A rubric converts taste into criteria. Keep it small. Use 4–6 criteria.

Recommended rubric criteria for creative work

Audience fit (will the target reader understand and value it)
Originality (not a cliché, distinct mechanism)
Feasibility (can you actually produce it within constraints)

Impact (would it noticeably improve learning or outcomes)
Risk (confusion, scope creep, wrong incentives)
Use a 1–5 scale with brief definitions:
1 = poor, 3 = acceptable, 5 = excellent
Optional weights if you want priorities:
Audience fit 25
Impact 25
Feasibility 20
Originality 20
Risk 10 (reverse scored)

Step 4: Score the 30 ideas quickly
Professional scoring should be fast. Do not overthink numbers. Each score needs a one-line justification.
Convergent scoring prompt (copy and paste)
"Convergent phase.
Input: the 30 ideas below.
Task:
Create a scoring table with columns:
ID | Idea | Audience fit (1–5) | Originality (1–5) | Feasibility (1–5) | Impact (1–5) | Risk (1–5, higher = riskier) | Total
Provide one short justification per idea (max 12 words).
Rank all ideas by Total (treat scores as directional).
Select the top 3. If two are very similar, replace one with the next best distinct idea.
For each selected idea, propose one improvement that reduces risk or increases feasibility.
Scoring rules:
Do not invent facts.
If unclear, score lower and note what is missing.
Avoid false precision: scores are approximate."
Paste the 30 ideas under this prompt.

Step 5: Refine the top 3 into "shippable" concepts
Now you turn three winners into complete, usable deliverables.
Refinement prompt (copy and paste)

"Refine these top 3 ideas into shippable concepts.
For each idea, produce:
Title
One-paragraph description (80–120 words)
Exact deliverable format (template, checklist, lab steps, worksheet)
Inputs needed from the user
Success criteria (how we know it worked)
Common failure and how to fix it
Rules:
Preserve the original core idea.
Do not expand scope beyond what is needed to ship."
This step transforms a ranked list into real assets.

Quality controls (so the process stays honest)

Control 1: Anti-duplication check

Before scoring, remove near-duplicates. In convergence, duplicates distort the ranking.
Prompt line:
"First, merge duplicates and keep the stronger version."

Control 2: "No new ideas during convergence"

Convergence should not invent new options. It should select and refine.
Prompt line:
"Do not introduce new ideas, only improve selected ones."

Control 3: Avoid false precision

Rubric totals can look scientific. They are directional.
Prompt line:
"Totals indicate preference, not certainty. Provide a sensitivity note."
Sensitivity note example:
"If feasibility is lower than expected, Idea #4 becomes the top choice."

Practice worksheet (what the learner should deliver)

At the end of this lab, the learner should have:
30 ideas in 6 categories, each with a risk line
A scoring table with rankings
The top 3 selected ideas
A one-paragraph refined concept for each

A short note explaining why these three won

Common failure modes (and fixes)

Failure: ideas are too generic

Fix:

Add bans:

"Avoid generic tips. Every idea must produce an artifact."

Failure: ideas repeat

Fix:

Enforce mechanism diversity:

"Each category must use different mechanisms."

Failure: scoring is inconsistent

Fix:

Define 1, 3, 5 for each criterion, then rescore.

Failure: top ideas are high-impact but unrealistic

Fix:

Increase feasibility weight, or add:

"Must be buildable in <time> with <resources>."

A complete end-to-end prompt pack (ready to paste)

Prompt 1, generate 30

"Generate 30 ideas for <target> …" (use the divergent prompt above)

Prompt 2, score and pick top 3

"Create a scoring table … select top 3 …" (use convergent scoring prompt)

Prompt 3, refine top 3

"Refine these top 3 ideas into shippable concepts …" (use refinement prompt)

This is a professional creative pipeline: explore widely, then narrow with criteria, then ship.

www.ingramcontent.com/pod-product-compliance
Ingram Content Group UK Ltd.
Pitfield, Milton Keynes, MK11 3LW, UK
UKHW020128290926
15471UKWH00003B/349

9 798295 509513